WHS

Teacher's resource

150 Numeracy Hour Lessons

YEAR 6

Contents | Page

First published 2001
exclusively for WHSmith by

Hodder & Stoughton Educational,
a division of Hodder Headline Ltd
338 Euston Road
London NW1 3BH

A CIP record for this book is available from the British Library.

Author: Robin Kearsley Bullen
Series editor: Paul Broadbent

ISBN 0340 79008 3

Impression number 10 9 8 7 6 5 4 3
2006 2005 2004 2003

Typeset by Servis Filmsetting Ltd
Printed and bound in Spain by Graphycems

Year 6

Summary of objectives

	Theme	Topics	Objectives – children will be taught to:
Autumn term			
1	**Mental calculation**	Understanding × and ÷ Mental calculation strategies (× and ÷)	***Consolidate all previous work.*** Understand and use relationships between the 4 operations, and the principles of the arithmetic laws. Use related facts and doubling or halving *e.g. halve an even number, double the other; multiply by 25, by ×100, then ÷ by 4.*
2	**Multiplication**	Pencil and paper procedures (× and ÷) Money and 'real life' problems Making decisions and checking results, including using a calculator	Approximate first. Use informal pencil and paper methods to support, record or explain × and ÷. Extend written methods to ThHTU × U and short multiplication involving decimals. Use all four operations to solve money or 'real life' word problems. Choose appropriate operations/calculation methods. Explain working. Check by estimating. Use inverse operation including with a calculator.
3	**Fractions and Decimals**	Fractions and decimals	***Consolidate all previous work.*** Change an improper fraction to a mixed number and vice versa. Recognise equivalent fractions. Reduce fractions by cancelling. Use decimal notation for tenths and hundredths; extend to thousandths for measurements. Know what each digit represents. Give a decimal lying between two others *e.g. 3.4 and 3.5.*
4	**Percentages, ratio and proportion**	Percentages, ratio and proportion	Understand percentage as the number of parts in every 100. Solve simple problems involving ratio and proportion.
5	**Handling data**	Handling data Using a calculator	***Consolidate all previous work.*** Use language of probability, including events with equally likely outcomes. Present and interpret grouped discrete data on a bar chart. Use prepared computer database to compare presentations of data. Find the mode and range of a set of data. Begin to find median and mean.
6	**Quadrilaterals**	Shape and space Reasoning about shapes	***Consolidate all previous work.*** Classify quadrilaterals using side/angle properties. Read and plot coordinates in all four quadrants. Recognise where a shape will be after two translations. Solve shape puzzles. Explain methods and reasoning orally and in writing.
7	**Measuring perimeters**	Measures, including problems	Calculate perimeter of rectangles and simple compound shapes. Use, read and write standard metric units of length, abbreviations and relationships. Convert larger to smaller units of length and vice versa. Know mile and km equivalents.
8	**Measures problems**	Measures, including problems	Appreciate different times around the world. Suggest suitable units/equipment to estimate or measure length. Record estimates/measurements from scales to suitable degree of accuracy. Use all four operations to solve measurement word problems, including time. Choose appropriate operations/calculation methods. Explain working.
9	**Problem-solving**	Mental calculation strategies (+ and −) Pencil and paper procedures (+ and −) Money and 'real life' problems Making decisions, checking results, including using a calculator	***Consolidate all previous work.*** Find a difference by counting up, and add/subtract a multiple of 10, 100, 1000 and adjust. If appropriate, use informal pencil and paper methods. Extend written methods to column + and − numbers involving decimals. Use all four operations to solve money or 'real life' word problems. Choose appropriate operations/calculation methods. Explain working.
10	**Number sequences**	Properties of numbers Reasoning about numbers	Recognise and extend number sequences such as square, triangular numbers. Count on/back in steps of 0.1, 0.2, 0.25, 0.5. and then back. Solve mathematical problems or puzzles. Recognise patterns, generalise.

Summary of objectives

	Theme	Topics	Objectives – children will be taught to:
Spring term			
1	**Negative numbers**	Place value, ordering, rounding Using a calculator	Find the difference between a positive and a negative integer, or two negative integers, in the context such as temperature or a number line. Order a set of negative integers. Develop calculator skills and use a calculator effectively.
2	**Multiplication and division**	Understanding × and ÷ Mental calculation strategies (× and ÷) Pencil and paper procedures (× and ÷)	***Consolidate all previous work.*** Use brackets. Use factors. Use closely related facts. Partition, *e.g.* 87×6, 3.4×3. Extend written methods to short division of TU or HTU (mixed number answer) and of decimals.
3	**Money problems**	Money and 'real life' problems Making decisions, checking results, including using a calculator	Use all four operations to solve money or 'real life' word problems. Choose appropriate operations/calculation methods. Explain working. Check by estimating. Use inverse operation, including with calculator.
4	**Fractions and decimals**	Fractions, decimals and percentages Using a calculator	***Consolidate all previous work.*** Order fractions by converting to common denominator, and position them on a number line. Use fractions as 'operators'; find fractions of numbers and quantities. Order a set of mixed numbers or measurements with up to 3 decimal places. Round a number to the nearest tenth or nearest whole number. Use a calculator effectively.
5	**Measuring angles**	Shape and space Reasoning about shapes	Recognise, estimate acute and obtuse angles. Use protractor to measure and draw acute/obtuse angles to 1°. Check angle sum of triangle is 180°. Calculate angles in triangle or around a point. Recognise where shape will be after 90° rotation about vertex. Recognise and explain patterns and relationships, generalise and predict.
6	**Area**	Measures including problems	***Consolidate all previous work.*** Use formula for area of rectangle. Calculate the area of a shape formed from rectangles, including using a calculator with memory.
7	**Mass**	Measures including problems Handling data	Use, read and write standard metric units of mass and abbreviations. Know relationships. Convert larger to smaller units and vice versa. Know approximate metric equivalents for pounds (lb) and ounces (oz). Suggest suitable units and equipment to estimate or measure mass. Read measurements from scales. Use all four operations to solve measurement word problems. Choose appropriate operations/calculation methods. Explain working. Represent, extract and interpret data in a line graph *(e.g. graph to convert kg to pounds)*. Recognise that intermediate points have meaning.
8	**Calculating with decimals**	Mental calculation strategies (+ and −) Pencil and paper procedures (+ and −)	***Consolidate all previous work.*** Extend written methods to column + and − of numbers involving decimals.
9	**Word problems**	Money and 'real life' problems Making decisions and checking results, including using a calculator	Use all four operations to solve word problems involving money or 'real life' measurement. Choose appropriate operations/calculation methods. Explain working. Check by adding in reverse order, including with a calculator.
10	**Properties of number**	Properties of numbers Reasoning about numbers	***Consolidate all previous work.*** Recognise multiples up to 10×10. Find simple common multiples. Know tests of divisibility. Recognise primes to at least 20. Find prime factors. Investigate products of odd/even numbers. Make general statements about them and give examples. Solve number puzzles and explain methods and reasoning.

	Theme	Topics	Objectives – children will be taught to:
Summer term			
1	**Multiplication and division**	Understanding × and ÷ Mental calculation strategies (× and ÷) Pencil and paper procedures (× and ÷)	***Consolidate all previous work.*** Express a quotient as a fraction, or as a decimal rounded to 1 decimal place. Dividing £ and pence by a two-digit number to give £ and pence. Round up or down after division depending on the context. Use known facts and place value to multiply and divide mentally. Use relationship between multiplication and division. Multiply HTU by TU. Division HTU by TU (long division, whole number answer).
2	**Problem solving**	Money and 'real life' problems Making decisions and checking results, including using a calculator	Use all four operation to solve word problems involving money or 'real life' including finding percentages and VAT. Choose appropriate operations/calculation methods. Explain working. Check using products of odd/even numbers or doing the inverse calculation, including using a calculator.
3	**Fractions, decimals and percentages**	Fractions, decimals and percentages	***Consolidate all previous work.*** Begin to convert fractions to decimal using division. Use a calculator to compare two fractions. Express simple fractions as percentages. Find simple percentages of whole number quantities, include using calculator.
4	**Ratio and proportion**	Ratio and proportion	Solve simple problems involving ratio and proportion.
5	**Handling data**	Handling data Using a calculator	***Consolidate all previous work.*** Extract information from a simple frequency table. and convert the data to percentages, using a calculator where appropriate. Interpret a simple pie chart, using fractions or percentages. Solve a problem by representing, extracting and interpreting data in frequency tables and bar charts with grouped discrete data.
6	**Reflection, translation and rotation**	Shape and space	Recognise where shape will be after reflection in a line not parallel to a side or in two mirrors at 90°. Consolidate work on translations and rotations.
7	**Investigating shapes**	Reasoning about shapes	Make and investigate a general statement about shapes.
8	**Measuring capacity**	Measures, including problems	Use, read and write metric units of capacity, including abbreviations. Know and use the relationships between them. Convert larger to smaller units of capacity, and vice versa. Know approximate metric equivalents for pint and gallon. Suggest suitable units and equipment to estimate or measure capacity. Read measurements from scales. Use all four operations to solve measurement word problems, including time. Choose appropriate operations/calculation methods. Explain working.
9	**Addition and subtraction**	Mental calculation strategies (+ and −) Pencil and paper procedures (+ and −) Money and 'real life' problems Making decisions and checking results, including using a calculator	Use number facts and place value to add and subtract mentally. Extend written methods to column addition and subtraction of numbers involving decimals. Use all four operations to solve word problems involving money or 'real life', including percentages. Choose appropriate operations/calculation methods. Explain working. Check using sums/differences of odd/even numbers or doing the inverse calculation, including using a calculator.
10	**Functions and formulae**	Properties of numbers Reasoning about numbers	Factorise numbers to 100 into prime factors. Investigate number sequences. Develop a generalised relationship in words; express it in a formula using symbols. Solve number puzzles and explain methods and reasoning.

Mental maths starters

1 Counting stick

Using a counting stick, designate the numbers at each end and ask the pupils to name the divisions, in order or at random.

2 Counting on

Count up or down from a specified number in units, twos, fives, tens etc.

3 Estimating measures

Ask the pupils to estimate the length/area/mass/capacity of various items that you or they suggest, e.g. *a bucket*: 'How tall, how wide, how heavy, how much does it hold etc.'

4 Visualising solids

Ask the pupils to visualise a 3D shape *(e.g. a cuboid, cone, tetrahedron etc.)*.

Ask various questions, e.g. *'How many faces/edges/vertices', 'If I cut it like this, what shape is exposed'* etc.

5 Time intervals

Pupils need clock faces or scrap paper to write on. Ask various questions, e.g. *'If a TV programme starts at 1730 and lasts for 45 minutes, when does it end?'* and equivalent questions where they have to find the time interval. Fast/slow clocks, e.g. *'A clock is 35 minutes fast. What time does it show now?'* and *'Imagine our clock is 20 minutes fast. What time is really?'*

6 Tables practice

Recitation of various multiplication tables, forwards and backwards. Rapid-fire interrogation of pupils on specific multiplications.

7 Division tables

Test recall of multiplication facts by posing inverse division questions, e.g. *48 ÷ 6, 63 ÷ 7 etc.*

8 Digit cards

Various questions on all four rules including multiplication and division by a power of ten. Pupils will pool their cards if necessary.

9 Combining shapes

Various questions such as, *'If I join two isosceles triangles together by an edge, what shape does it make (answer could be a rhombus, parallelogram of kite)?', 'If I cut a square out of another square, what shape is left?'* etc.

10 Mystery numbers

Various 'puzzle' questions, e.g. *'50% of a number is 10. What's the number?', 'My number is even and a multiple of 9. What could it be?'* etc.

11 Doubling and halving

Quick-fire questions asking pupils to double or halve numbers, answering with digit cards.

12 Arrow cards (including decimals)

Various questions such as 'Show me a number between … and …', 'Show me a number that rounds to …, to the nearest ten/whole number' etc.

Theme 1 Mental calculation

Objectives
- To understand and use relationships between the four operations
- To combine known facts, extending the range of mental calculations available

Vocabulary
add, subtract, multiply, divide, plus, minus, times, decimal, digit, place, double, halve, ten, hundred, thousand

Resources
Copymasters 1 and 2, digit cards, arrow cards, hundred grids

Homework Copymaster 1

Mental maths starters 6, 7

Assessment
At the end of this theme is the pupil able to:
- Recall multiplication facts to 10×10 and deduce associated division facts;
- Halve and double numbers with up to three digits;
- Multiply and divide by a power of ten and by single-digit multiples of powers of ten;
- Combine addition and subtraction with multiplication and division to extend the range of mental calculations he/she can do?

Lesson 1

Introduction — 5 mins
Each pupil needs a set of digit cards. Do rapid multiplication table drill, the pupils holding up the answers to questions you give them.

Activities — 30 mins
Chains of facts (whole class)
Work round the class in batches of six like this: two pupils produce a multiplication fact, the next two give an associated division fact, the next two the converse division fact.
An example might run: *'3 × 10', '= 30'. '30 ÷ 10', '= 3'. '30 ÷ 3', '= 10'.*
Tables on grids (individual)
Pupils need a number of 10×10 grids with the numbers from 1 to 100 on them.
Ask the pupils to colour in all the squares that 'belong' to the (say) 3× table. They should continue the pattern until all possible squares have been filled in.
Repeat with other tables. Ask the pupils to spot similarities between the patterns created. Large versions of these make a useful wall display.

Differentiation
Low Attainers – Cut the grids in half and use numbers 1–50 only.
High Attainers – Could be asked to investigate what happens on a 12×12 grid, or predict which tables above 10× could exhibit the same type of similarities as the ones they have already produced.

Plenary — 5 mins
Check that pupils have filled in their grids correctly.
Discuss the links between the patterns: 2 matches 8, 3 matches 7 etc.

Lesson 2

Introduction — 10 mins
Discuss how numbers can be doubled. Use a grid-type presentation if desired, *e.g. 24 × 2*:

×	20	4	
2	**40**	**8**	40 + 8 = **48**

Stress that this should always be done mentally.
Start with 2-digit numbers with both digits below 5, then make the units digit more than 5, the tens etc. Move on to 3-digit numbers and decimals.
Work on halving in the same way, *e.g. 15.4 ÷ 2*:

÷	10	5	0.4	
2	**5**	**2.5**	**0.2**	5 + 2.5 + 0.2 = **7.7**

Move on to multiplication and division by 4 and 8, using repeated doubling or halving.

Activities — 25 mins
Operation chains (whole class)
Pick an 'adding number', say 10, to start with. One pupil starts with an **even** number. Work round the class, each pupil applying an operation as follows: double, add 10, halve, add 10, double…
Repeat the exercise with different adding numbers.
Introduce subtraction.
Change to doubling twice in order to multiply by 4 etc.
Practice (individual)
Issue Copymaster 1. This gives practice in multiplying and dividing by 2, 4 and 8 mentally, and in identifying when numbers are connected by doubling or halving.

Differentiation
Low Attainers – Tailor the starting/adding numbers to be smaller.
High Attainers – Could devise their own doubling/halving picture, as in part 2 of the copymaster.

Plenary — 5 mins
Mark the copymaster and check that the pictures are correct.

Lesson 3

Introduction **10 mins**
Ask a group of five pupils to come to the front of the room. Ask one to bring his/her chair, give him/her a round object such as a tennis ball to represent the decimal point and seat him/her in a suitable place. Give the others digit cards. Ask them to make a number between 1 and 10.
Ask the other pupils to issue instructions such as 'multiply by 10' etc. The pupils with digit cards must move to make the answer. The seated decimal point must not move!
Get extra pupils to hold zero cards if the calculation demands it.

Activities **25 mins**
Multiplication/division facts and place value (whole class/group)
Discuss how to use multiplication table facts to multiply, say, 20 by 30, or to divide 12 000 by 40.
Go round the class as follows: the first pupil calls out a multiplication fact (*e.g.* $6 \times 8 = 48$). To the next pupil, give an instruction such as 'first number 10× bigger'. He/she must then respond with '$60 \times 8 = 480$'. Build on this, altering one number at a time by a power of 10. Decimal answers are fair game! Move on to divisions.
Factorising (individual/pairs)
Write some numbers on the board that can be factorised in a number of ways using powers of 10, such as 48 000. The pupils must write down as many different ways of making the number using multiplication as possible, *e.g.* 6000×8, 600×80 *etc.* Repeat with division.

Differentiation
Low Attainers – Reduce the size of the numbers involved.
High Attainers – Ensure that decimal answers are included.

Plenary **5 mins**
Examine the answers obtained to some of the factorising puzzles. Try to find the largest and smallest numbers used by members of the class.

Lesson 4

Introduction **10 mins**
Look at multiplying a 2-digit number by 9 (*e.g.* 36×9).
Discuss how you can use 36×10 and then subtract. Try a few examples out with the class. You could use arrow cards to show the results.
Repeat for 36×11. Try a few examples out with the class.

Activities **25 mins**
One more, one less (whole class)
Ask individual pupils how they think they could multiply by the following:
99, 101, 90, 110
19, 29, 39 etc.
21, 31 etc.
Try examples out as you go.
Squares (individual)
Ask pupils to work out the squares of 11, 21, 31 etc.
Repeat with 9, 19, 29, 39 etc.
Ask them to find the differences between 9^2 and 11^2, 19^2 and 21^2 etc. and to write down any patterns they notice in the answers.

Differentiation
Low Attainers – Pick some tables, such as 19×, 41× etc. and ask them to write them out.
High Attainers – Look at multiplication by 12, 22, 32 etc. and at 8, 18, 28 etc. They could try the squares activity on these. An overall pattern may suggest itself to the most able.

Plenary **5 mins**
Check that pupils have found the patterns in the 'Squares' activity (multiples of 40).

Lesson 5

Introduction **10 mins**
Ask what might be an easy way to multiply a number by 5, *e.g. by multiplying by 10 and halving the result.* Try some examples with the pupils. You could use arrow cards to show the results.
Repeat with division by 5.
Ask individual pupils how they think they could multiply or divide by 50 and 25.

Activities **25 mins**
More methods (whole class)
Look at a calculation that can be split, *e.g.* 34×15: *multiply by 10, then add half of the result.*
To multiply by 75, multiply by 50, then add half of the result, or multiply by 150 and halve the answer.
Practice (individual)
Issue Copymaster 2. This gives practice in multiplying and dividing by 5, 50, 25, 75, 150 etc. Pupils should be encouraged to make jottings as they work to help them.

Differentiation
Low Attainers – Keep to operations involving 5 and 50.
High Attainers – Could be asked to devise and test some new rules for multiplying by other numbers.

Plenary **5 mins**
Mark the copymaster. Review the strategies used by the pupils to answer the questions.

Theme 2 Multiplication

Objectives
- To consolidate knowledge of written methods of multiplication
- To understand the value of approximating answers

Vocabulary
multiply, divide, times, decimal, digit, place, column, approximate, rough, estimate

Resources
Copymasters 3 and 4, calculators

Homework Copymaster 2

Mental maths starters 6, 10, 11

Assessment
At the end of this theme is the pupil able to:
- Approximate the answer to a multiplication;
- Use the grid method to multiply numbers up to 4 digits by a single digit;
- Use a formal column method to multiply numbers up to 4 digits by a single digit;
- Use the above methods to solve problems?

Lesson 1

Introduction **10 mins**
Write a number on the board, say 542. Ask a pupil to round it. Don't specify the type of rounding required. Ask another pupil to round the same number. Ask which answer is the 'roundest'.
Repeat with other numbers. Progress to four digits.
Write a calculation on the board. Ask a pupil to say the calculation out loud, but to round the numbers. Ask another pupil to supply the answer. Explain that this is an **estimate** of the answer to the original calculation.

Activities **25 mins**
Rounding chain (whole class)
Work round the class. One pupil should think of a number, the next should give an operation and another number. The next pupil should repeat the calculation, using rounded numbers, and the next should estimate the answer. An example might be: *'253', '×48', '300', '×50', '= 15 000'.*

Calculator activity (pairs)
Write a number of rounded calculations on the board. The pupils should work out the approximate answers and write them down.
Pupils need their calculators. One between two is adequate. In pairs, they should investigate the smallest and largest numbers that, when rounded, produce the approximate calculation on the board. An example might be $400 \div 20$, giving the answer 20. The smallest answer is given by $350 \div 25 = 14$. The largest answer is given by $450 \div 15 = 30$. Work through an example of this type with the pupils first.

Differentiation
Low Attainers – Stick to numbers with three digits or less.
High Attainers – Use some five- and six-digit numbers.

Plenary **5 mins**
Check through the answers to the 'calculator activity', pointing out where mistakes have been made.

Lesson 2

Introduction **10 mins**
Discuss the grid method of multiplying by a single digit, *e.g.* 24×7:

×	20	4	
7	**140**	**28**	140 + 28 = **168**

Stress that multiplying two digits like this should always be done mentally.
Extend the method to three- and four-digit numbers.

Activities **25 mins**
Practice (individual)
Give out Copymaster 3. This contains some questions with predefined grids and some with squares for guidance.
Investigation (individual)
Write four digits on the board. Two of them should be five or less, the other two more than five. The pupils use the digits as follows: take three digits to make a three-digit number. Multiply this number by the remaining digit. Try different combinations to find the largest and smallest possible answers, *e.g. 2, 4, 5 and 7 give* $457 \times 2 = 914$ *and* $542 \times 7 = 3794$.

Differentiation
Low Attainers – Use three digits that are five or less and one more than five.
High Attainers – Use five digits or more.

Plenary **5 mins**
Check that the pupils have found the smallest and largest answers. They can use their calculators to check their answers by division.

Lesson 3

Introduction **10 mins**
Work through some examples of short multiplication in columns. Check that the pupils understand the principles involved.

Activities **25 mins**
Cross multiplying (individual)
Ask five pupils to make up numbers with three or four digits. Write them on the board, randomly distributed inside a circle or cloud shape. Ask another pupil to give you five single digits. Write these inside another circle or cloud. The pupils should multiply all the numbers in the first cloud by each of the digits in the second cloud, and then write down separately the largest and smallest answers.

Differentiation
Low Attainers – Stick to numbers with three digits, and possibly reduce the number of numbers in the clouds.
High Attainers – Use larger numbers in the first cloud.

Plenary **5 mins**
The pupils can use their calculators to check their answers by division.

Lesson 4

Introduction **10 mins**
Ask a pupil to give you a decimal with two decimal places. Ask another pupil for a single digit. Write on the board the decimal multiplied by the single digit. Carry out the multiplication with the pupils' help using the grid method, *e.g.* 6.27×4:

$\times$	6	0.2	0.07	
4	**24**	**0.8**	**0.28**	$24 + 0.8 + 0.28 = \mathbf{25.08}$

The idea is to show that this is unwieldy.
Repeat the calculation, setting it out in columns. Discuss why this is easier.
Do two or three more with the pupils.

Activities **25 mins**
Cross multiplying (individual)
Ask five pupils to make up numbers with three or four digits. Write them on the board, randomly distributed inside a circle or cloud shape. Ask another pupil to give you five single digits. Write these inside another circle or cloud. The pupils should multiply all the numbers in the first cloud by each of the digits in the second cloud, and then write down separately the largest and smallest answers.

Differentiation
Low Attainers – Stick to numbers with three digits, and possibly reduce the number of numbers in the clouds.
High Attainers – Use larger numbers in the first cloud.

Plenary **5 mins**
The pupils can use their calculators to check their answers by division.

Lesson 5

Introduction **5 mins**
This is largely a practice lesson. Explain to the pupils that they will be using all of their multiplying skills to answer questions, and that they can use whichever written method they prefer.

Activities **30 mins**
Practice (individual)
Give out Copymaster 4. This contains a list of prices and other information for wholesale ordering. Pupils need to answer various questions based on this information.

Differentiation
Low Attainers – Work through the questions, deciding with the pupils what information is required and what to do with it.
High Attainers – Could introduce some additional items, working in pairs, to test each other.

Plenary **5 mins**
Mark the copymaster. Check that the correct strategies were used by the pupils.

Theme 3 Fractions and decimals

Objectives
- To consolidate knowledge of the meaning of fractions
- To understand equivalent fractions and lowest terms
- To understand and use place value in numbers with up to 3 places of decimals, and to apply this to metric unit conversion

Vocabulary
fraction, numerator, denominator, equivalent, improper, mixed, cancel, simplify, decimal, place, convert

Resources
Copymasters 5 and 6, digit cards, squared paper (5 mm or 1 cm), fraction dominoes, scrap A4 paper

Homework Copymaster 3

Mental maths starters 7, 10, 11

Assessment
At the end of this theme is the pupil able to:
- Identify the fraction represented by a diagram;
- Generate equivalent fractions, identify when fractions are equivalent and cancel fractions to lowest terms;
- Order numbers with up to 3 places of decimals;
- Convert between metric units, multiplying or dividing by a suitable power of ten?

Lesson 1

Introduction **10 mins**
Review the meaning of the numerator and denominator in a fraction. Check that the pupils are familiar with these words.
Each pupil needs a set of digit cards. Draw several fraction diagrams on the board: circles, rectangles etc., divided into various numbers of equal parts, with some parts coloured or shaded in. As you draw each diagram, ask the pupils to hold up two digit cards, one above the other, showing the numerator and denominator of the fraction.

Activities **25 mins**
Practice (whole class)
Give out Copymaster 5. This contains further examples similar to those on the board.
Halving and quartering (individual)
Give out sheets of squared paper. Ask the pupils to draw as many 4 cm × 4 cm squares as they can fit on the sheet. The task is to find as many different ways as possible of dividing the squares into halves. One half of each diagram should be coloured.
The exercise can then be repeated with quarters.

Differentiation
Low Attainers – Restrict the last activity to halving only.
High Attainers – Select other fractions to be illustrated in various ways.

Plenary **5 mins**
Mark the copymaster. Ask the pupils to check each others' 'Halving and quartering' work.

Lesson 2

Introduction **10 mins**
Draw a number of squares on the board and divide each in half with a vertical line. Shade one half of each. By drawing horizontal lines in each square, divide them into different numbers of equal parts to demonstrate that various fractions are equivalent to $\frac{1}{2}$.
Repeat the exercise with other starting fractions.
Discuss with the pupils what it means for fractions to be equivalent, and for a fraction to be in lowest terms.

Activities **25 mins**
Equivalent fraction chains (whole class)
Work round the class as follows: a pupil names a fraction. The next pupil names an equivalent fraction, the next another, and so on. When you see fit, stop the chain of equivalent fractions and start a new one.
Fraction tennis (pairs)
One pupil names a fraction, not in lowest terms. The other pupil names an equivalent fraction with a smaller denominator. If this is done successfully, one point is scored. If the fraction is in lowest terms, an extra point is scored and a new round begins. If it is not in lowest terms, the first pupil cancels it further. The longer the rally, the more points are scored. Pupils should keep a record of the fractions named and the points scored. Deduct a point for a non-equivalent fraction.

Differentiation
Low Attainers – Fraction dominoes can help.
High Attainers – Modify the game so that intermediate steps between the starting fraction and the final fraction in lowest terms count as errors.

Plenary **5 mins**
Review the results of the fraction tennis game, asking pupils to read out some of the more interesting rallies. Go over the rules for fractions.

Lesson 3

Introduction **10 mins**

Draw two circles on the board, divided into quarters. Add another quarter. Ask, 'How many pies have I drawn?' (Answer: $2\frac{1}{4}$.) Ask, 'How many people could have a quarter each?' (Answer: 9.) Write up the improper fraction $\frac{9}{4}$ and discuss the significance of the numerator and denominator. Repeat this with different denominators and whole numbers.

Activities **25 mins**

Improper fraction chains (whole class)

Work round the class in groups of four as follows: the first pupil gives a numerator. The second chooses a denominator (less than the numerator). The third pupil works out how many wholes will be in the mixed fraction and the fourth provides the fractional part. An example might be, *'twenty...', 'thirds...', 'equals six...', 'and two-thirds'*. If the conversion leads to a whole number, the fourth pupil should say 'exactly'.

Investigation (individual)

Give the pupils a set of three digits to use *(e.g. 3, 4, 5)*. They must make as many different improper fractions as possible with the digits *(e.g.* $\frac{34}{5}, \frac{43}{5}, \frac{35}{4}, \frac{53}{4}, \frac{45}{3}, \frac{54}{3}$*)*, then convert these to mixed fractions. The pupils should then make as many valid mixed numbers as possible *(e.g.* $3\frac{4}{5}, 4\frac{3}{5}, 5\frac{3}{4}$*)*. Pupils can then choose their own sets of digits. What happens if identical digits are allowed.

Differentiation

Low Attainers – Use 1, 2 and 3 as the starting digits.
High Attainers – Extend to four digits.

Plenary **5 mins**

Mark the investigation. With three distinct digits, pupils should find six improper fractions and three mixed fractions; with two identical digits, three improper fractions and one mixed are possible; with three identical digits, only one improper fraction, equal to 11.

Lesson 4

Introduction **10 mins**

Revise the meaning of the first three decimal places. Give each pupil a piece of scrap A4 paper. Ask them to write on it, in large numerals, a 3dp number between 1 and 10. Ask pupils questions such as, *'hold up your number if it's between 4.5 and 5.5... bigger than 8...'* etc.

Activities **25 mins**

Position game (pairs)

The first pupil names a decimal number. The second pupil names another number. Scoring now begins. On his/her turn, each pupil has to name a number between the last two numbers called. If this is done successfully, a point is scored. Numbers can have at most 3 decimal places. Pupils should record all the numbers and their scores on each turn. A round is over when a pupil can't go. An example might be (second pupil in italics): 3, *5*, 4, *4.2*, 4.1, *4.06*, 4.08, *4.081* (player 2 wins). If a pupil makes a mistake (i.e. goes outside the target range) a point is lost and the turn is forfeited. It is probably best to play a couple of sample games with pupils.

Investigation (individual)

Pupils must use the digits 1, 2 and 3, three zeroes and a decimal point. They must make a complete list of all the numbers that can be made using these, then order the list. All the components must be used in all the numbers. Note that numbers with leading trailing zeroes (such as 0012.30) can't be used. Whole numbers can't be used as the decimal point would appear at the end, with nothing after it.

Differentiation

Low Attainers – Restrict the number of decimal places allowed in the game.
High Attainers – Allow pupils to use more decimal places in the game.

Plenary **5 mins**

Check the results of the investigation.

Lesson 5

Introduction **10 mins**

Revise the connections between the metric units of length, mass and capacity. Ask questions like 'How many centimetres are there in a metre?' and ask the class to respond '100' together verbally.
Go over how to convert units, e.g. *when converting to a smaller unit, there are more of them, so multiply by the correct power of ten*. Ask questions like 'How do I change millilitres into litres?', asking the pupils to reply 'divide by 1000'.

Activities **25 mins**

Conversion chains (whole class)

Work round the class like this: a pupil starts by calling out a measurement. The next few pupils give as many different equivalents as possible, using related units. If a pupil thinks all the equivalents have been given, but you know there are more, prompt him/her. An example might be: *'3 km', '3000 m', '3 000 000 mm', (prompt: centimetres...) '300 000 cm'*.

Practice (individual/pairs)

Give out Copymaster 6. This contains further examples similar to those in the last activity.

Differentiation

Low Attainers – Avoid km/cm or km/mm conversions.
High Attainers – Some small group work on converting area and volume units would be useful.

Plenary **5 mins**

Mark the copymaster. Discuss the most **sensible** unit to use for each item.

Theme 4 Percentages, ratio and proportion

Objectives
- To understand and use language associated with ratio and proportional quantities
- To understand and use the equivalence between 'in every' and 'to every' statements
- To understand percentage as a ratio 'in every 100' and to find simple percentages of multiples of 100
- To use the above skills in solving simple problems concerning proportional quantities

Vocabulary
ratio, in every, to every, simplify, percentage, per cent, equivalent

Resources
Copymasters 7 and 8, hundred grids or squared paper, digit cards, 2 mm graph paper

Homework Copymaster 4

Mental maths starter 10

Assessment
At the end of this theme is the pupil able to:
- Use statements of the form '1 in every 3' or '2 to every 3' and convert between them;
- Understand percentage as a ratio 'in every 100';
- Find equivalent ratios and simplify them where possible;
- Solve simple problems concerning proportional quantities?

Lesson 1

Introduction **10 mins**
Draw on the board a row of 5 squares. Shade in 2 of the squares. Make several copies of the pattern by replicating sideways, up-and-down or in a 'skewed' direction. Discuss the fact that 2 in every 5 squares are shaded.
Ask pupils to come to the board to draw other groupings and replicate them.

Activities **25 mins**
Shading grids (individual)
Give out blank 100 grids to the pupils, or squared paper. Write a list of various ratio statements such as '3 in every 4' on the board. The pupils should make a 'unit' diagram, then copy this, square by square, onto the 100 grid, 'wrapping round' as they come to the end of a row.

Differentiation
Low Attainers – Keep to simple numbers such as 'in every 5', 'in every 10' and perhaps 'in every 4'.
High Attainers – Could be asked to choose a ratio statement and work out how many of the 100 squares will be shaded in, then colour these as a block.

Plenary **5 mins**
Neighbours can check that they have similar diagrams. You could discuss the fact that certain statements such as '1 in every 3' can't be represented exactly on a grid of 100 squares, and why this is.

Lesson 2

Introduction **10 mins**
Prepare a diagram as in Lesson 1: draw on the board a row of 5 squares. Shade in 2 of the squares. Make several copies of the pattern by replication. Remind the pupils that 2 in every 5 squares are shaded. Discuss the fact that this means there are 2 shaded squares to every 3 unshaded ones. Try this with other combinations.

Activities **25 mins**
Ratios and numbers (whole class)
Discuss the equivalence of statements such as '4 in every 10' and '2 in every 5'.
Each pupil needs a set of digit cards. First say, 'These ratios are for dividing things between you and me.' Give the pupils a ratio statement such as 'I have 2 in every 3'. Ask them 'How many do *you* have in every 3?' The pupils hold up '1'. Then say 'I'm going to hold up how many I have.' Hold up '8'. Ask 'How many do you have?' The pupils hold up '4'. Repeat this with with 'I have 2 *to* every 3. How many do you have to every 2?' The pupils hold up '3'. Hold up '8'. Ask 'How many do you have?' The pupils hold up '12'. Repeat the whole questioning scheme with other ratios and numbers.
Matching ratios (individual)
Give out Copymaster 7. This contains sets of equivalent statements that the pupils have to identify. The sheets will be used again in Lesson 4.
Explain how to use the sheet: each group has two sets of four ratios, all mixed up. Copy them into two lists. Each list should only have ratios that mean the same thing. So a list could have '1 in every 2' and '4 to every 4', but '1 in every 3' would have to go into another list.

Differentiation
Low Attainers – Use counters, a pegboard etc.
High Attainers – Explore three-way proportional divisions.

Plenary **5 mins**
Mark the copymaster. Discuss any wrong answers and why the pupils made them.

Lesson 3

Introduction **10 mins**

Pupils need blank 100 grids. Discuss the fact that 'per cent' means 'in every 100'. Select some numbers and ask the pupils to colour in that percentage of a grid *(e.g. 35%, colour 35 squares)*.

Activities **25 mins**

Shading squares (individual)

Pupils need 2 mm graph paper. They need to be able to see the 2 cm squares clearly. Check that they understand that there are 100 small squares in a big square. Ask them to draw the outline of 1 large square and shade in 30% of it. Then ask them to outline a square 2 cm $\times$ 4 cm ('2 big squares') and to shade 30% of that, and so on.

Repeat with a selection of percentages and numbers of squares. The questions could be written on the board.

Differentiation

Low Attainers – Keep to multiples of 10%, with small numbers of squares.

High Attainers – Ask them to shade fractions of a square, *e.g. 20% of* $2\frac{1}{2}$ *squares.*

Plenary **5 mins**

Check through the questions, making sure that pupils have shaded the correct numbers of small squares in each case. Discuss any wrong answers and why the pupils made them.

Lesson 4

Introduction **15 mins**

Start with a percentage, *e.g.* 40%. Write it on the board. Remind the pupils that this means '40 in every 100'. Ask for any other ratio statements that are equivalent. If the numbers start to go up *(e.g. 80 in every 200 etc.)*, explain that you would really like to have **smaller** numbers. Write the pupils' suggestions on the board. Ask the pupils which answer they think is the simplest. Hopefully, '2 in every 5' will be there, otherwise, take the simplest and ask if it can be made any simpler.

Use other starting ratios, *e.g. '18 in every 24'*.

Activities **20 mins**

Ratio chains (whole class/group)

Work round the class in the following way: a pupil starts with a percentage or ratio. The next pupil simplifies it, and so on until the simplest form is reached.

Simplest ratios (individual/pairs)

Give out Copymaster 7, or ask the pupils to get them out again if they retained them after Lesson 2. If the simplest form of a ratio is in the outline, they should ring it. For example, in question 1, '1 to every 2' should be ringed. The corresponding simplest 'in every' statement, '1 in every 3', is missing, so the pupils should write this in the outline themselves and ring it. The two rings should then be joined with a line to show that they are equivalent ratios.

Differentiation

Low Attainers – Just ring the simplest available in each group.

High Attainers – Where possible, add an equivalent percentage to each group. They could use a calculator for this.

Plenary **5 mins**

Mark the copymaster. Discuss, particularly, those cases where the simplest ratios were missing.

Lesson 5

Introduction **10 mins**

Give some examples of ratio problems, for example, a recipe for 4 could be adapted for 6, by working out the quantities for 1 person first.

Activities **25 mins**

Practice (individual)

Give out Copymaster 8. This contains a variety of applications of the theories explored in the first four lessons.

Differentiation

Low Attainers – Give assistance where required.

High Attainers – Question 5 on the copymaster is only recommended for high attainers, as it is an example of inverse proportion.

Plenary **5 mins**

Mark the copymaster and examine any common errors.

Theme 5 Handling data

Objectives
- To collect and display data, manually and using ICT
- To group data values logically and understand when this is necessary
- To calculate the common statistics: mode, range, median, mean
- To review the concept of probability as related to equally likely outcomes

Vocabulary
probability, likely, unlikely, even, certain, impossible, equally likely, chance, data, survey, collect, process, group, tally, bar chart, average, mode, range, median, mean

Resources
Copymasters 9 and 10, scrap card or paper, drawing pins or paper-fasteners, pre-prepared database or spreadsheet, calculators

Homework Copymaster 5

Mental maths starter 3

Assessment
At the end of this theme is the pupil able to:
- Group data using suitable class intervals;
- Conduct a probability experiment and analyse the results in terms of equally likely outcomes;
- Calculate the common statistics: mode, range, median, mean;
- Use ICT to display data in various ways and to do this manually when required?

Lesson 1

Introduction 15 mins
You will need a means of measuring the pupils' heights, as not all will know how tall they are. Some may be able to give a height in feet and inches, which can be converted. Discuss making a bar chart of the heights of pupils in the class. Collect the data and begin to draw the axes for the bar chart on the board, with one bar for each different height in cm. Encourage the pupils to come to the conclusion that it won't be much use like this.
Look at groupings for the data and design tally tables to record the frequencies. Use 10 cm groups for one tally table and 5 cm groups for another. Discuss the fact that groups must not overlap.

Activities 20 mins
Height bar charts (whole class/group)
Pupils should make a list of the heights, then tally the data and produce a bar chart for the 10 cm grouping. They should then repeat the procedure for the 5 cm grouping. Pupils who finish this task early can choose another grouping of their own to work with.

Differentiation
Low Attainers – Decide on one method only of dividing up the data and work with that.
High Attainers – Ask them to work out the connection between the two sets of tally figures.

Plenary 5 mins
Check that the pupils have arrived at the same set of frequencies for each grouping.
Give out Copymaster 9. This is a form onto which pupils can enter their personal data. A space has been left for an additional data item. Pupils may not have all the data to hand, and can fill it in as homework. Insist that it is completed for the following day, as you will need time to collate the data, ready for Lessons 3–5.

Lesson 2

Introduction 10 mins
Review the probability scale with the pupils, placing phrases such as 'unlikely', 'certain' etc. along it. Talk about well-known events like flipping a coin and rolling a die; discuss the fact the each outcome of these events is equally likely.

Activities 25 mins
Spinners (pairs)
Each pair should make a spinner with four identical regions (a square divided by its diagonals is easy to design). These can be labelled or coloured. If you plan to pool the results later, standardise the colour schemes. Discuss the anticipated results from 100 spins of the spinner. Record these.
Pairs should now do the experiment, spinning 100 times. A narrow card triangle mounted on a drawing pin or paper fastener makes a good pointer. The results should be tallied and, perhaps, made into a bar chart.
Any pairs who have time could repeat the experiment with a different spinner design (say, three equal regions).

Differentiation
Low Attainers – Divide the spinner into 2 identical regions.
High Attainers – Experiment with non-equal divisions, predicting the results before carrying out the experiment.

Plenary 5 mins
Review the results of the experiment: see if anyone got equal numbers of 'hits' on the four regions. Discuss why the results, in general, are not exact. If there is time, the number of hits could be collected together for the whole class.

Lesson 3

Introduction **10 mins**

Give out Copymaster 10. This is a table into which the results of the class survey can be entered. It is re-used in Lessons 4 and 5. Alternatively, to save time in this lesson, you could enter the relevant data onto the form yourself, then distribute copies of the completed form to the pupils. You might want to enter the data into a spreadsheet or database in preparation for Lesson 5. However you decide to tackle it, the pupils need copies of the class data.

Remind the pupils of the meaning of mode and range. Deduce these quantities for the height data from Lesson 1. Discuss the modal class for the groupings undertaken in that lesson.

Activities **25 mins**

Processing the survey data (individual/pairs)

Pupils should calculate the mode and range of the various data items on the survey sheet. If any equal modal frequencies are found, stop the lesson and discuss multiple modes.

Differentiation

Low Attainers – Work with, say, the first 10 data rows on the sheet.

High Attainers – Group the mass and house number data and find the modal class.

Plenary **5 mins**

Compare answers. Try to find out why discrepancies have occurred.

Lesson 4

Introduction **10 mins**

Pupils will need their calculators. Remind the pupils of the meaning of median and mean. Deduce these quantities for the shoe size data.

Activities **25 mins**

Processing the survey data (individual/pairs)

Calculate the median and mean of the various numerical data items on the survey sheet.

Differentiation

Low Attainers – Work with, say, the first 10 data rows on the sheet.

High Attainers – Calculate the mean from a frequency table.

Plenary **5 mins**

Check that pupils have obtained matching results.

Lesson 5

Introduction **10 mins**

In this ICT-based lesson, you will either have prepared a spreadsheet or database of the class survey data, or the pupils will be entering the data themselves (this is counter-productive as it is not the point of the lesson). Familiarise the pupils with the data set and remind them how to call up the graphing/charting functions available.

Activities **25 mins**

Find the best graph (individual/pairs)

Pupils should pick a couple of data items and experiment with the different graph and chart types available. They should attempt to determine which chart shows the data in the clearest way and justify why they think so. Pupils could print the best charts.

Differentiation

Low Attainers – Use non-numeric data.

High Attainers – They could attempt to scatter height against mass and/or shoe size.

Plenary **5 mins**

Discuss which graphs pupils found most helpful, and which options they found they had to alter to get the best results.

Theme 6 Quadrilaterals

Objectives
- To recall the names of the different types of quadrilateral
- To ascertain and learn angle, side and symmetry properties of quadrilaterals
- To understand the relationships and connections between the different types of quadrilateral
- To explore combinations of shapes possible through superposition and juxtaposition

Vocabulary
quadrilateral, square, rectangle, rhombus, parallelogram, (isosceles) trapezium, kite, side, angle, parallel, line symmetry, rotational symmetry, triangle, pentagon, hexagon etc.

Resources
Copymasters 11 and 12 (2 copies per sheet) tracing paper, squared paper, square dot grid paper, scissors

Homework Copymaster 6

Mental maths starters 4, 9

Assessment
At the end of this theme is the pupil able to:
- Understand the relationships and connections between the different types of quadrilateral;
- Identify quadrilaterals from descriptions of their properties?

Lesson 1

Introduction — 10 mins
Brainstorm as many names of quadrilaterals as the pupils can remember. Ask pupils to sketch these on the board as you go. Pick one example *(e.g. a rhombus)*. Discuss the side, angle, line and rotational symmetry properties of the chosen quadrilateral.
Introduce or review the conventions for illustrating right angles, equal angles, equal sides, parallel lines and lines of symmetry on a diagram. Apply these to the quadrilateral under discussion.

Activities — 25 mins
Properties of quadrilaterals (individual/pairs)
The pupils should work through the various types of quadrilateral, making a careful drawing (preferably quite large) of each one and marking it up with all the relevant information. They should also write a summary of the facts as a caption to the diagram *(e.g. four equal sides etc.)*.

Differentiation
Low Attainers – Constructing the quadrilaterals out of linkable strips or on a geo-board may help.
High Attainers – Could also look at the properties of the diagonals of the quadrilaterals.

Plenary — 5 mins
Run through the properties of each quadrilateral. Any that have been missed by the pupils can be added at this stage.

Lesson 2

Introduction — 10 mins
Discuss the idea that some quadrilaterals are special examples of more general types. A good starting example is that a rhombus is a type of kite, and then to list the extra properties that are achieved when a kite 'becomes' a rhombus *(e.g. all sides become the same length, another pair of opposite angles becomes equal, there is an extra line of symmetry)*.

Activities — 25 mins
Relationships between quadrilaterals (individual/pairs)
Pupils should proceed by writing down questions such as, 'Is a rhombus a type of kite?', then working out whether the answer is yes or no. If it is 'yes', they should list the extra properties as in the introduction.

Differentiation
Low Attainers – Give them a specific list of pairs of quadrilaterals to investigate, e.g. *square/rectangle, rectangle/parallelogram etc.*
High Attainers – Could draw a 'flow diagram' showing which quadrilaterals are types of others.

Plenary — 5 mins
Run through the results, asking pupils to say which questions had 'yes' answers. Correct any errors.

Lesson 3

Introduction **10 mins**
Review plotting coordinates and associated language.

Activities **25 mins**
Practice (individual)
Give out Copymaster 11 and squared paper. This contains a variety of sets of coordinates which, if plotted and joined correctly, will produce recognisable quadrilaterals.
Investigation (pairs)
Give out some square dot grid paper (squared paper if you don't have any). The pupils have to draw as many different squares as possible. The 'catch' is, although they must use the grid points for the vertices of the squares, the sides of the squares are not allowed to be parallel to the grid lines.

Differentiation
Low Attainers – Stick to squares oriented at 45° to the grid lines.
High Attainers – Progress to drawing rotated rectangles as well.

Plenary **5 mins**
Mark the copymaster. Examine some of the efforts from the investigation. Make sure everyone has at least seen the rotated squares.

Lesson 4

Introduction **10 mins**
Give out 2 sheets of tracing paper to each pupil. Ask them to draw a large, accurate square on each sheet (both should be the same size). Place the squares exactly one on top of the other. Show how, by offsetting the two squares from one another, a new, smaller square can be created. If you have access to an OHP, it is ideal for demonstrating this.

Activities **25 mins**
Investigation (individual/pairs)
The pupils should try to make as many shapes as possible by experimenting with their squares. They should record the results.
After they have found out as much as they can using two congruent squares, pupils can work with two squares of different sizes.

This activity can be carried out using a computer graphics package.

Differentiation
Low Attainers – Restrict the activity to identical squares.
High Attainers – Extend the activity to three squares or two rhombi.

Plenary **5 mins**
Check that the pupils have been able to make right-angled and isosceles right-angled triangles, squares, rectangles and kites, and also irregular pentagons, hexagons, heptagons and octagons.

Lesson 5

Introduction **10 mins**
Give out Copymaster 12. This is best copied onto card or coloured paper. Pupils will need scissors to cut the parts out carefully. They should reassemble the square once they have cut out the pieces.

Activities **25 mins**
Tangrams (individual/pairs)
The pupils should attempt to make as many triangles, quadrilaterals etc. as they can using all the pieces. This activity can be carried out using a computer graphics package.

Differentiation
Low Attainers – Allow them to use fewer than all the pieces.
High Attainers – Aim to produce results with rotational symmetry.

Plenary **5 mins**
Demonstrate how to produce a range of shapes, with the pupils' help. On OHP is useful for this.

Theme 7 Measuring perimeters

Objectives
- To understand the concept of perimeter and to carry out measurements
- To use relationships between the sides of a shape to facilitate calculations of perimeter
- To find missing lengths

Vocabulary
perimeter, side, equal, length, millimetre, centimetre, metre, kilometre, inch, foot, yard, mile

Resources
Copymasters 13 and 14, 1 cm and 5 mm squared paper, measuring equipment (rulers, metre sticks, tape measures, trundle wheel), ordnance survey map and/or atlas

Homework Copymaster 7

Mental maths starter 3

Assessment
At the end of this theme is the pupil able to:
- Evaluate perimeters by measurement and calculation;
- Find missing lengths using available information?

Lesson 1

Introduction **5 mins**
Review the meaning of **perimeter**. Draw a few examples of shapes on the board, labelled with lengths, and discuss their perimeters.

Activities **30 mins**
Fixed perimeter (individual)
Give out 1 cm squared paper. Pupils have to design as many shapes as possible that have a perimeter of 12 cm. Advise them to begin with rectangles before they branch out into other shapes. Some pupils may think that the diagonals of the grid squares are allowable as 1 cm. If this becomes widespread, you may want to interrupt the work to discuss it (a diagonal is $\sqrt{2} \approx 1.4$ cm).

Differentiation
Low Attainers – Could simply confine themselves to rectangles.
High Attainers – Could use plain paper to design shapes that have decimal lengths. They don't need to draw them accurately but should label all measurements.

Plenary **5 mins**
Review the rectangles with whole number sides (1×5, 2×4, 3×3 etc.). Discuss whether, for example, 2×4 should be counted as different to 4×2. Ask pupils to draw some of their results on the board for everyone to see.

Lesson 2

Introduction **10 mins**
Ask the pupils to draw a rectangle 10 cm $\times$ 3 cm in their books or on squared paper. Ask them to write down what they think the perimeter is. Ask various pupils what they wrote and establish a consensus.
Ask various pupils how they arrived at the answer. Aim to draw out three methods:
- Just add all four sides in order.
- Double the length, double the width and add.
- Add the length and width, then double this.

Move on to discuss how to find an unknown side in a rectangle, where the perimeter and one side are known. Illustrate with a suitable example.
- Double the known side, subtract this from the perimeter, then halve the answer.
- Halve the perimeter and subtract the known side.

Activities **25 mins**
Practice (individual)
Give out Copymaster 13. This has a number of rectangles on it whose perimeters the pupils have to find, and some missing lengths to determine.
Growing rectangles (individual)
Give out 1 cm squared paper. Ask the pupils to draw a small rectangle and to work out its perimeter. Then ask them to draw another rectangle whose sides are exactly 1 cm outside the first rectangle and measure its perimeter. Carry on this process until a pattern emerges. Does the same happen with different starting rectangles?

Differentiation
Low Attainers – Could start with squares.
High Attainers – Could try varying the distance between the successive rectangles.

Plenary **5 mins**
Mark the copymaster and discuss the results of the investigation. Make sure that everyone has found the pattern.

Lesson 3

Introduction **10 mins**
Draw an L-shape on the board. Mark in some measurements, but not all. Discuss how it's possible to find the missing measurements by subtraction.
Use a rectangle or parallelogram to illustrate the use of peck-marks in diagrams to indicate equal lengths.

Activities **25 mins**
Practice (individual)
Give out Copymaster 14. This has a number of rectangles on it whose perimeters the pupils have to find.
Take a bite (individual)
Ask the pupils to draw any rectangle and to find its perimeter. Draw the same rectangle again, but take a rectangular 'bite' out of one corner (not the middle of a side – this is very important!). What is the perimeter of the 'L' shapes thus formed? What happens if you take another 'bite' out of a different corner? How many times can you do this? Does it work for any rectangle?

Differentiation
Low Attainers – Stick to a single 'bite'.
High Attainers – Try to explain **why** the results are as they are. Try a 'bite' out of the middle of a side.

Plenary **5 mins**
Mark the copymaster and discuss the results of the investigation. Make sure that everyone understands the rule.

Lesson 4

Introduction **10 mins**
Discuss the issues involved in measuring perimeters: having a suitable measuring instrument, recording measurements as you work, calculating the final result.
Discuss how to measure the perimeter of a curved object (tape measure or use a piece of string).

Activities **20 mins**
Practical perimeters (pairs or small groups)
Have available a number of measuring devices: rulers, metre sticks, tape measures, trundle wheel.
Decide in advance on a number of objects whose perimeters are to be determined, *e.g. book, desk, room, blackboard, hall, games court, pupil's head, outline of hand, object on Ordnance Survey map (field, village, coastline etc.).*
Make sure that some of the objects will be measured by everybody.

Differentiation
Low Attainers – Use only objects in the classroom, so that you are available to help at all times.
High Attainers – Try to determine the true perimeters for the map objects. Perhaps also use an atlas and do an American state or a country.

Plenary **10 mins**
Compare results on objects that were common to all pupils. Invite pupils to read out some of their other results. Discuss how to calculate the true perimeters of objects on the map.

Lesson 5

Introduction **10 mins**
Brainstorm as many 'old' imperial units of length as possible. See if the pupils know roughly how big each unit is. Establish the relationships between the imperial units (12 in = 1 foot, 3 ft = 1 yard, 1760 yards = 1 mile).
Construct a list of metric equivalents (1 inch = 2.54 cm so 1 cm = 0.39 in – work from this).

Activities **25 mins**
Perimeters with old units (individual, pairs or same small groups as Lesson 4)
Pooling the data from the previous lesson, convert the perimeters measured into imperial units. Pupils will have to select the most appropriate unit for each object.
Pupils will need their calculators and will need to round answers. You should determine a suitable level of accuracy for your group.

Differentiation
Low Attainers – Round all calculator displays to the nearest whole number.
High Attainers – If you have some old rulers marked in inches, they could re-measure some of the objects and compare the results with their calculations.

Plenary **5 mins**
Check the results and that people agree on the answers. If anyone has made any measurements in inches, they could present their findings.

Theme 8 Measures problems

Objectives
- To understand and use the relationships between metric units of length and mass
- To read decimal scales calibrated in units of length and mass and to estimate these quantities
- To solve open-ended length and mass problems
- To use global time zones to find the time in a different part of the world
- To use bus and train timetables

Vocabulary
millimetre, centimetre, metre, kilometre, gram, kilogram, tonne, estimate, scale, measure, weigh, second, minute, hour, time zone, timetable

Resources
Copymasters 15 and 16, kitchen and bathroom scales, local bus/train timetables

Homework Copymaster 8

Mental maths starters 1, 3, 5

Assessment
At the end of this theme is the pupil able to:
- Understand and use the relationships between metric units of length and mass, read decimal scales and estimate the size and mass of an object;
- Establish a means of approaching problems;
- Understand and use global time zones;
- Use bus and train timetables?

Lesson 1

Introduction **10 mins**
Ask what the pupils understand by **estimation**. Draw out the idea that estimation is not just guessing, but making a comparison with certain 'standard' items, such as knowing that a door is usually just over 2 m in height, that the mass of a bag of sugar is about 1 kg etc. Build up a bank of comparison objects for each unit (mm, cm, m, km, g, kg, t).

Activities **20 mins**
Estimation chain (whole class)
Work round the class in fives as follows: one pupil thinks of an object. The second picks an appropriate unit of length. The third estimates the size of the object using that unit. The fourth and fifth do the same thing with mass.
Match the measurement (pairs)
Write on the board a number of different measurements, *e.g. 3 m, 50 g, 10 km etc.* The pupils try to find as many different things as possible that match the measurements.

Differentiation
Low Attainers – Ask for just a single example for each measurement
High Attainers – Include some more 'extreme' measurements such as 1 000 000 km, 0.1 g etc.

Plenary **10 mins**
Ask pupils to read out some of their results. Use these to 'mark' the rest of the class. Proceed by asking for any additional answers.

Lesson 2

Introduction **10 mins**
Draw 4 copies of the same scale with major divisions marked 0, 1, 2, 3. Subdivide the four scales into 2, 4, 5 and 10 minor divisions respectively *(e.g. a mark every 0.5, 0.25, 0.2, 0.1)*. Discuss the differences between the scales, how relatively easy they are to use, the difficulty of interpolation (particularly on the 0.25 scale) etc.

Activities **25 mins**
Spot the scale (whole class)
Draw a variety of scales on the board. These should be 'calibrated' in various ways. Decide on a major division type *(e.g. 10 kg, 1 cm etc.)*, then use the various subdivisions. Give various pupils scale readings and ask them to come to the board to mark the positions on the correct scale.
Reverse the activity, marking the scales yourself and asking the whole class to call out the readings.
Weighing (pairs)
If you have a set of kitchen scales, pairs of pupils, in turn, could weigh two or three items while the class activity is proceeding. With a set of bathroom scales, they could weigh themselves.

Differentiation
Low Attainers – Use scales with 5 or 10 subdivisions only.
High Attainers – Could introduce a scale with 8 subdivisions.

Plenary **5 mins**
Give out the correct masses for the objects the pupils have weighed.

Lesson 3

Introduction **5 mins**
Discuss very briefly how problems involving length and mass are solved: make sure you have enough information, plan what calculations will be needed, that answers are sensible etc.

Activities **30 mins**
Hiking (pairs)
Dictate the following question:
Three friends are going hiking. They have to carry this equipment. Radio (3 kg), first aid kit (10 kg), tent (20 kg), cooking gear (5 kg), food (5 kg), maps (1 kg), water (4 kg), 3 sleeping bags (2 kg each). Who should carry what, so the weight is shared fairly?
Car park (pairs)
Dictate the following question:
A plot of land for a new car park is 30 m by 20 m. Design a plan of the car park. Remember that it should hold as many cars as possible. Cars have to be able to get in and out of the parking spaces, and in and out of the car park. Assume that a car is 3 m long and 1.5 m wide.

Differentiation
Low Attainers – Stipulate the positions of the entrance and exit.
High Attainers – Increase the size of the car park.

Plenary **5 mins**
Discuss some of the solutions to the two problems.

Lesson 4

Introduction **10 mins**
Discuss the fact that the sun rises at different times for people in different countries and why this is. Explain that, so that 12 noon is in the middle of the day for everyone and 12 midnight is in the middle of the night, different countries set their clocks to different times. The world is divided into **time zones**. Issue Copymaster 15. Discuss the meaning of the map.

Activities **25 mins**
Questions (whole class)
Invent questions for the class of increasing difficulty as follows:
It's 12 noon in London. What time is it in ...? In which city is it ... am/pm?
It's 1 pm in London. What time is it in ...? In which city is it ... am/pm?
It's ... in London. What time is it in ...? In which city is it ... am/pm?
It's 12 noon in .... What time is it London? What time is it in ...?
It's ... in .... What time is it in London? What time is it in ...?
What is the time difference between ... and ...?
Which two cities are ... hours different?

Differentiation
Low Attainers – Use the first two question lines only.
High Attainers – Could use an atlas to find the names of other places in various time zones. Could work out the relationship between longitude and time zone.

Plenary **5 mins**
With the map, review the meaning of the time zones. Discuss the international date line and what this means.

Lesson 5

Introduction **5 mins**
Give out some copies of local bus/train timetables. Discuss the way that they are organised, what the symbols mean etc.
Work through some examples of finding the length of a journey.
Work through some examples of arriving at a stop/station at a certain time, then calculating the waiting time for the next bus/train.

Activities **25 mins**
Local timetables (whole class)
Give questions to the pupils based on your local timetables. They should give the answers out loud. Examples might include: *What time does the ... from ... arrive at ...? How long does it take to get from ... to ...? If I want to be at ... by ..., what time would I leave ...?*
Other timetables (individual)
Give out Copymaster 16. This includes a class timetable, a rail timetable and a bus timetable. Questions on the school timetable might include: When does registration begin? How long is one lesson? What time is the lunch break? If you went to the dentist's and arrived at ..., what lesson would you be joining?
Give questions to the pupils based on these. They should write down the answers for later checking. It is best to prepare your questions in advance.

Differentiation
Low Attainers – Use stops on the timetables that are close to each other to ease reading.
High Attainers – Could also plan a day trip using local services.

Plenary **5 mins**
Mark the questions you set on Copymaster 16. Investigate and correct errors.

Theme 9 Problem solving

Objectives
- To employ the four operations correctly when solving real-life problems

Vocabulary
add, subtract, multiply, divide, decimal, money

Resources
Copymasters 17 and 18, calculators

Homework Copymaster 9

Mental maths starters 10, 12

Assessment
At the end of this theme is the pupil able to:
- Select the correct operation for a given question;
- Carry out necessary calculations correctly using mental, paper or calculator methods as appropriate?

Lesson 1

Introduction **10 mins**
Select a 'ceiling' number (perhaps start with 100). Answers above this number are not allowed. Give the pupils a starting number, then work round the class as follows: a pupil gives a number, the next has to decide whether to add or subtract and then carry out the calculation. Change the 'ceiling' number from time to time. You could also introduce a 'floor' number below which the answer is not allowed to drop.

Activities **25 mins**
Geometry problems (whole class)
Use geometrical facts to generate problems, e.g. *supplementary angles on a straight line adding up to 180°; angle sum of a triangle = 180°; angles round a point add up to 360°*. Use 'find the missing angle' and 'is this possible?' questions. Discuss the methods used to add and subtract mentally. Ask pupils to explain how they answered the questions.
Happy numbers (individual)
The rule for this investigation is 'square the individual digits of the number, add the squares together and write down the new number'. If the chain finishes at 1, the number is 'happy'.
Example: $\mathbf{32} \rightarrow 3^2 + 2^2 = \mathbf{13} \rightarrow 1^2 + 3^2 = \mathbf{10} \rightarrow 1^2 + 0^2 = \mathbf{1}$, so 32 is 'happy'.
Questions: Are all numbers happy? If there are any 'sad' numbers, why are they sad?

Differentiation
Low Attainers – A list of the squares for them to refer to would be useful.
High Attainers – Challenge them to make a diagram showing all the happy and sad numbers.

Plenary **5 mins**
Ask for some examples of 'happy' and 'sad' numbers. Review what happens to 'sad' numbers.

Lesson 2

Introduction **10 mins**
Discuss and demonstrate the different methods of addition and subtraction. Work through a few examples with the pupils.

Activities **25 mins**
World facts (whole class or individual)
Give out Copymaster 17. This contains a number of facts relating to countries of the world. Use it to ask questions such as 'What's the total area of…?', 'How many more people live in … than in …?' etc. This could be tackled orally, question by question, by dictation or by writing a list of questions on the board.

Differentiation
Low Attainers – Use only the smaller numbers, e.g. *the areas.*
High Attainers – Bring in some multiple calculations.

Plenary **5 mins**
Mark the questions you set. Discuss any difficulties the pupils experienced.

Lesson 3

Introduction **10 mins**
Discuss the similarities and differences between adding and subtracting whole numbers and using these operations with decimals. Work through some examples.

Activities **25 mins**
Decimal anagrams (whole class/individual)
Write the letters *S*, *T*, *A*, *I*, *N*, *E*, *D* one above the other on the board. Ask pupils for six decimal numbers. Set the letters equal to these *(e.g. S = 2.4)*. Make sure you have numbers with different amounts of 'precision', *e.g. 1, 2 and 3 decimal places*. Write simple words on the board, with the letters connected by plus and minus signs, such as *N* + *E* – *T*, for the pupils to evaluate. Allow them to make up some words of their own (the letters have been chosen to allow a large number of anagrams).

Decimal target (pairs)
Each pupil in the pair should contribute a decimal with two places. Give the class a target, *e.g. 5*. By adding and subtracting their two decimals as often as they like, the pairs have to try to make the target number.

Differentiation
Low Attainers – Confine activities to 1 or 2 decimal places.
High Attainers – Allow numbers with 3 decimal places, and/or work in threes on Decimal target, using 3 numbers.

Plenary **5 mins**
Check the answers to 'Decimal anagrams'. See who got closest to the target number and how they did it.

Lesson 4

Introduction **10 mins**
Discuss the terms **credit**, **debit** and **balance** with the pupils, and what items might appear on a bank statement in connection with them.

Activities **25 mins**
Bank statements (individual)
Give out Copymaster 18. This contains two bank statements with blanks to be calculated and filled in by the pupils.
Find them all (individual)
Using the numbers 3, 0.2 and 0.01 once each, and any operations desired, how many different answers can be made?

Differentiation
Low Attainers – Restrict the operations to addition and subtraction.
High Attainers – Could investigate what happens with other sets of starting numbers.

Plenary **5 mins**
Mark the copymaster and discuss the answers to Find them all.

Lesson 5

Introduction **5 mins**
Discuss how, sometimes, people lay long lines of coins as a way of collecting money for charity. Ask the pupils to write down the following information:

Coin	1p	2p	5p	10p	20p	50p	£1
Diameter (mm)	20.32	25.91	18.00	24.5	21.4	30.0	22.5
Mass (g)	3.56	7.13	3.25	6.5	5.0	13.5	9.5

Work through an example, *e.g. 'A line of 2p pieces is worth £32.50. How long is the line?'* Also discuss converting units at the end, as mm will not be suitable for the size of the answer. Also discuss rounding.

Activities **30 mins**
Lines of coins (whole class or individual)
Pupils will need calculators. Write or dictate questions of this type:

How long would a line of pennies worth £50 be?
How much would a line of 5p pieces 200 m long be worth?
If £652 worth of 50p pieces is collected, what does this weigh?
What would 3 kg of £1 coins be worth?
Which would make the longest line: 5 kg of pennies, 5 kg of 2p's etc.?

Differentiation
Low Attainers – Keep to simple questions where the number of coins is known or to be calculated from the amount.
High Attainers – Could draw a graph showing length of line against amount. Several coins could be represented by different lines on the same graph.

Plenary **5 mins**
Mark the questions you set. Analyse wrong answers.

Theme 10 Number sequences

Objectives
- To carry on a sequence by finding the term-to-term rule
- To find the position-to-term rule for linear sequences
- To generate terms of a sequence from a given rule
- To recognise certain well-known sequences: square numbers, triangular numbers, Fibonacci numbers

Vocabulary
sequence, position, term, difference, grow, ascending, descending

Resources
Copymasters 19 and 20

Homework Copymaster 10

Mental maths starters 1, 2, 11

Assessment
At the end of this theme is the pupil able to:
- Analyse a linear sequence, find the next term and calculate a term in any position;
- Generate terms of a sequence using a rule;
- Recognise important named sequences?

Lesson 1

Introduction **10 mins**
Revise counting up in equal whole numbers from zero, and down from a given starting point, round the class.

Activities **25 mins**
Decimal counting (whole class/group)
Count round the class in units of 0.1, 0.2, 0.3 etc.
Progress to 0.01, 0.02 etc.
Progress to 1.3, 2.1 etc.
Hidden whole numbers (individual)
Pupils should write down a number of sequences like the ones they have been counting in the previous activity and analyse how often a whole number appears. Are there any rules governing this?

Differentiation
Low Attainers – Restrict the activities to numbers with 1 decimal place.
High Attainers – Use more decimal places or more significant figures.

Plenary **5 mins**
Review the results of Hidden whole numbers. See if any pupils have formulated rules.

Lesson 2

Introduction **10 mins**
Write the first five terms of a sequence of numbers on the board whose common difference is a fixed whole number *(e.g. 2, 5, 8, 11, 14, …)*. Work through finding the 10th term with the pupils, by extending the sequence. Make sure the pupils understand the terminology: sequence, term, position etc.
Work through finding the 20th term by adding 10 times the common difference. Find the 100th term.

Activities **25 mins**
Practice (individual)
Give out the **top half** of Copymaster 19. For each sequence, the pupils have to identify the common difference, continue the sequence to 10 terms and find the 20th and 100th terms through reasoning using the common difference.
Sequence swap I (pairs)
Pupils can make up their own sequences to test each other.

Differentiation
Low Attainers/High Attainers – The copymaster is graded in difficulty. Pupils will set sequences for their partners commensurate with their abilities.

Plenary **5 mins**
Mark the copymaster. Check over any errors. 'Sequence swap' should be self-marking, but ask if there were any problems.

Lesson 3

Introduction **15 mins**

Write the first five multiples of 3 on the board as a sequence. Write the position numbers (1, 2, 3, 4, 5, ...) above the terms. Demonstrate that because the terms count up 3 times as fast as the positions, multiplying the position by 3 gives the term. Illustrate this with a function machine diagram of the form *position* $\rightarrow \times 3 \rightarrow$ *term*. Write the sequence 2, 5, 8, 11, 14, ... on the board and label the positions. Demonstrate that $\times 3$ is still required to make the numbers count up fast enough, but that an additional +2 is needed as well to get the starting number right. This yields *position* $\rightarrow \times 3 \rightarrow + 2 \rightarrow$ *term.*
Work through finding the 10th, 20th and 100th term by using the function machines on the position numbers. Try a few more examples, including some with negative differences.

Activities **20 mins**

Practice (individual)
Give out the **top half** of Copymaster 19. For each sequence, the pupils have to find the position-to-term rule and find the 10th, 20th and 100th terms by applying the rule.

Sequence swap II (pairs)
Pupils can make up their own sequences to test each other, as in lesson 2. However, they should invent the **rule** first and generate the terms from that. Check that no-one is over-complicating the rules!

Differentiation

Low Attainers/High Attainers – The copymaster is graded in difficulty. Pupils will set sequences for their partners commensurate with their abilities.

Plenary **5 mins**

Mark the copymaster. Check over any errors. 'Sequence swap' should be self-marking, but ask if there were any problems.

Lesson 4

Introduction **15–20 mins**

Give examples of sequences with differences that change in a regular way. The square and triangular numbers should be specifically mentioned: their differences are the odd numbers and the counting numbers, respectively. Ask the pupils to give you a starting number, then to make up a set of differences by working round the class. Continue each sequence on to 10 terms. Demonstrate that it is difficult to predict terms further into the sequence as the rules aren't obvious.
Give some examples of power sequences that evolve multiplicatively, such as 3, 6, 12, 24, 48, ... where each term is double the last.

Activities **15–20 mins**

Sequence swap III (pairs)
Pupils can make up their own sequences to test each other, as in Lessons 2 and 3. Pupils should merely extend their partners' sequences to the 10th term, to demonstrate that they have understood the rule in each case.

Differentiation

Low Attainers – Avoid the power sequences entirely.
High Attainers – Ask them to look at the sequence of cube numbers to see how the differences between terms work.

Plenary **5 mins**

Ask pupils to demonstrate some of the sequences they have designed. Try them out on the whole class.

Lesson 5

Introduction **5 mins**

Give out Copymaster 20. Read through the sheet with the pupils and answer any questions.

Activities **30 mins**

Investigation (individual/pairs)
The pupils should proceed to investigate the problem. You may wish to extend this over more than one lesson.

Differentiation

Low Attainers – Should simply find all the possible ways for different sized staircases.
High Attainers – Should identify the Fibonacci sequence from their results.

Plenary **5 mins**

Go over the results of the investigation and reveal the solution.

Theme 1 Negative numbers

Objectives
- To understand the meaning of negative numbers on a number line and in a simple context (temperature)
- To carry out simple calculations involving negative numbers
- To use negative values when reading and plotting coordinates

Vocabulary
positive, negative, above/below zero, minus, plus, plot, point, coordinates

Resources
Copymasters 21 and 22, squared paper, cards with positive and negative numbers on them

Homework Copymaster 11

Mental maths starters 1, 2

Assessment
At the end of this theme is the pupil able to:
- Use positions on a number line to understand negative numbers;
- Carry out additions and subtractions, starting from a negative number or yielding a negative answer;
- Read and plot coordinates in all four quadrants?

Lesson 1

Introduction — 10 mins
Draw a line on the board. Mark 0 in the centre and add marks for 1, 2, 3, 4, 5 etc. Discuss with the pupils what belongs on the other half of the line. Add negative number marks.

Activities — 25 mins
Number lines (whole class)
Give out Copymaster 21. The centre mark is longer on each line to make it easy to find. Give the pupils a number with which to label the centre line, then give the gap between divisions on the scale. They then have to label the rest of the line. For example, centre 0, gap 2 on the first line would give {−10, −8, −6, −4, −2, **0**, 2, 4, 6, 8, 10}. Repeat for other lines. Use more copies of the sheet if you wish.

Differentiation
Low Attainers – Always centre on zero and use whole numbers.
High Attainers – Use decimal values, and large numbers.

Plenary — 5 mins
Mark the number lines. Discuss any difficulties.

Lesson 2

Introduction — 10 mins
Issue a number of pupils with cards bearing a selection of positive and negative numbers. Ask them to stand at the front of the class. Other pupils should suggest one movement at a time that will bring the numbers into the right order.
Introduce or revise the order symbols < (less than) and > (greater/more than).

Activities — 25 mins
More or less? (whole class)
Ask pairs of pupils for two numbers, positive or negative. Write them on the board in such a way that the correct order symbol can be inserted between them, then ask the whole class to say which symbol, 'less than' or 'greater/more than', should go between the numbers. Repeat for different number pairs.

Ordering (whole class/individual)
Draw four large ovals on the board. Work round the class, each pupil supplying a positive or negative number until you have 6–8 numbers in each oval. Pupils should then work to put the numbers from each oval into order.

Differentiation
Low Attainers – Use whole numbers of small magnitude.
High Attainers – Use larger numbers and decimals or fractions.

Plenary — 5 mins
Check the answers to 'Ordering'.

Lesson 3

Introduction **10 mins**
Draw a number line on the board, or pupils could use their completed number lines from Lesson 1. Ask various questions about the difference between two numbers chosen from the line.

Activities **25 mins**
Temperature differences (whole class)
Write this data on the board:

London 6°C	Cape Town 21°C
Leningrad −13°C	Sydney 27°C
Helsinki −7°C	Tokyo 14°C
Mexico City 31°C	Shackleton (Antarctica) −36°C

Ask various questions, e.g. *'What's the difference in temperature between …?', 'How much colder is … than …?' etc.*

Matching differences (individual)
Ask the pupils to make lists of pairs of numbers with a given difference. For each difference, they should ensure that they have at least two pairs where the numbers are both positive, two where they are both negative and two where they are of opposite sign, e.g. *difference 10 could give (3, 13), (1, 11); (−6, −16), (−2, −12); (−5, 5), (−8, 2).*

Differentiation
Low Attainers – Restrict differences to small numbers.
High Attainers – Use decimals as well as integers.

Plenary **5 mins**
Ask pupils to call out some of their answers to 'Matching differences'. Mark by swapping with a partner.

Lesson 4

Introduction **10 mins**
Use a number line to illustrate the results of calculations $a + b$ and $a - b$, where a can be positive or negative but b must be positive.

Activities **25 mins**
Calculations (whole class)
Ask a number of questions of the above type. Pupils may give the answers out loud or may write them down. Mark them before moving on.
What's the question? (individual)
Give the pupils a number of answers. They have to produce three questions for each answer, as defined in the introduction, e.g. $3 = 1 + 2 = 6 - 3 = -4 + 7$. A negative starting number with a subtraction will never give a positive answer, so this type is ruled out.

Differentiation
Low Attainers – Keep the numbers small.
High Attainers – Use larger numbers and decimals.

Plenary **5 mins**
Ask pupils to call out some of their answers to 'What's the question?'. Mark by swapping with a partner.

Lesson 5

Introduction **10 mins**
Draw a small 4-quadrant coordinate grid on the board. Mark various points in each quadrant. The pupils should call out the coordinates of points you indicate.
Ask individuals to come to the board and mark points whose coordinates you give them.

Activities **25 mins**
Practice (individual)
Give out Copymaster 22. Pupils should follow the instructions to read and plot coordinates on the grid.
Diagonal lines (individual/pairs)
Pupils will need to draw a coordinate grid like that on Copymaster 22. They should plot and join the points (−7, 10) and (10, −7) to make a straight line. They should investigate the coordinates of points along this line. When they have found the connection, they should draw another, parallel, line on the grid and test to see if the rule works for points on this line.

Differentiation
Low Attainers – Just find the rule for the first line.
High Attainers – Could try lines perpendicular to those already drawn.

Plenary **5 mins**
Mark the copymaster and see if pupils have found the rule from the investigation.

Theme 2 Multiplication and division

Objectives

- To consolidate written methods of multiplying and dividing by a single digit
- To multiply by two-digit numbers, by using their factors split the calculation into two or more stages
- To appreciate the effect of bracketing parts of a calculation

Vocabulary

multiply, divide, times, factor, decimal, digit, place, column, digit sum (digital root)

Resources

Copymasters 23 and 24, calculators

Homework Copymaster 12

Mental maths starters 6, 7, 8, 11

Assessment

At the end of this theme is the pupil able to:

- Multiply and divide numbers of any size, including decimals, by a single digit;
- Split up calculations involving multiplication by invoking factorisation;
- Carry out calculations involving brackets?

Lesson 1

Introduction **10 mins**

Stress that multiplying two digits by a single digit should always be done mentally. Do a few examples with the pupils.

Discuss the grid method of multiplying a three-digit number by a single digit, *e.g.* 542×8:

×	500	40	2
2	**4000**	**320**	**16**

4000 + 320 + 16 = **4336**

Extend the method to four-digit numbers and beyond. This lesson consolidates previous work.

Activities **25 mins**

Make a million (individual)

Start with 2. Double it. Double this answer. Double that etc. until the total exceeds a million. How many doublings are needed? The first few can be done mentally, then the grid method can be used.

Go on to 3. Multiply by 3. Multiply by 3 again etc. How many times do you have to multiply to make a million? Work through more numbers and record the results in a table. Is there a pattern?

Differentiation

Low Attainers – Differentiation will be by degree of progress and accuracy of results.

High Attainers – Could make a graph of starting number against number of multiplications.

Plenary **5 mins**

Check the results of the investigation.

Lesson 2

Introduction **10 mins**

Work through some examples of short multiplication in columns. Check that the pupils understand the principles involved. Make sure to include some decimals.

Introduce or revise the concept of digit sum or digital root.

Activities **25 mins**

Digit sums (individual)

Pupils should begin with any two-digit integer, then multiply it by its digit sum. Multiply this number by **its** digit sum, and so on until a pattern has developed. Try different starting numbers. What rules operate?

Differentiation

Low Attainers – Simply carry out the multiplications.

High Attainers – Obtain an answer for starting numbers with any given digital root.

Plenary **5 mins**

The pupils can use their calculators to check their answers by division.

Lesson 3

Introduction **10 mins**

Pick an example three-digit number. With the pupils, work through demonstrating that multiplication by 6 can be achieved by first doubling, then multiplying by 3, or vice versa. Discuss the implications. Repeat the demonstration using a decimal starting number.
Remind the pupils that multiplication by 10, 100 etc. is straightforward.

Activities **25 mins**

Chain multiplication (individual)
Give out Copymaster 23. This asks the pupils to design strategies for multiplying by a two-digit number, by using its single-digit factors.

Differentiation

Low Attainers – Will need help in deciding which combinations of numbers will work.
High Attainers – Could be asked to design strategies for some larger multipliers and test them.

Plenary **5 mins**

Pupils can check their answers with a calculator, by division.

Lesson 4

Introduction **10 mins**

Review the techniques used in short division, emphasising the need for good knowledge of multiplication tables. Use at least one example with an integer answer (*e.g.* $364 \div 7 = 52$), then move on to divisions with remainders presented as the fractional part of the answer (*e.g.* $360 \div 7 = 51\frac{3}{7}$). Remember to do some examples where the fraction needs to be cancelled at the end (*e.g.* $1144 \div 6 = 190\frac{4}{6} = 190\frac{2}{3}$).

Activities **25 mins**

Practice (individual)
Give out Copymaster 24. This contains a mixture of questions with integer and mixed fractional answers.
Self-testing (pairs)
Pupils should now have the idea of how the questions from the copymaster are structured. They should make up their own pairs of questions and try them out on a neighbour.

Differentiation

Low Attainers – Some guidance in choosing divisors may be needed.
High Attainers – Could try to produce some triple chains.

Plenary **5 mins**

Mark the copymaster. Pupils can check the answers to 'Self-testing'.

Lesson 5

Introduction **10 mins**

Remind pupils of the precedence order of operations. Demonstrate how this can be interfered with using brackets: use a combination of +/− with × at first.
Also discuss what happens with bracket combinations of the types $a \div (b \times c)$ and $a \div (b \div c)$.

Activities **25 mins**

Number crunching (individual)
Give the pupils 3 numbers, say, 2, 3 and 4. Using any operations and one pair of brackets, the pupils have to generate as many different answers as possible. Non-integer division results should be presented as fractions.

Differentiation

Low Attainers – Will not be expected to try all combinations in a logical order.
High Attainers – Should find all 24 possible answers.

Plenary **5 mins**

Check the results of the investigation. Pupils could check each other's calculations. See who has found the greatest number of different answers (24 are theoretically possible, though some choices of starting number may introduce duplication).

Theme 3 Money problems

Objectives
- To use the four operations with money in a variety of contexts
- To round amounts to the nearest penny where appropriate

Vocabulary
pounds, pence, add, subtract, multiply, divide, round, balance income, expenditure, quantity

Resources
Copymaster 25 (divided into two halves: **(a)** Balance sheet and **(b)** Order form) and Copymaster 26 (divided into two halves: **(a)** Lottery winners and **(b)** Funny money), and plastic or card money, imitation banknotes, catalogues

Homework Copymaster 13

Mental maths starter 12

Assessment
At the end of this theme is the pupil able to:
- Select the correct operation to tackle a problem involving money;
- Round answers to the nearest penny where appropriate?

Lesson 1

Introduction **10 mins**
Review the decimal representation of amounts of money. Go over decimal addition and subtraction on the board, using amounts with three digits of pounds, and pence. Introduce/revise the terms **income** and **expenditure**.

Activities **25 mins**
Balance sheet (individual)
Give out Copymaster 25(a). Pupils should copy this into their books or onto paper, then calculate the missing amounts. If the pupils have previously completed the Bank statements activity (Autumn Term, Theme 9, Lesson 4), they will find the context reasonably familiar.

Differentiation
By outcome.

Plenary **5 mins**
Mark the copymaster.

Lesson 2

Introduction **10 mins**
Ask for the 100-complements of various numbers. All pupils should answer out loud, simultaneously. So '32' would yield the response '68', 75 would yield '25' etc.

Activities **25 mins**
Change (whole class)
Work round the class as follows: one pupil states an amount of money up to £10; the next pupil gives the amount that is to be tendered (£5 or £10); the next gives the change from that amount.
After a fair amount of practice, increase the limit to a maximum of £20 (or £50 if this is suitable for your group).
Efficient coins (pairs)
Each pupil needs a set of coins: 1p, 2 × 2p, 5p, 10p, 2 × 20p, 50p, 4 × £1

The first player makes an amount with his/her coins; the second has to make the change for this amount from £5. Players should check together that the total value of all the coins played is £5. If it is not, the first player scores a point. Repeat, with the roles reversed, then carry on. The winner is the player who has made the fewest mistakes!

Differentiation
Low Attainers – Make the total in Efficient coins £1 or £2.
High Attainers – Add £5, £10, 2 × £20 notes to the 'arsenal': the pupils can choose an arbitrary number of pounds as the total (not necessarily a note value).

Plenary **5 mins**
Go over the rules for calculating change (i.e. the pence sum to 100 and the pounds to one less than the required total). Discuss any difficulties encountered in the game.

Lesson 3

Introduction **10 mins**
Revise multiplication of money as decimal column multiplication (though pupils may, of course, use the grid method if they prefer it).
Do some oral exercises with the class where they have to calculate a multiple of an amount 1p short of a whole number of pounds.

Activities **25 mins**
Order form I (individual)
Give out Copymaster 25(b). This is a standard order form where item totals and a grand total are to be calculated.
Order form II (pairs)
Pupils should design their own order forms, then give them to a neighbour to complete.

Differentiation
Low Attainers – Use the same items and prices as on the copymaster.
High Attainers – Use a real catalogue as the basis for their work.

Plenary **5 mins**
Mark the copymaster. Pupils can mark each other's work from Order form II.

Lesson 4

Introduction **10 mins**
Revise division of money as decimal short division.
Decide what to do when the number of pence is not an integer.

Activities **25 mins**
Lottery syndicates (individual)
Give out Copymaster 26(a). Pupils should work out how much money each member of the syndicate wins.
Share a million (individual)
Work out how much each person would win if £1 000 000 were divided equally between various numbers of people.

Differentiation
Low Attainers – Do not go beyond 10 winners in Share a million.
High Attainers – Could work out what the nearest amount is to that given on the copymaster, that would give a whole number of pounds to each winner.

Plenary **5 mins**
Mark the copymaster and the amounts from 'Share a million'.

Lesson 5

Introduction **5 mins**
Discuss the fact that different countries use different currencies. Ask for names of currencies and whether the pupils know which countries they belong to.

Activities **20 mins**
Funny money I (individual)
Give out Copymaster 26(b). Pupils will need their calculators.
Funny money II (pairs)
Pupils could make up their own Country and Currency, answering similar questions to those above.

Differentiation
Low Attainers – Adjust the Monar exchange rate to be more 'pupil-friendly', e.g. *M̶1 = £1.25.*
High Attainers – Produce a currency conversion graph.

Plenary **10 mins**
Mark the set questions and review what the pupils have invented themselves. If you have some extra time, the pupils could present their currencies to the rest of the class.

Theme 4 Fractions and decimals

Objectives

- To find equivalent fractions and cancel to lowest terms.
- To calculate fractions of quantities
- To change a set of fractions to a common denominator and thereby order them
- To change terminating decimals to fractions in lowest terms

Vocabulary

fraction, numerator, denominator, equivalent, improper, mixed, cancel, simplify, decimal place, convert, order

Resources

Copymasters 27 and 28, cards with fractions and decimals written on them, dice

Homework Copymaster 14

Mental maths starters 1, 7, 8, 12

Assessment

At the end of this theme is the pupil able to:

- Find equivalent fractions, convert decimals to fractions and order sets of fractions;
- Calculate a fraction of a quantity?

Lesson 1

Introduction **10 mins**

Ask the pupils to draw fraction diagrams to illustrate a number of simple fractions you give them. Include some fractions that are equivalent to each other. Use these to discuss/revise the meaning of equivalent fractions.

Activities **25 mins**

Dicey fractions (pairs)

Each pair needs two dice. Taking turns, pupils roll both dice twice to make a fraction. The first roll gives the numerator, the second gives the denominator. Pupils should note down the fractions as they are made, and rewrite them in lowest terms if possible. Score as follows: pupil cancels fraction to lowest terms, 1 point; lowest terms is also a unit fraction, 2 points; fraction is improper, 1 point. If the fraction is proper and already in lowest terms, the opponent can score a bonus point by naming correctly any equivalent fraction. Set a winning target, say 20 points. Play best of three if there is time.

Differentiation

Low Attainers – Use a single die.

High Attainers – Could use three dice, or use the product of two dice instead of the sum.

Plenary **5 mins**

Review who won the games. Find out who had the fraction with the biggest denominator, the smallest etc., who got the biggest integer (6 is possible) etc.

Lesson 2

Introduction **10 mins**

Give a group of five pupils cards with the fractions $\frac{1}{2}, \frac{3}{4}, \frac{2}{5}, \frac{7}{10}, \frac{3}{5}$ written on them. Ask them to stand in front of the class, in the order given. Discuss with the class the fact that the only way to put the fractions into order easily is to convert them to the same type. Introduce/revise the term **common denominator**. Ask which denominator will be best. Suggestions of 40, 100 etc. may come up. Stress that you want to find the smallest number that will work, to keep the calculations easy. When 20 has been agreed on, each pupil can write the equivalent fraction on the back of the card and display it to the class ($\frac{10}{20}, \frac{15}{20}, \frac{8}{20}, \frac{14}{20}, \frac{12}{20}$). The pupils can then ask them to change places until the fractions are in the right order. They should then re-display the original side of their cards.

Activities **25 mins**

Choosing denominators (whole class/group)

Give out Copymaster 27. With the class, choose the correct denominators for the first two questions. Work through the conversion and ordering with them.

Practice (individual)

The pupils have to order the fractions on the sets of flags.

Differentiation

By outcome.

Plenary **5 mins**

Mark the copymaster. Review any difficulties the pupils experienced.

Lesson 3

Introduction **10 mins**

Discuss how to find a unit fraction by division. Make up examples such as '$\frac{1}{5}$ of £30', '$\frac{1}{4}$ of 20 kg' etc. The pupils should reply together, out loud.
Discuss how to find non-unit fractions, by division and subsequent multiplication. Carry on with similar examples.

Activities **25 mins**

Investigation (individual/pairs)

Specify an answer (12 is a good starter). Pupils should try to make as many fraction statements as possible with this answer, such as '$\frac{1}{2}$ of 24', '$\frac{3}{4}$ of 16' etc. Set a target of, say, 10 statements. Pupils could then pick their own answer, find as many statements as possible that fit it, and try it out on a neighbour.

Differentiation

Low Attainers – Set a lower target, say half a dozen statements.
High Attainers – Could try a decimal answer, *e.g. 4.5*.

Plenary **5 mins**

Review and mark the results for '12', then get the pupils to mark each others' efforts.

Lesson 4

Introduction **10 mins**

The object of the lesson is to convert decimals into fractions. Review the meaning of decimals with 1 decimal place, *e.g.* $0.1 = \frac{1}{10}$, $0.2 = \frac{2}{10} = \frac{1}{5}$ *etc.*
Move on to 2 decimal places. Present these as $\frac{?}{10} + \frac{?}{100}$, or directly as $\frac{?}{100}$. Cancel to lowest terms.
Do a couple of examples with 3 decimal places.

Activities **25 mins**

Pick a decimal (whole class)

Get the pupils to invent decimals with up to 3 decimal places.
Write these on the board, with enough space to do the conversions.
Work round the class, asking pupils to perform various stages of the conversion to fractions. Pupils can copy these when they are correct, for future reference.

'Consecutive' decimals (individual)

Each pupil should pick five 'consecutive' two decimal place numbers *(e.g. 0.34, 0.35, 0.36, 0.37, 0.38)* and convert them to fractions. How many are already in lowest terms? How many cancel? Try it with a different 'consecutive' set. Are the answers the same?
Try the same exercise with 3 decimal place numbers.

Differentiation

Low Attainers – Try 1dp 'consecutive' decimals.
High Attainers – Try more decimal places, or try a run of ten.

Plenary **5 mins**

Mark 'Consecutive' decimals.

Lesson 5

Give a group of five pupils cards with the following fractions and decimals on them: $\frac{3}{5}$, 0.64, 0.61, $\frac{2}{3}$, 0.66. Ask them to stand in front of the class, in the order given. Explain that, to put the amounts into order, the decimals should be converted to fractions, then the fractions compared using a common denominator as in Lesson 2. When 300 has been agreed on, each pupil can write the equivalent fraction on the back of the card and display it to the class ($\frac{180}{300}, \frac{192}{300}, \frac{183}{300}, \frac{200}{300}, \frac{198}{300}$). The pupils can then ask them to change places until the fractions are in the right order. They should then redisplay the original side of their cards.

Activities **25 mins**

Choosing denominators (whole class/group)

Give out Copymaster 28. With the class, choose the correct denominators for the first question. Work through the conversion and ordering with them.

Practice (individual)

The pupils have to order the fractions and decimals on each belt.

Differentiation

By outcome.

Plenary **5 mins**

Mark the copymaster. Review any difficulties the pupils experienced.

Theme 5 Measuring angles

Objectives
- To estimate angles and measure them to the nearest degree
- To draw angles to the same accuracy
- To understand that the angle sum of a triangle is 180° and to use this fact to determine unknown angles
- To carry out rotations of shapes that are multiples of 90°, around their vertices

Vocabulary
angle, vertex, arm, degree, estimate, measure, protractor, base, baseline, centre, scale, acute, right, obtuse, straight, reflex, round, triangle, angle sum, rotation, centre of rotation, rotational symmetry

Resources
Copymasters 29 and 30, tracing paper, squared paper, geo-strips, isometric paper, protractors, OHP useful

Homework Copymaster 15

Mental maths starter 4

Assessment
At the end of this theme is the pupil able to:
- Estimate, draw and measure angles;
- Use the angle sum of a triangle to determine unknown angles;
- Carry out and recognise rotations through multiples of 90° with varying centres?

Lesson 1

Introduction **10 mins**
Pupils need geo-strips, a pair of 30 cm rulers, or 2 pencils. Discuss the meaning of angle as turn. Work through the different types of angle using the strips (acute, right, obtuse, straight, reflex, round) and the ranges of numbers of degrees these involve. The pupils should copy your movements.
Revise/introduce the terminology **vertex (vertices)** and **arms**.

Activities **25 mins**
Shapes to order (individual/pairs)
Give the pupils various sets of instructions for drawing shapes.
Examples: *a triangle with one obtuse angle, a pentagon with two reflex angles, a quadrilateral with two right angles, two right-angled triangles joined along a side etc.*

The pupils can work in pairs, devising sets of instructions for each other.

Differentiation
Low Attainers – Restrict the activity to triangles and quadrilaterals.
High Attainers – Use greater numbers of sides in polygons.

Plenary **5 mins**
Draw examples of the shapes you defined for the pupils to mark from. Ask if anyone produced impossible instructions. If not, devise some *(e.g. a quadrilateral with 3 obtuse angles)*.

Lesson 2

Introduction **15–20 mins**
Issue the pupils with tracing paper. They should draw a cross on it, then roughly bisect the right angles, giving eight 45° angles. They should be able to estimate angles to within 10° using this. Practise this with a few angles on paper, then draw some angles on the board and tell the pupils that they are to **imagine** the tracing paper being used.
Revise/introduce the **base**, **centre** and **scales** of the protractor. A board protractor would be useful for demonstration. Draw some angles on the board and measure them. Emphasise the need to estimate first, so that they know which scale to read. The pupils should now measure accurately the angles they drew for estimation purposes earlier.
Discuss measuring reflex angles. Some pupils will have circular protractors; others will need to subtract from 360°.

Activities **15–20 mins**
Estimating and measuring (pairs)
Each pupil should draw ten angles, covering all types. These should then be estimated by the other member of the pair and returned. The first pupil should then measure them accurately. For each angle, they should then work out the difference between the estimated and actual angle. The total of these ten differences is a rating of how good the second pupil's estimations have been. For example, a total of 100° or less is excellent, over 300° is not very good. Any 'silly' totals may mean that reflex angles have been wrongly dealt with.

Differentiation
Low Attainers – Omit reflex angles and/or allow them to use their tracing paper.
High Attainers – After the main activity, investigate the fact that angles at a point add up to 360°.

Plenary **5 mins**
Review the pupils' scores from 'Estimating and measuring'. Investigate any very high totals.

Lesson 3

Introduction **10 mins**
Demonstrate drawing angles using a protractor: baseline, radial mark from protractor scale, draw second arm. It is recommended that pupils do not measure from the end of the baseline, but put a small reference mark **near** the end and measure from there. This improves accuracy considerably.

Activities **25 mins**
Drawing angles (individual)
Give the pupils a range of angles to draw, including reflex angles.

Differentiation
Low Attainers – Omit reflex angles.
High Attainers – Could draw some triangles, given a baseline of 10 cm and an angle at either end.

Plenary **5 mins**
Pupils should mark each others' work by careful measuring. A cumulative difference score like that in Lesson 2 could be awarded.

Lesson 4

Introduction **10 mins**
Ask the pupils to draw two different triangles, one acute-angled, one obtuse-angled, and to measure the angles carefully. They may want to turn their work round so that one arm of the angle being measured always appears 'horizontal'. Ask them to total the angles in each case. Carry out a survey of the results.
Discuss the fact that, with very careful measuring, the total should always be 180°.
Do a couple of examples of using this to find missing angles in triangles. Include an example of an isosceles triangle where both base angles are missing.

Activities **25 mins**
Practice (individual)
Give out Copymaster 29. The pupils have to measure and verify the 180° total in some triangles, then calculate missing angles in other triangles.

Investigation (individual)
Pupils should draw a number of different quadrilaterals and find the angle sum by measurement.

Differentiation
High Attainers – Could look at pentagons/hexagons if time allows.

Plenary **5 mins**
Mark the copymaster. Check the results of the investigation for closeness to 360°.

Lesson 5

Introduction **10 mins**
An Ottp is ideal for demonstrating rotations.
Give each pupil a piece of tracing paper and some squared paper. They should draw an 'L' shape on the squared paper and trace it onto the tracing paper.
Superimposing the tracing paper on the squared paper, select one vertex of the 'L' shape and 'fix' it by placing a pencil point onto it. Introduce the term **centre of rotation**. The pupils can now rotate the shape about that vertex. They should draw the image after rotations of 90°, 180° and 270°, giving a design with fourfold rotational symmetry (point this out). They should repeat this for the other vertices, making a fresh diagram each time.

Activities **25 mins**
Rotating (individual)
Give out Copymaster 30. This specifies various other shapes for rotation. The pupils should copy the shapes and repeat the introductory exercise for each. Larger versions of these diagrams could make an interesting display.
Outside points (individual)
Pupils can investigate the effect of different centres of rotation on their shapes. Points inside the shape tend to produce confusing and crowded pictures, but those outside are comparatively easy to draw.

Differentiation
Low Attainers – Just use vertices of the shapes as centres of rotation.
High Attainers – Investigate rotations on isometric paper.

Plenary **5 mins**
Mark the work: pupils could hold up their designs as these are easy to check for rotational symmetry, or a neighbour could check them.

Theme 6 Area

Objectives

- To use the formula for the area of a rectangle, and find unknown sides, given the area and another side
- To find areas of simple shapes made from rectangles
- To find areas of right-angled triangles

Vocabulary

area, covers, surface, rectangle, side, edge, length, width, height, triangle, square, millimetre, centimetre, metre, kilometre, mm^2, cm^2, m^2, km^2

Resources

Copymasters 31 and 32, measuring equipment (rulers, tapes, trundle wheel), square dot grid paper, plain paper, 2 mm graph paper, digit cards

Homework Copymaster 16

Mental maths starters 3, 7, 9

Assessment

At the end of this theme is the pupil able to:

- Calculate areas of rectangles and right-angled triangles;
- Calculate unknown sides in rectangles, given the area and the other side;
- Calculate areas of shapes made by combining up to 3 rectangles, or by removing one rectangular area from another?

Lesson 1

Introduction **10 mins**

Check that the pupils understand the concept of area and the units involved. Draw a rectangle representing 5 cm by 4 cm on the board. Divide this into unit squares. Discuss the fact that the area can be evaluated by counting the squares. Ask if anyone knows an easier way to work out the area. Check that the pupils remember how to use the area formula as follows: draw some rectangles with measurements. Ask the pupils to raise their hands if they think an area is: >10 cm^2, >20 cm^2 etc. until the correct area is arrived at.

Activities **25 mins**

Measure an object (whole class)

Pick an object such as an exercise book. Ask the pupils to measure and record the length and width. They should then calculate the area, and round to the nearest cm^2. Check that answers are similar across the class.

Rectangles around the class or school (pairs)

Give the pupils a list of rectangular objects. There should be a range of small desktop items *(e.g. book, eraser, pencil case, calculator)*, larger classroom objects *(e.g. board, wall, window, desk, computer monitor)*, and possibly outdoor items *(netball court, dining room etc.)*.

They should record the length and width of each object (perhaps in a suitable table), then calculate its area, rounding to a suitable degree of accuracy. Calculators may be used.

Differentiation

Low Attainers – Prepare a number of cut-out rectangles with whole-unit sides.

High Attainers – Estimate the areas before any measurements are made.

Plenary **5 mins**

Compare results for the same objects across the class. Try to find out the cause of any anomalous results.

Lesson 2

Introduction **10 mins**

Draw a diagram on the board to illustrate this problem: 'Mary wants to build a rectangular pig pen for Snorter, her pet pig. She is going to use the wall of the cow shed as one side of the pen. She has 35 m of wire netting for the other three sides, and as many posts as she needs. How wide should the pen be to give Snorter the most space?'

Choose a width for the pen, say 3 m. Discuss how to calculate the length (29 m) of the pen once a width has been decided, then work out the area (87 m^2).

Activities **25 mins**

Solve the pig pen problem (individual/pairs)

Pupils should investigate the effect of different pen widths on the length, and therefore the area.

Differentiation

Low Attainers – Use a shorter length of netting, *e.g. 12 m, to start with.*

High Attainers – Find a more accurate solution using a decimal search, and generalise the solution to deal with any available length of netting.

Plenary **5 mins**

Discuss the results. Those who found the best integer solution will have a pen $9\text{ m} \times 17\text{ m}$, having area 153 m^2. The exact solution to the problem is $8.75\text{ m} \times 17.5\text{ m}$, having area 153.125 m^2. Discuss this if time allows. The general solution for any length of netting is a rectangle $\frac{1}{4}$ the length by $\frac{1}{2}$ the length.

Lesson 3

Introduction **10 mins**

Pupils need digit cards. Draw a rectangle on the board. Mark inside it '24 cm^2'. Ask the pupils to hold up cards that could be the length and width of the rectangle. Replace '24 cm^2' with '50 cm^2'. Repeat the exercise. Discuss how the pupils knew what to hold up.
Repeat with other areas. Specify lengths or width and ask the pupils to find the other measurements.

Activities **25 mins**

Practice (individual)

Issue Copymaster 31. The pupils are asked to calculate missing lengths and widths, then to use their answers to calculate the perimeters of the rectangles. The last three questions involve a mixture of units.

Investigation (individual or pairs)

Draw a rectangle on the board. Mark inside it '180 cm^2'. Ask the pupils to find as many rectangles as they can with this area. Which one has the smallest perimeter? Which one has the largest perimeter?

Differentiation

Low Attainers – Omit questions 9–12 from the copymaster. Reduce the area of the rectangle in the investigation to a number with fewer factors, say 100 cm^2.
High Attainers – Find a more accurate solution to the smallest perimeter using a decimal search. Investigate the largest perimeter more fully.

Plenary **5 mins**

Mark the copymaster and compare the results of the investigation. Discuss the fact that the smallest perimeter is not given by a whole number at all, and that the perimeter can be made as large as you like by choosing smaller and smaller widths.

Lesson 4

Introduction **15 mins**

Draw an 'L' shape on the board, with all measurements marked. Discuss how it can be split up into rectangles (two ways into 2, one way into 3). Work through the area calculation with the class.
Using two dotted lines, mark the extended sides required to see the 'outer' rectangle of which the 'L' shape is part. Discuss how the area can be calculated as a rectangle with a rectangular 'bite' taken out.
Repeat for a 'U' shape.

Activities **15 mins**

Initials (individual)

Ask everyone to draw their initials in rough, using combinations of rectangles.
Issue square dotted grid paper (squared paper will do, but makes it too easy to count squares!). Ask everyone to draw their initial designs neatly onto the paper. They should then mark all the measurements carefully and calculate the area of each letter.

Differentiation

Low Attainers – Specify some letters with simple decompositions, such as C, J, L, O, T, U.
High Attainers – Use plain paper, or 2 mm graph paper.

Plenary **10 mins**

Go through the alphabet, asking pupils who used each letter, how they drew it and how they decomposed it to evaluate the area.

Lesson 5

Introduction **10 mins**

Prepare some card or paper rectangles. Draw a diagonal on one side of each. Show the rectangle to the pupils, keeping the side with the marked diagonal towards you. Tell the pupils that the width is 10 cm and the height 5 cm, then ask them what the area is.
Cut the rectangle in two along the marked diagonal. Discuss the fact that the two resulting triangles are congruent and right-angled, and that each must have half the area of the rectangle.
Repeat this for other rectangles, giving new measurements each time.
Discuss the resulting method for finding the area of a right-angled triangle.

Activities **25 mins**

Practice (individual)

Issue Copymaster 32. The pupils are asked to calculate the areas of a number of triangles. Questions 10–12 involve combining triangles.

Investigation (pairs)

Ask the pupils to find as many right-angled triangles as they can with an area of 12 cm^2.

Differentiation

Low Attainers – Omit question 8 and questions 10–12.
High Attainers – Discuss the implications of questions 11 and 12. Ask them to see if they can discover a rule that will work for triangles like this.

Plenary **5 mins**

Discuss the results of the investigation. Ask pupils how they arrived at their results and what the relationship is between the two measurements of each triangle.

Theme 7 Mass

Objectives
- To understand and use the metric system of mass units
- To know and use common imperial equivalents and to construct conversion graphs
- To carry out calculations involving masses

Vocabulary
metric, mass, weight, gram, kilogram, tonne, milligram, imperial, ounce, pound, stone, ton, conversion graph

Resources
Copymasters 33 and 34, scrap paper, weighing scales, sealed envelopes containing scrap paper, list of current postal charges

Homework Copymaster 17

Mental maths starters 1, 3

Assessment
At the end of this theme is the pupil able to:
- Convert between metric units of mass and decide which is the most appropriate for a given measurement;
- Use imperial units and convert to and from metric units;
- Select the correct operations to solve problems involving mass?

Lesson 1

Introduction **10 mins**
Brainstorm the different units of mass. Divide them into two groups: **metric** and **imperial**. Keep the list of imperial units for use in Lessons 4 and 5.
Discuss the relationships between the different metric units, perhaps drawing up a table. Be sure to include tonnes and milligrams.

Activities **25 mins**
Equivalence chains (whole class)
A pupil starts with a mass. The next few pupils give its equivalents in as many different units as possible. An example might be, '15 kg', '15 000 g', '0.015 t'. You can prompt pupils with any units that have been missed out. Start with amounts with only one significant figure.
Ordering masses (pairs)
Discuss briefly how to order a group of masses by converting them all to the same type of unit. Pupils need small pieces of scrap paper. Each member of the pair contributes three masses written on three scraps. The six masses are then mixed up and laid out on the table at random. The pupils should agree on what unit will be best to work in for the comparison. They should then convert each mass to the correct unit and write it on the back of each scrap. These can then be ordered on the table, and the scraps turned over again when the ordering is complete. Pupils should then record the answer. Encourage them to make things harder by using large and small numbers, and ones with similar groups of significant figures.

Differentiation
Pair pupils by ability.

Plenary **5 mins**
Review the metric units and their relationships.
Ask the pupils to describe their work to the rest of the class, or write their masses on the board and work through the ordering with the class.

Lesson 2

Introduction **10 mins**
Review the use of scales for weighing. Write a few examples of scales on the board. Point to positions on the scales and ask pupils to read the value at each position. Give readings to various pupils and ask them to indicate the correct point on the relevant scale.

Activities **25 mins***
Weighing (small groups)
Decide on a list of objects that are to be weighed. These can include common classroom objects such as books, pens, bags etc., the pupils themselves, their shoes, a football, and so on. You could also prepare some special 'benchmark' objects for them to measure, such as a model made from cubes or a bottle of water. Pupils will need to rotate through using the various weighing devices.
Postal charges (pairs)
Prepare some envelopes containing varying amounts of scrap paper. These should be sealed and labelled 'Package A', 'Package B' etc. Pairs of pupils should weigh the packages carefully, then consult a list of current postal rates to determine how much it would cost to post each one (1st and 2nd class). *This activity will need to be split over more than one lesson, as it takes quite a while to cycle an entire class through it!

Differentiation
Low Attainers – When marking the 'benchmark' objects, allow more leeway.
High Attainers – Insist on greater accuracy in their measurements.

Plenary **5 mins**
Mark the results for your 'benchmark' objects and check that everyone has similar answers. Compare results for similar objects from the various groups.
*Mark 'Postal charges': this may have to be later in the week!

Lesson 3

Introduction **5 mins**

Review problem-solving techniques for measures: make sure you have enough information, plan what calculations will be needed, that answers are sensible, what unit should be used for the final answer etc.

Activities **30 mins**

Practice (individual)

Give out Copymaster 33. This contains questions about various foods and their contents. Pupils will need their calculators.

Not enough weights? (pairs)

Give the pupils this problem: you have a pair of scales with pans for weights. You have one each of the following weights: 1 g, 2 g, 5 g, 10 g, 20 g, 50 g. The biggest mass you can balance is obviously 88 g, but can you balance **every** whole number of grams up to that amount? Investigate.

Differentiation

Low Attainers – Omit the last question on the copymaster.
High Attainers – Give them the information that 1 l of orange juice actually weighs 1.1 kg (the truth). They should recalculate the figures for 100 g and see if it affects the 'league tables'.

Plenary **5 mins**

Mark the copymaster and review the 'Not enough weights?' activity.

Lesson 4

Introduction **10 mins**

Use the list of imperial units made in Lesson 1, or brainstorm them again. Examine the relationships between the imperial units.

Activities **25 mins**

Metric equivalents (individual)

Pupils need their calculators. Tell them that 1 oz = 28.3 g. Ask them to work out the metric equivalents for 1 lb, 1 st, 1 ton. Round these off sensibly at the end, so that the pupils have a useful list of equivalents.

Practice (individual/pairs)

Give out Copymaster 34. Each item has a mass in metric or imperial units. The pupils must convert and fill in the equivalents.

Differentiation

Low Attainers – Could be restricted to the first 10 questions, which use the equivalents 'forwards'.
High Attainers – Should round off answers to sensible accuracy.

Plenary **5 mins**

Mark the practice exercise. Investigate any problems.

Lesson 5

Introduction **10 mins**

Introduce or revise the idea of a conversion graph. Concentrate on practical considerations, such as the scaling of the axes, the best number of data points to plot etc.

Activities **25 mins**

Graph plotting (individual)

Individuals should choose two pairs of units for which to plot conversion graphs. These pairs could be g/oz, g/lb, kg/lb, kg/st, kg/ton, t/ton. Pupils will need their calculators.

Questions (pairs)

Once graphs have been plotted, the pupils should think of half a dozen conversion questions to be answered using their graphs, and prepare the answers for them. They should then swap graphs and questions with their partners.

Differentiation

Low Attainers – Recommend that they tackle g/oz and kg/lb only.
High Attainers – Could investigate other, less frequently used units of mass (pennyweights, drams, hundredweights etc.) if you have reference materials available, and make a conversion graph.

Plenary **5 mins**

Pupils should mark the answers to the questions they set each other. Resolve any problems. Ask pupils who chose the same conversions to compare their graphs.

Theme 8 Calculating with decimals

Objectives
- To consolidate the meaning of the decimal point and of digits after it
- To order sets of decimals
- To extend mental and written methods for adding and subtracting whole numbers to decimals
- To multiply and divide decimals by a power of ten and use the results to carry out other calculations

Vocabulary
decimal place, column, move, order, add, subtract, multiply, divide

Resources
Copymasters 35 and 36, scraps of paper (about 10 per pupil), calculators, cards with decimals written on them, cards for order symbols

Homework Copymaster 18

Mental maths starters 1, 10, 12

Assessment
At the end of this theme is the pupil able to:
- Use decimal notation confidently and know which of two decimals is the larger;
- Use facts from integer mental arithmetic in a decimal context;
- Add and subtract decimals using a suitable written method?

Lesson 1

Introduction — 10 mins
Write a number of decimals on cards (suggestions: 4, 4.1, 4.2, 4.01, 4.02, 4.12, 4.21, 4.4 – add 3dp numbers at your discretion). Each pupil needs a card with the '>' symbol on it. On the back of the card, at the top, should be written 'greater than'. They should then turn the card upside down and write 'less than' at the top. The card can then be shown to you as > or < easily. Pick two of the decimal cards and show them to the pupils. They have to hold up the correct inequality sign. Discuss how you tell which number is greater *(e.g. with 4.2 and 4.12)*.
Finally, order the whole set of numbers with the pupils' help. They could hold the cards and be given instructions for 'shuffling' themselves, or you could blu-tak them to the board.

Activities — 25 mins
Making and ordering (individual)
Tell the pupils that they can use two zeroes, a decimal point and the digits 1 and 4. Not all the digits have to be used at once, but they must use the decimal point. They have to **(a)** make as many different numbers as possible using the digits available; **(b)** order the set of decimals they have created. It simplifies things if numbers like '1.0' and '14.00' are not allowed. Those who finish should add an extra zero and an extra digit, say, 5.

Differentiation
Low Attainers – Add an extra zero, only.
High Attainers – Should be encouraged to structure their work in a logical fashion so that groups of possibilities are recognized and tackled exhaustively.

Plenary — 5 mins
Mark 'Making and ordering'. Try to determine which numbers have been consistently missed, if any.

Lesson 2

Introduction — 10 mins
Revise counting up in equal whole numbers from zero, and down from a given starting point, round the class.

Activities — 25 mins
Decimal counting (whole class)
Count round the class in units of 0.1, 0.2, 0.3 etc.
Progress to 0.01, 0.02 etc.
Progress to 1.3, 2.1 etc.
Decimal zig-zags (individual)
Pupils should pick a number with a digit in the first decimal place *(e.g. 0.4)* and a number with a digit in the second decimal place *(e.g. 0.07)*. The 1dp number should be used to count up and the 2dp number to count down, making a decimal 'zig-zag'. These can be illustrated on number lines (The examples given would generate 0.4, 0.33, 0.73, 0.66, 1.06, 0.99, …). Also, a second counting sequence should be apparent: the 'multiplication table' of the difference between the two numbers (0.33 in the example).
Pupils can experiment with various combinations of starting numbers.

Differentiation
Low Attainers – May only have time to tackle one zig-zag.
High Attainers – Could plot a line graph of position against value (which will show why these are called zig-zags!)

Plenary — 5 mins
Review the results of 'Decimal zig-zags'. See if any pupils have formulated rules.

Lesson 3

Introduction **10 mins**

Review mental methods for adding and subtracting whole numbers and do some quick-fire, round-the-class testing.
Discuss how these methods are carried over into the decimal realm, using numbers with up to 3dp.

Activities **25 mins**

Calculation chains (whole class)

Work round the class as follows: give a starting number, then alternate pupils give an instruction, followed by the answer (an example might proceed: '2.1', 'add 3.6', '5.7', 'subtract 0.75', '4.95' etc.).

Decimal targets (pairs)

Each member of the pair needs 6 small scraps of paper, on which they should write decimals of their own choice: two each with 1, 2 and 3dp. At the start of each game, one player should specify a whole-number 'target', and the 'running total' is reset to 0. Players should lay down their decimals alternately, stating whether they want to add to or subtract from the running total. Both players should record the calculation and the running total at each stage. The winner is the player who laid the number that brought the running total closest to the target. If at any time the target is matched exactly, that game is over. Pupils should play several games. They may decide to replace some of their numbers before each game begins, but not after the new target has been declared.

Differentiation

Low Attainers – Use three each of 1dp and 2dp numbers.
High Attainers – Add an extra card of each type.

Plenary **5 mins**

Ask if anyone managed to hit their target exactly. Ask these pupils to describe the sequence of operations that led to this.

Lesson 4

Introduction **10 mins**

Review the written methods for adding and subtracting integers. Discuss how these are extended to decimals. When using formal 'column' methods, pay particular attention to the case where numbers to be added or subtracted have differing numbers of decimal places, and how adding 'padding' zeroes to these numbers makes the question easier to understand.

Activities **25 mins**

Practice (individual)

Give out Copymaster 35. This contains a number of simple drill and practice exercises.

Sums and differences (individual)

Put a number of circles on the board. Inside each, write two decimal numbers. Explain that the two numbers in each circle represent the sum and the difference of two **other** numbers that the pupils have to identify. There is a rule to be discovered!

Differentiation

Low Attainers – Restrict the number of decimal places used in Sums and differences.
High Attainers – Encourage them to find the rule and apply it to numbers with more decimal places.

Plenary **5 mins**

Mark the copymaster and board activity. Discuss any problems the pupils had and try to discover the reasons for incorrect answers.

Lesson 5

Introduction **10 mins**

Review the effect of multiplying and dividing whole numbers by 10, 100, 1000. Ask a pupil to begin with a simple multiplication or division *(e.g.* $3 \times 4 = 12$*)*. The next pupil should give another calculation based on this one *(e.g.* $0.3 \times 4 = 1.2$*)*, and this should carry on until the complexity is too great to be useful or instructive. Then restart. Make sure multiplications and divisions are covered, so that the effect of division by numbers smaller than 1 can be observed and discussed.

Activities **25 mins**

Practice (individual)

Give out Copymaster 36.

Investigation (individual or pairs)

Give pupils a number such as 2.4. They should find as many different ways as possible of making this number by multiplication.
Perform a similar task to this using division, with a target of, say, 0.4.

Differentiation

Low Attainers – Restrict the activity to multiplication.
High Attainers – Progress to expressions involving two operations.

Plenary **5 mins**

Mark the copymaster and give examples of the correct answers to the investigation. Make sure the pupils write down at least one example from each 'family' of answers.

Theme 9 Word problems

Objectives
- To think clearly about the parameters and variables involved in solving problems
- To formulate strategies for dealing with the variables
- To select the correct mathematical techniques to carry out their solutions

Vocabulary
length, mass, currency, exchange rate, graph, axes, scale, area, time

Resources
Copymasters 37 and 38, newspaper with current exchange rates, graph paper, calculators

Homework Copymaster 19

Mental maths starter 10

Assessment
At the end of this theme is the pupil able to:
- Approach a wide variety of (possibly open-ended) problems involving measures, money and mensuration, formulate and carry out strategies for their solution, selecting the correct mathematical techniques?

Lesson 1

Introduction 5 mins
You need a newspaper containing exchange rates for various currencies.
Discuss the concept of exchange rate with the pupils and write half a dozen of these on the board.
Recall the features of a conversion graph. If you worked through Theme 17, Lesson 5, the pupils should have an example to look at. Explain that they will be making conversion graphs for some of the currencies you have listed.

Activities 25 mins
Conversion graphs (individual)
Pupils need graph paper and their calculators. Pupils should select two currencies and prepare a conversion graph with Sterling, for each. Minimal input should be given at the start *(e.g. in choosing scales for the axes)* – act as a troubleshooter.

While this is taking place, write a number of questions on the board, such as, 'Convert 14 Deutschmarks to £'. Pupils should attempt to answer these, either from a graph they have drawn, or by borrowing one that contains the correct currency and has a suitable scale.

Differentiation
Low Attainers – One graph may be sufficient – you may wish to choose the currency for them.
High Attainers – Could make a graph connecting two non-Sterling currencies.

Plenary 5 mins
Mark the questions. If any answers are wrong, identify the graph that produced the wrong answer and try to work out why this is so.

Lesson 2

Introduction 5 mins
Give out Copymaster 37 (this will be needed again for Lesson 5). Explain that it contains some information about the distance from the Sun of various objects.

Activities 30 mins
Astronomical units (individual)
Pupils need their calculators. Their job is to use the information given to convert all the distances into **astronomical units**. 1 astronomical unit (au) is equal to the distance of the Earth from the Sun. The issue of rounding may come up: encourage pupils to choose the degree of rounding appropriately.

Differentiation
This will be by outcome. High attainers could look up some more objects in an encyclopaedia and add them to the list.

Plenary 5 mins
Mark the copymaster. Discuss the rounding issue and see what solutions have been arrived at.

Lesson 3

Introduction **5 mins**
Give out Copymaster 38 (this will be needed again for Lesson 4).

Activities **30 mins**
House plans (individual/pairs)
Pupils need their calculators. The problem is to find as many different ways as possible to make the L-shaped house and its garden, so that the area covered by the garden is exactly twice that covered by the house.

Differentiation
Low Attainers – Supply them with the area of the house at the start of the activity.
High Attainers – Should select the best solution they have found, and justify this choice.

Plenary **5 mins**
Review the pupils' solutions. Can any be ruled out on grounds of practicality *(e.g. rooms too narrow etc.)*?

Lesson 4

Introduction **5 mins**
Give out Copymaster 38.

Activities **30 mins**
Mass of a house (pairs)
Pupils need their calculators. Pupils should then be asked the question: How much do the walls of the house that they designed in Lesson 3 weigh? They should be encouraged to think first about what additional information they will need in order to answer the question.

Differentiation
Low Attainers – Help them with the mortar problem (i.e. changing the size of the basic 'unit' in a wall).
High Attainers – Encourage them to think about whether they could make a better choice from their solutions to Lesson 3 that would reduce the mass.

Plenary **5 mins**
This will be impossible to 'mark' as such, but a poll of answers should reveal an overall similarity, and answers that are wildly wrong should be obvious. Discuss the problems such as how to include the mortar, what the height of the walls should be etc.

Lesson 5

Introduction **10 mins**
Give out Copymaster 37.

Activities **25 mins**
Travelling light (individual)
Pupils need their calculators. Tell them that their job is to calculate how long the Sun's light takes to reach the objects given in the table.

Differentiation
Low Attainers – May need to be reminded that the results from Lesson 2 will be useful.
High Attainers – Include any additional objects they used in Lesson 2. Find the speed of light in km/s.

Plenary **5 mins**
Mark the copymaster. Allow some leeway with answers to account for rounding at intermediate stages.

Theme 10 Properties of numbers

Objectives
- To reinforce the concepts of odd, even, multiple and prime
- To provide quick multiple tests
- To introduce the concept of common multiple
- To use the above skills, and others, to solve number puzzles

Vocabulary
odd, even, multiple, factor, prime, common multiple, inverse

Resources
Copymasters 39 and 40

Homework Copymaster 20

Mental maths starters 8, 10

Assessment
At the end of this theme is the pupil able to:
- Identify odd and even numbers, prime numbers and multiples of a given number;
- Identify or generate common multiples of numbers;
- Solve number puzzles of various types?

Lesson 1

Introduction **10 mins**
Review the meaning of **multiple**.
Introduce or review the concept of digit sum (or digital root) with a few examples.

Activities **25 mins**
Investigation (individual)
Ask the pupils to write down the following:

multiples of **2**	58, 74, 102, 50, 46, 282
multiples of **5**	75, 305, 200, 130, 155, 550
multiples of **10**	80, 150, 400, 530, 1000, 370
multiples of **3**	87, 210, 249, 303, 705, 966
multiples of **4**	64, 100, 240, 304, 396, 516
multiples of **9**	81, 90, 234, 504, 333, 1350
multiples of **6**	72, 138, 174, 420, 612, 702

They should investigate the connections between the numbers in each group: look at their final digits, their digit sums etc. and try to find rules for determining when a number is a multiple of one of the given numbers. Make sure that everyone has a correct list of tests at the end.
Practice (individual)
Write a collection of numbers on the board at random with pupils' prompting. The pupils have to identify which numbers are which type of multiple.

Differentiation
Low Attainers – Direct them to the fact that the multiple tests for 3, 6 and 9 involve the digit sums.
High Attainers – Ask them to look at multiple tests for 20, 25, 50, 100… and 7.

Plenary **5 mins**
Go through the numbers from 'Practice'. Various pupils could supply the answers, together with the reasons for their conclusions.

Lesson 2

Introduction **10 mins**
Ask two pupils each to think of two numbers less than 10.
Ask various pupils to give the multiples of these numbers in order: make two lists.
Identify the numbers that are common to both lists.
Introduce the concept of common multiple.

Activities **25 mins**
Fizzbuzz (whole class, or smaller groups)
Select two numbers, a 'fizz' number and a 'buzz' number. Work round the class as follows: count up, out loud, from 1. If a number is a multiple of the 'fizz' number, say 'fizz'. If it is a multiple of the 'buzz' number, say 'buzz'. If it is a common multiple, say 'fizzbuzz'. (Some versions of the game require that the direction of play is reversed at every 'fizzbuzz'. Don't do this if the whole class is playing!)

Example: 2 = *fizz*, 3 = *buzz (actually quite hard!) gives 'One, fizz, buzz, fizz, five, fizzbuzz, seven, fizz, buzz, …'*
Variation: Try the game with three numbers: 'fizzbuzzjazz'!
Practice (individual)
Draw several circles on the board. Inside each circle, write a pair of numbers. The pupils should make lists of the first 5 common multiples for each pair. Make sure you have some pairs where the lowest common multiple of the numbers is not obtained simply by multiplying them *(e.g. 10 and 12)*, as this 'rule' can be erroneously established by a poor choice of examples.

Differentiation
Low Attainers – Keep the practice numbers small.
High Attainers – Move on to common multiples of three numbers.

Plenary **5 mins**
Mark the 'Practice' exercise. Identify any problems and correct them.

Lesson 3

Introduction **10 mins**
Review the meaning of **factors**. Ask various pupils to reply with factors of a given number.
Review the meaning of a **prime number**. Ask pupils to supply examples of prime numbers.
Ask if there are any factors of 330 that are prime numbers. Do the same with some other starting numbers.
Put across the idea of identifying a number's prime factors.

Activities **25 mins**
Practice (individual)
Give out Copymaster 39. In this, the pupils have to identify the prime numbers from a list and find prime factors of various numbers.
Prime factorisation (pairs)
The copymaster shows an example of prime factorisation. Pupils should work up through the counting numbers attempting to factorise each number in turn.

Differentiation
Low Attainers – The final activity is probably not suitable.
High Attainers – Could attempt prime factorisation of the numbers from the copymaster.

Plenary **5 mins**
Mark the copymaster and any additional activities. Make sure that pupils who have missed some of the 'larger' prime numbers realise their mistakes.

Lesson 4

Introduction **5 mins**
Make sure pupils know the definitions of **odd** and **even**.
Review the multiple tests from Lesson 1.

Activities **30 mins**
Odd and even (individual)
Draw two circles on the board. In one of them, write five even numbers. In the other, write five odd numbers.
Below, write the four statements 'even × even', 'even × odd', 'odd × even', 'odd × odd'. Ask the pupils to investigate what kind of answer results from each statement, by trying examples using numbers from the circles.
Multiplying multiples (individual)
Write some further statements, such as 'multiple of 3 × even', 'multiple of 5 × odd', 'multiple of 3 × multiple of 4' etc. and ask the pupils to find out as much about the answers as possible.

Differentiation
Low Attainers – The Odd and even activity may be sufficient.
High Attainers – Ask them to try to find a reason for the 'odd and even' rule. A hint would be to examine the prime factors of the numbers involved.

Plenary **5 mins**
Mark the 'Odd and even' activity and elicit as many rules as possible from the second activity. Someone may have found an overall rule for statements of this type. If so, discuss it.

Lesson 5

Introduction **10 mins**
Try out some questions of the form 'I think of a number, double it, add 5 to the answer and the result is 57. What was the number?' Remind the pupils that they need to use inverse operations to find the answers.

Activities **30 mins**
Puzzles (individual)
Give out Copymaster 40. This contains questions of the 'think of a number' type, and some harder ones where numbers have to match two criteria.

Differentiation
Low Attainers – The harder, 'cross-matching' questions could be omitted. They could then make up some of their own 'think of a number' puzzles.
High Attainers – Encourage them to make up some of their own 'multiple plus' questions to try out on others.

Plenary **5 mins**
Mark the copymaster. If there is time, try out some of the examples the pupils have thought of.

Theme 1 Multiplication and division

Objectives
- To consolidate knowledge of written and mental methods of multiplication and division
- To round quotients to 1dp or express them as fractions
- To extend these into decimals with 2dp and to apply this to money

Vocabulary
multiply, divide, fraction, numerator, denominator, decimal, round, money, place value, digit

Resources
Copymasters 41 and 42

Homework Copymaster 21

Mental maths starters 6, 7, 8, 11

Assessment
At the end of this theme is the pupil able to:
- Multiply and divide whole numbers by whole numbers with one or two digits, expressing the answer as a fraction or rounded decimal;
- Use multiplication tables and place value movement to perform a wide range of simple multiplications and divisions mentally;
- Apply these techniques to money?

Lesson 1

Introduction **10 mins**
With the pupils, look at some examples of divisions that have remainders. Discuss the meaning of this and how the remainder represents a fraction *(e.g.* $6 \div 4 = 1\frac{2}{4} = 1\frac{1}{2}$*)*. A visual aid such as dividing up circles or rectangles on the board could be useful.
Also show how a division of this kind can lead to a decimals answer *(e.g. $6 \div 4 = 1.5$, done using short division across the decimal point)*. Demonstrate that rounding to 1dp can be imposed on the answer if desired, once the 2nd decimal place has been calculated.

Activities **25 mins**
Division chains (whole class)
Work round the class as follows: a pupil starts with a division, the next pupil supplies the whole number part of the answer, the next the fractional part.
Example: *'seven divided by four', 'equals one', 'and three-quarters'.*
Practice (individual)
Write a set of suitable divisions on the board. Pupils should carry out these divisions, giving the answers as fractions and as decimals, rounded to 1dp if necessary.

Differentiation
Low Attainers – Restrict the questions to two-digit dividends.
High Attainers – Could investigate some divisions leading to recurring decimals.

Plenary **5 mins**
Mark the questions from the board. Ascertain the reasons for wrong answers and correct them.

Lesson 2

Introduction **10 mins**
Spend a few minutes doing a quick-fire round of multiplications and divisions based on multiplication tables.
Review the effect of multiplying and dividing whole numbers by 10, 100, 1000.

Activities **25 mins**
Calculation families (whole class)
Ask a pupil to begin with a simple multiplication or division *(e.g.* $7 \times 3 = 21$*)*. The next pupil should give another calculation based on this one *(e.g.* $70 \times 3 = 210$*)*, and this should carry on until the complexity is too great to be useful or instructive. Then restart. Make sure multiplications and divisions are covered.
Practice (individual)
Give out Copymaster 41. This contains several pairs of circles with a multiplication or division symbol between each pair. Pupils must carry out the operation on **every pair** of numbers they can identify from each set (so three numbers in each circle would generate nine answers).

Differentiation
Low Attainers – Omit the triple multiplications on the copymaster.
High Attainers – Give some addition questions, extending multipliers and divisors into the teens.

Plenary **5 mins**
Mark the copymaster, making sure that pupils have identified all the pairs of numbers.

Lesson 3

Introduction **10 mins**
Review written methods for multiplying three digits by two digits: the grid method and standard long multiplication, for example.

Activities **25 mins**
Number crunching I (individual)
Pupils can use the digits 2, 4, 7, 7 and 9. From these they can make various combinations of two- and three-digit numbers. They should attempt to find out which combinations give the largest answer when multiplied, and the smallest.
They can then pick their own set of digits to use.

Differentiation
High Attainers – Investigate the effects of multiple digits as opposed to single ones.

Plenary **5 mins**
Mark Number crunching I. Make sure that everyone found the smallest and largest answers. Pupils' own work could be checked by a neighbour, or they could check by division, using a calculator.

Lesson 4

Introduction **10–15 mins**
Review the long division method for dividing by a two-digit number.

Activities **20–25 mins**
Number crunching II (individual)
Pupils can use the digits 2, 4, 7, 7 and 9. From these they can make various combinations of two- and three-digit numbers. They should attempt to find out which combinations give the largest answer when divided, and the smallest.
They can then pick their own set of digits to use.

Differentiation
High Attainers – Investigate the effects of multiple digits as opposed to single ones.

Plenary **5 mins**
Mark 'Number crunching II'. Make sure that everyone found the smallest and largest answers. Pupils' own work could be checked by a neighbour, or they could check by multiplication, using a calculator.

Lesson 5

Introduction **10 mins**
Review the extension of the written techniques for integers to decimals with 2dp. Discuss how this is useful in manipulating amounts of money.

Activities **25 mins**
Practice (individual)
Give out Copymaster 42. This contains a number of multiplications and divisions of money. Note that all amounts divide exactly, so no rounding is required.

Differentiation
By outcome.

Plenary **5 mins**
Mark the copymaster. You may want to work through some of the questions for correction purposes. Pupils would check results by working backwards on their calculators.

Theme 2 Problem solving

Objectives
- To use select and apply relevant mathematical procedures to solve problems
- To obtain and present valid solutions from data given

Vocabulary
length, mass, area, capacity, units, round, table, density, diameter, circumference, radius, diagonal, discount

Resources
Copymasters 43 and 44

Homework Copymaster 22

Mental maths starter 10

Assessment
At the end of this theme is the pupil able to:
- Identify the correct strategy for solving a given problem;
- Select and apply relevant mathematical procedures;
- Obtain the relevant information from data supplied;
- Present solutions appropriately worded, in sensible units and to a sensible degree of accuracy?

Lesson 1

Introduction **5 mins**
Discuss the relationship between the shape of the Earth and a map of it.

Activities **30 mins**
Measure the Earth (whole class)
Using a map of the world, determine the circumference of the equator by measurement and scaling. Then, using the approximate formula, diameter = circumference ÷ 3, find the diameter of the Earth to the nearest 1000 km (*Answer: 13 000 km*).
Solar system (individual)
Using the following data, calculate the diameters of the other planets in the solar system. Each planet's diameter is given as a multiple of Earth's, to 1dp.

Planet	Mercury	Venus	Mars	Jupiter	Saturn	Uranus	Neptune	Pluto
Diameter (Earth = 1)	0.4	0.9	0.5	11.2	9.4	4.1	3.9	0.5

Draw a set of circles to represent the planets, choosing a suitable scale. Assistance may be required with choosing the scale and calculating the radii to use for the circles. The circles could be concentric, or drawn separately. There are possibilities for a wall display.

Differentiation
Low Attainers – Round the figures given in the table to 1sf.
High Attainers – Could find out about the Moon and Sun in comparison to the Earth, and add these to their drawings.

Plenary **5 mins**
Mark the exercises. Discuss the fact that the data table alone is sufficient to draw the circles.

Lesson 2

Introduction **5 mins**
Introduce the tea urn problem: you have two buckets that hold 5 litres and 3 litres, respectively. The tea urn holds up to 50 litres, is filled from the top and emptied by a tap on the bottom. How can you use these to measure 1 litre of water into the urn?
Work through the solution with the pupils.

Activities **30 mins**
Tea urn (individual or pairs)
The object of the exercise is to work out how to measure as many different amounts of water into the urn as possible.

Differentiation
Low Attainers – Start with simpler capacities, say, 2 l and 3 l.
High Attainers – After solving the first problem up to, say, 30 l, ask them to think up their own capacities for the two buckets and investigate the results.

Plenary **5 mins**
Work through the solutions to the problem. You may find that pupils have found alternative solutions, but there will always be a most efficient solution involving the fewest pourings.

Lesson 3

Introduction **10 mins**

Discuss the concept of density (you may be able to refer to some work in science), concentrating on the fact that if you wish to compare two materials to see 'how heavy' they are, you need to look at the same amount of each material. Work through the following examples with the pupils (they will need their calculators). Find the mass of 1 cm^2 in each case, and hence the density in g/cm^2.
1 l of water weighs 1 kg.
A 10 cm^2 pendant made of iron weighs 39.3 g.
1 m^2 of balsa wood weighs 97 kg.

Activities **25 mins**

Densities (individual)

Give out Copymaster 43. This contains pictures of substances with volumes and masses. The object of the exercise is to produce a table of the substances, ordered by density. Include the substances from the introduction.

Differentiation

Low Attainers – Assist them with the changes of unit required to deal with the liquids and gases.
High Attainers – Given that 1 m^2 of average paper weighs 80 g, make measurements to calculate the density of paper.

Plenary **5 mins**

Mark the copymaster. Discuss the 'extreme' values, and those that are similar to water.

Lesson 4

Introduction **5 mins**

Discuss the meaning of the diagonal of a rectangle. Review the meaning of perimeter.

Activities **30 mins**

Diagonals (individual)

Given that a rectangle's perimeter is 24 cm, find the dimensions that give the shortest diagonal. Which measurements give the longest diagonal?
What if the area of the rectangle is fixed, instead of the perimeter (20 cm^2, say)?

Differentiation

Low Attainers – Omit the second question.
High Attainers – Make sure that fractional values for the rectangles' sides are considered.

Plenary **5 mins**

Mark Diagonals and interpret the results. You may wish the pupils to write a proper conclusion at the end of their work.

Lesson 5

Introduction **10 mins**

Give out Copymaster 44. Review the extraction of data from tables by asking a few simple questions about the data.

Activities **25 mins**

Day trips (individual/pairs)

The pupils should work through the questions on the copymaster. You may have to point out to them that in questions 1 and 3, the number of child ride tickets is '6 or more'. Watch out for pupils who miss out the volume discounts.
Question 2 deliberately doesn't mention whether Toni is an adult or a child. The answer covers both cases.

Differentiation

Low Attainers – Start with question 2.
High Attainers – Could look at data for your class and work out the cost of a day/cost per person.

Plenary **5 mins**

Mark the copymaster, breaking down the costs into categories and discussion where people may have misread tables.

Theme 3 Fractions, decimals and percentages

Objectives
- To understand the relationships between fractions, decimals and percentages
- To convert between fractions, decimals and percentages
- To calculate simple percentages of quantities

Vocabulary
fraction, numerator, denominator, decimal place, divide, round, percent, percentage, compare, order, greater than, less than

Resources
Copymasters 45 and 46, calculators

Homework Copymaster 23

Mental maths starters 1, 7

Assessment
At the end of this theme is the pupil able to:
- Convert between fractions, decimals and percentages;
- Calculate simple percentages of quantities;
- Order a set of fractions by converting them to decimals?

Lesson 1

Introduction **10 mins**
Review division of whole numbers by one- or two-digit numbers, with the remainder interpreted as a decimal.

Activities **25 mins**
Quarters (whole class)
Work through the derivation of the decimal equivalents for $\frac{1}{4}$ and $\frac{3}{4}$, dividing 1 and 3, respectively, by 4.
Demonstrate that $\frac{6}{8}$ is equivalent to $\frac{3}{4}$ by dividing 6 by 8 and comparing decimal equivalents.
Practice (individual)
Write a number of fractions on the board that the pupils are to write as decimals. None of the decimals must recur! Suitable denominators under 100 are 2, 4, 5, 8, 10, 16, 20, 25, 32, 40, 64 and 80.

Differentiation
Low Attainers – Keep to denominators not greater than 20.
High Attainers – Introduce some 3-digit denominators.

Plenary **5 mins**
Mark the practice questions. Ask pupils if they have noticed any patterns in the answers.

Lesson 2

Introduction **10 mins**
Demonstrate how to derive a recurring decimal from a fraction by division and introduce the dot notation for indicating repeated groups of digits. Explain that the number of digits in the repeated group is called the **period** of the decimal.
Use $\frac{1}{3}$ and $\frac{6}{11}$ as examples.

Activities **25 mins**
Denominators (individual)
Pupils should work through complete sets of fractions, looking for patterns and using them to make progress.
$\frac{1}{3}, \frac{2}{3}$
$\frac{1}{7}, \frac{2}{7}, \frac{3}{7}$ etc.
$\frac{?}{6}$
$\frac{?}{9}$
$\frac{?}{11}$

Differentiation
Low Attainers – Perhaps avoid 7ths.
High Attainers – Investigate the relationships between 3rds, 6ths and 12ths.

Plenary **5 mins**
Mark the activities (pupils could use their calculators). Discuss the fact that a calculator often can't help with work like this, because there aren't enough digits to show the patterns.

Lesson 3

Introduction **10 mins**
Demonstrate how to order a set of fractions by converting them to decimals first. Pupils may use their calculators. Discuss the fact that usually a calculator will show enough digits to order a set of fractions.

Activities **25 mins**
Practice (individual)
Give out Copymaster 45. This contains pairs of fractions which need inequality symbols between them and groups of fractions to be ordered.
Investigation (pairs)
Each member of the pair thinks of a fraction. They make a new fraction as follows: its numerator is the sum of their two numerators, and the denominator is the sum of their two denominators. What happens when you arrange all three fractions in order of size? Try this with different pairs of fractions. What happens if the two starting fractions are identical or equivalent?

Differentiation
Low Attainers – Restrict the sizes of numerators and denominators.
High Attainers – Try to think of a reason for the results.

Plenary **5 mins**
Mark the practice exercise and check the results of the investigation. Ask if anyone has an explanation of the conclusion.

Lesson 4

Introduction **10 mins**
Review the relationship between decimals and percentages. Demonstrate how recurring decimals can be expressed as percentages with a fractional component (*e.g.* $\frac{1}{3} = 0.3333\ldots = 33.33\ldots\% = 33\frac{1}{3}\%$) or with a decimal component, rounded if necessary (*e.g. 33.3% to 1dp*). Demonstrate how to convert a percentage to a fraction, by writing it with denominator 100 and cancelling if possible.

Activities **25 mins**
Practice (individual)
Use Copymaster 45. Pupils should convert the fractions in questions 1–12 into percentages and check that their orderings are still valid.
Investigation (individual or pairs)
When converting a whole number percentage to a fraction, various denominators are possible when cancelling has taken place. What is the connection between the number of per cent and the final denominator?

Differentiation
Low Attainers – Should simply investigate a number of cases.
High Attainers – Should produce a final statement encapsulating the result of the investigation.

Plenary **5 mins**
Mark the copymaster questions and discuss the results of the investigation.

Lesson 5

Introduction **10 mins**
Review calculation of a fraction of a quantity (start with a unit fraction and progress to non-unit fractions). Demonstrate the application of this to the determination of a percentage of a quantity.

Activities **25 mins**
Practice (individual)
Give out Copymaster 46. This contains various percentages of quantities to be calculated, in a variety of contexts.
Fifties (pairs)
Pairs should make up as many percentage statements as possible containing the number 50.
Examples: *50% of 30 is 15. 20% of 250 is 50. 46% of 50 is 23 etc.*
When they have amassed a collection of statements, they should choose their own number to work with.

Differentiation
Low Attainers – May need assistance to devise statements other than '50% of x is y'.
High Attainers – Could investigate a fractional percentage.

Plenary **5 mins**
Mark the copymaster and examine statements from the pairs. Investigate any errors that have occurred.

Theme 4 Ratio and proportion

Objectives
- To understand and use the equivalence between 'in every' and 'to every' statements
- To use the above skills in solving simple problems concerning proportional quantities
- To solve problems involving proportional division.
- To understand in an informal way, situations in which inverse proportion applies

Vocabulary
ratio, in every, to every, simplify, equivalent, proportional, divide, share

Resources
Copymasters 47 and 48

Homework Copymaster 24

Mental maths starters 1, 10

Assessment
At the end of this theme is the pupil able to:
- Use statements of the form '1 in every 3' or '2 to every 3' and convert between them;
- Find equivalent ratios and simplify them where possible;
- Solve simple problems concerning proportional quantities and proportional division;
- Demonstrate an empirical grasp of situations where inverse proportion applies?

Lesson 1

Introduction **10 mins**
Review the meaning of 'in every' and 'to every' with respect to ratios. Discuss the equivalence of statements such as '4 in every 10' and '2 in every 5'.

Activities **25 mins**
Numbers from ratios (whole class)
Each pupil needs a set of digit cards. First say, 'These ratios are for dividing things between you and me.' Give the pupils a ratio statement such as 'I have 3 in every 4'. Ask them 'How many do **you** have in every 4?' The pupils hold up '1'. Then say 'I'm going to hold up how many I have.' Hold up '9'. Ask 'How many do you have?' The pupils hold up '3'.
Repeat this with with 'I have 3 **to** every 4. How many do you have to every 8?' The pupils hold up '6'. Say 'I'm going to hold up how many I have.' Hold up '12'. Ask 'How many do you have?' The pupils hold up '16'.
Repeat the whole questioning scheme with other ratios and numbers.
Ratio families (individual)
Give the pupils the starting ratio '5 in every 8'. Ask them to write down the equivalent 'to every' ratio.
They should then write down as many equivalent ratios of both types as possible.
After a suitable time interval, pupils may choose their own starting ratio.

Differentiation
Low Attainers – Make starting ratio simpler, *e.g.* '*2 in every 3*'.
High Attainers – Ask them to find the unitary forms of their chosen ratio.

Plenary **5 mins**
Ask the pupils to read out their equivalents for '5 in every 8'. Equivalents for pupils' own ratios could be checked by a neighbour.

Lesson 2

Introduction **10 mins**
Introduce a pair of proportional quantities, such as '5 kg of apples cost £3'. By asking questions, explore the relationship between the two quantities. Aim to arrive at statements such as 'if you double the amount of apples, you double the cost'. Explain that this kind of relationship means that the two amounts are proportional to each other. Make up a table of values for this relationship, like this:

Mass of apples	1 kg	2 kg	3 kg	4 kg	**5 kg**	10 kg	20 kg	50 kg
Cost	£0.60	£1.20	£1.80	£2.40	**£3**	£6	£12	£30

Activities **25 mins**
Proportional amounts (whole class)
Ask the pupils for further examples of quantities that could be related proportionally. Take some suitable examples and calculate reasonable tables of values for them.
Graphs (individual)
Pupils should pick a pair of quantities from the list available and plot a graph to show the relationship.
Repeat with another pair of quantities if you have time.

Differentiation
Low Attainers – Could omit the graphing activity.
High Attainers – Could use a graph to predict values not in the tables.

Plenary **5 mins**
Examine the pupils' graphs, making sure they are all straight lines.

Lesson 3

Introduction **10 mins**

Introduce the concept of proportional division with an example such as: *'Martyn wants to share £100 between his two nieces, Toni and Michelle. The amount he gives each one is proportional to their ages. Toni is 6 and Michelle is 4. How much does each receive?'* Discuss the fact that because Toni receives £6 to every £4 Michelle receives, there are 10 'shares' to be divided up altogether, so one 'share' must be £10.

Activities **25 mins**

Shares (whole class)

Repeat the example with different amounts to be divided. Vary the ages of the recipients, and hence the ratio of division.

Practice (individual)

Give out Copymaster 47. This contains various problems using proportional division.

Differentiation

Low Attainers – Omit the questions with more than two parts to their ratios.

High Attainers – Could be taught to use ratio notation (*e.g.* 6 : 4).

Plenary **5 mins**

Mark the copymaster. Discuss any questions with which pupils had difficulty.

Lesson 4

Introduction **10 mins**

Introduce the idea of inverse proportion with an example such as: *'There are 60 sweets in a bag. If you share out the sweets equally between 2 people, how many will each get?'* Repeat the example for different numbers of people. Build up a table like this.

Number of people	1	2	3	4	5	6	10	12	15	20	30	60
Sweets each	60	30	20	15	12	10	6	5	4	3	2	1

Activities **25 mins**

Inversely proportional quantities (whole class)

Ask the pupils for further examples of quantities that could be related by inverse proportion (suggestions: time taken for a journey and average speed of the journey; time taken to complete a task and the number of people who work on it; number of people who win the lottery and the amount each receives). Take some suitable examples and calculate reasonable tables of values for them.

Graphs (individual)

Pupils should pick a pair of quantities from the list available and plot a graph to show the relationship. Repeat with another pair of quantities if you have time.

Differentiation

Low Attainers – Could omit the graphing activity.

High Attainers – Could use a graph to predict values not in the tables.

Plenary **5 mins**

Check the pupils' graphs. They should all have a similar curved shape.

Lesson 5

Introduction **10 mins**

Give out Copymaster 48, or use an OHT version of it. Talk about the first row of examples with the pupils. Ask questions such as: *'If the grey wheel turns once, how many times does this wheel turn?'*

Activities **25 mins**

Gear problems (whole class)

The copymaster contains various configurations of interlocking gears. Pupils can model the gear arrangements by drawing circles and writing the number of teeth inside.

Ask various questions about each arrangement, such as: *'If this wheel turns clockwise, which way will this wheel turn?'*; *'If this wheel turns 10 times, how many times does this wheel turn?' etc.*

Gear rings (pairs)

Each member of the pair should design a gear ring, similar to that in the last question on the copymaster. They should then check each others' rings carefully to make sure that they 'work'.

They can also design an 'impossible' one in which the gears would lock.

Differentiation

Low Attainers – Gear rings may be too difficult and could be omitted.

High Attainers – Could investigate the relationship between this activity and a 'Spirograph' pattern.

Plenary **5 mins**

Mark the copymaster. 'Gear rings' should be self-checking. Ask pupils to demonstrate any particularly interesting examples.

Theme 5 Handling data

Objectives

- To consolidate knowledge of frequency tables and bar charts
- To understand the use of pie charts; to produce and interpret simple examples

Vocabulary

frequency, group, table, chart, bar, pie, circle, centre, sector, angle, protractor

Resources

Copymasters 49 and 50, calculators, protractors

Homework Copymaster 25

Mental maths starter 5

Assessment

At the end of this theme is the pupil able to:

- Place data into suitable groups and illustrate the frequency distribution with a bar chart;
- Draw a simple pie chart from given data;
- Read and interpret a pie chart, measuring the angles of the sectors?

Lesson 1

Introduction **10 mins**

Use Copymaster 9 to record some information about members of the class, unless you have already done so in Autumn Term, Theme 5, in which case, use the consolidated data. Revise the placement of data into groups (use height, weight etc.). If there is more than one Year 6 group in your school, you could swap data with them.

Activities **25 mins**

Practice (pairs)

Present the class with the following data. It shows the speed, in miles per hour, of 100 cars passing a radar checkpoint.

31	56	41	63	59	61	49	58	74	65	60	52	68	43	57	68	38	76	71	80
72	66	69	64	32	52	33	69	40	56	71	63	57	69	56	44	75	48	52	68
63	48	61	55	70	53	66	44	53	67	50	35	66	51	75	69	47	67	63	77
54	77	60	47	68	74	43	61	42	68	80	54	75	62	45	51	54	78	54	66
75	58	62	56	57	65	66	62	70	42	79	46	46	73	74	52	73	37	79	65

The pairs should group the data sensibly. They may choose their own class widths.

Charts (individual)

Pupils should produce bar charts to illustrate their groupings.

Differentiation

Not applicable.

Plenary **5 mins**

Check that the pupils have tallied the frequencies correctly. Get neighbours to check the axes and scale of their bar charts.

Lesson 2

Introduction **10 mins**

Use data as in the introduction to Lesson 1.
Work through the eye colours, making a frequency table. Discuss how these can be converted to percentages and discuss the accuracy to be used (nearest % is recommended at this stage). Work through the calculation. Verify that the percentages sum to 100% and discuss the effect of rounding errors (1 decimal place could be tested to see if it eradicates them).

Activities **25 mins**

Practice (individual)

Pupils should calculate the percentages allocated to various data items from the class survey. They should use their calculators.

Differentiation

Low Attainers – Use discrete or non-numeric data only.

High Attainers – Could work to a higher accuracy if rounding errors occur.

Plenary **5 mins**

Cross-check the frequencies and percentages between pupils. Discuss any rounding errors that have occurred.

Lesson 3

Introduction **10 mins**
Discuss why pie charts are used (i.e. to compare fractions of a whole). Use an example such as: *'A bag has 25 fruit sweets in it, 10 mints and 5 toffees. Draw a pie chart to show this.'* Work through finding the total and then the fraction for each type of sweet. Draw this roughly on the board.

Activities **25 mins**
Drawing pie charts (whole class)
Give out Copymaster 49. This contains various 'skeletons' for pie charts with different numbers of subdivisions. Concoct various data sets to be illustrated using some of these skeletons. Discuss which type of subdivision will be best for each set.

Differentiation
Low Attainers – Keep to examples requiring only a few subdivisions, say up to 12.
High Attainers – Could examine how to illustrate data from the class survey – this will probably involve an 'awkward' number of degrees per pupil.

Plenary **5 mins**
Check that pupils have coloured or shaded sectors using the correct number of subdivisions for each pie chart.

Lesson 4

Introduction **10 mins**
Review the use of a protractor to measure angles. The pupils should draw and measure a few different angles and have these checked by their neighbours.

Activities **25 mins**
Reading pie charts (whole class)
Give out Copymaster 50. This contains various pie charts. Work through the first chart with the pupils. Determine what fraction of the chart is taken up by each sector, and calculate the frequency for each sector from the information given.
Practice (individual)
The pupils should now work through the other pie charts.

Differentiation
Low Attainers – May need assistance in measuring the angles and determining the fractions.
High Attainers – Could find a pie chart in a book or newspaper and interpret it in the same way.

Plenary **5 mins**
Mark the copymaster. Encourage the pupils to self-check by looking at totals.

Lesson 5

Introduction **10 mins**
Draw a bar chart on the board as follows, or prepare it in advance on an OHT: the chart represents a survey of cars passing a checkpoint. The number of people in each car was recorded, giving the following data. Do not display the frequencies, as finding these is part of the pupils' work.

Number of people in car	1	2	3	4	5
Number of cars	66	26	14	8	6

Activities **25 mins**
Tasks (individual or pairs)
Set the pupils the following tasks:
1 Make a frequency table from the bar chart.
2 Work out how many cars there were altogether.
3 Work out how many people there were in **all** the cars.
4 Calculate the mean number of people per car.
5 Draw a pie chart to show this information.

Differentiation
Low Attainers – Steps **3** and **4** may be omitted.
High Attainers – Could calculate the number of people who drove alone and the number of people who shared a car, and draw a new pie chart to show this data.

Plenary **5 mins**
Mark the tasks and discuss any difficulties the pupils had in making progress.

Theme 6 Reflection, translation and rotation

Objectives
- To consolidate knowledge of translation and rotation
- To recognise line symmetry and impose it on simple designs
- To recognise rotational symmetry and impose it on simple designs

Vocabulary
reflect (reflection), translate (translation), rotate (rotation), clockwise, anticlockwise, angle, symmetry, line of symmetry, order of rotational symmetry, coordinates

Resources
Copymasters 51 and 52, squared paper, tracing paper

Homework Copymaster 26

Mental maths starter 9

Assessment
At the end of this theme is the pupil able to:
- Rotate, reflect and translate shapes;
- Recognise lines of symmetry and orders of rotational symmetry?

Lesson 1

Introduction **10 mins**
Review the meaning of line symmetry. Brainstorm shapes and objects that have line(s) of symmetry.

Activities **25 mins**
Practice (individual)
Give out Copymaster 51. This contains a number of shapes, onto which the pupils should draw any lines of symmetry they find.
Alphabet (pairs)
Ask the pupils to draw the alphabet carefully in capital letters. They should then mark the lines of symmetry on each one.

Differentiation
Low Attainers – Check that they have included all the interesting types of triangles and quadrilaterals. They could use paper-folding to help them.
High Attainers – Ask them to think about what kind of symmetry a solid shape could have.

Plenary **5 mins**
Mark the copymaster. Check the results of 'Alphabet'. Discuss variations in answers due to different styles *(e.g. X, Q)*.

Lesson 2

Introduction **10 mins**
Draw an 8×8 grid of squares on the board. Shade or colour a pattern of 4 squares, which should have no obvious symmetry of its own. Use another colour to mark a line (vertical, horizontal or 45° diagonal, not necessarily passing through the centre of the grid). This line will become a line of symmetry. Ask various pupils to add a square at a time, reflecting one of the existing squares. Repeat with a pair of symmetry lines at right angles.

Activities **25 mins**
Investigation (individual)
Pupils need 5 mm squared paper. Each pupil should draw his or her own pattern of squares. How many different designs can be produced from the pattern by varying the position and number of the lines of symmetry? Some tracing paper might be useful for those who have difficulty 'seeing' the reflections.

Differentiation
Low Attainers – May find it easier to work with 1 cm squares.
High Attainers – Could progress to patterns of triangles on isometric paper.

Plenary **5 mins**
Ask pupils to examine each others' work. It should be obvious if errors have been made.

Lesson 3

Introduction **10 mins**
Review the meaning of translation. Illustrate with diagrams if necessary.

Activities **25 mins**
Translation grids (individual)
Pupils need 1 cm squared paper. They should draw a coordinate grid with x- and y-axes from 0 to 10. They should then draw the small quadrilateral with vertices at (0, 2), (1, 0), (2, 1) and (2, 2).
Their tasks are as follows:

1 Draw a translation of the quadrilateral anywhere on the grid.
2 Write down the coordinates of the object quadrilateral.
3 Write down the coordinates of the image quadrilateral.
4 Investigate what has happened to each pair of coordinates. Write a conclusion.
5 Repeat steps 1–4 with another translation.
6 Write an overall conclusion about what happens to the coordinates. Try more examples if necessary. Make a prediction and test it.

Differentiation
Low Attainers – Check that they have carried out the translations correctly – mistakes will make it impossible to 'guess the rule'.
High Attainers – Could be taught how to describe translations using column vectors.

Plenary **5 mins**
Go through the pupils' results. You may wish them all to write a formal conclusion dictated by you.

Lesson 4

Introduction **10 mins**
Work through rotating a small shape on squared paper about one of its vertices. Show the results when the rotation is 90° clockwise, 90° anticlockwise or 180°. Demonstrate to the pupils how to use tracing paper to accomplish the rotation (an OHP is useful for this).

Activities **20 mins**
Rotating Ls (individual)
Ask the pupils to draw an L shape on squared paper. They should use each vertex in turn as the centre for a 90° clockwise rotation, drawing a new diagram for each one.
Repeat with 90° anticlockwise rotations.
Repeat with 180° rotations.

Differentiation
Low Attainers – Rotating about the vertex with the reflex angle could be omitted.
High Attainers – Could try rotating about a point which is not a vertex.

Plenary **10 mins**
Pupils can check each others' work by tracing.

Lesson 5

Introduction **10 mins**
Ask the pupils to recreate their L shape from Lesson 4. Ask them to pick a vertex about which to rotate. They should then perform 90° clockwise, 90° anticlockwise and 180° rotations on the same diagram. The result should be a design with order 4 rotational symmetry and no line symmetry.
Ask them to trace this shape. Discuss how many different positions this can be rotated into and look the same. Explain that this means the shape has rotational symmetry and that the **order** is 4.
They should then look back at their 180° rotations from Lesson 4. Establish that these designs have rotational symmetry of order 2.

Activities **25 mins**
Practice (individual)
Give out Copymaster 52. The pupils have to identify the order of rotational symmetry for each shape on the sheet.
Designs (individual)
Pupils should design a starting shape and produce order 4 rotational symmetry patterns from them. These can form the basis for a wall display.

Differentiation
Low Attainers – Use starting shapes with right angles for their designs.
High Attainers – Could be asked to investigate the angles of rotation for the various orders of rotational symmetry.

Plenary **5 mins**
Mark the copymaster and examine the pupils' designs.

Theme 7 Investigating shapes

Objectives
- To understand that the angle sums of triangles and quadrilaterals are 180° and 360°, respectively
- To calculate missing angles in triangles when other angles are known
- To calculate an exterior angle of a triangle
- To investigate angle and other properties of shapes, generating and recording results systematically, making inferences and generalisations, and testing them appropriately

Vocabulary
triangle, quadrilateral, pentagon, hexagon etc., polygon, angle, acute, right, obtuse, straight, reflex, isosceles, equilateral, tetromino, pentomino, diagonal

Resources
Copymaster 53: *Angles in triangles*
Copymaster 54: *Diagonals*
Scrap paper, protractors, squared paper

Homework Copymaster 27

Mental maths starters 3, 9

Assessment
At the end of this theme is the pupil able to:
- Remember the angle sums of triangles and quadrilaterals;
- Calculate missing angles in triangles when other angles are known;
- Pursue a shape investigation systematically?

Lesson 1

Introduction **5 mins**
Review the different types of angle: acute, right, obtuse, straight, reflex. Make sure the pupils know the ranges of degrees allowed for each type.

Activities **30 mins**
Paper tearing (whole class)
Pupils need scrap paper, scissors and glue. Each pupil should draw a (large) triangle on a piece of paper, then cut it out carefully. They should then tear off the three corners. Place the corners together to form a straight angle. Make sure the pupils understand that this represents 180°.
Repeat with another triangle. The torn-off corners could be stuck down in a book or onto another sheet of paper.
Angle measuring (individual)
Pupils should draw a number of different triangles on plain paper, measure the angles and add them up. You could even award points for proximity to 180°!

Differentiation
Low Attainers – Check that pupils are writing down degree values that reflect the type of angle correctly, i.e. using the correct scale. Allow more leeway for the measurements.
High Attainers – They should ensure that some of their triangles have obtuse angles.

Plenary **5 mins**
Check that pupils are obtaining results within a few degrees of 180°. Investigate any that are too far out.

Lesson 2

Introduction **10 mins**
Demonstrate how an unknown angle in a triangle can be found by subtracting the sum of the known angles from 180°.
Also demonstrate how to find the base angle in an isosceles triangle given the apex angle.

Activities **25 mins**
Practice (individual)
Give out Copymaster 53. This contains a number of 'unknown angle' problems.
Exterior angles (individual)
The final diagram on Copymaster 53 demonstrates how to extend one side of a triangle to make an exterior angle. Pupils should investigate the sizes of exterior angles in various triangles that they draw.

Differentiation
Low Attainers – Omit Exterior angles.
High Attainers – Could attempt an explanation of the Exterior angles result.

Plenary **5 mins**
Mark the copymaster. Ask if anyone can calculate the exterior angle shown on Copymaster 53. Ask them to explain how they did it.

Lesson 3

Introduction **5 mins**
Explain that the pupils will be testing the angles in quadrilaterals in the same way as the triangles in Lesson 1.

Activities **30 mins**
Paper tearing (whole class)
Pupils need scrap paper, scissors and glue. Each pupil should draw a (large) quadrilateral on a piece of paper, then cut it out carefully. They should then tear off the four corners. Place the corners together to fill up the angular space around a point. Make sure the pupils understand that this represents 360°.
Repeat with another quadrilateral. The torn-off corners could be stuck down in a book or onto another sheet of paper.

Angle measuring (individual)
Pupils should draw a number of different quadrilaterals on plain paper, measure the angles and add them up. You could, as with the triangles, award points for proximity to 360°!

Differentiation
Low Attainers – Check that pupils are writing down degree values that reflect the type of angle correctly, i.e. using the correct scale. Allow more leeway for the measurements.
High Attainers – They should ensure that some of their quadrilaterals have reflex angles.

Plenary **5 mins**
Check that pupils are obtaining results within a few degrees of 360°. Investigate any that are too far out. These are usually caused by using the wrong scale on a protractor.

Lesson 4

Introduction **10 mins**
Ask pupils what shapes a domino is made from. Introduce the idea of a tromino and explore how many arrangements of three squares are possible

Activities **25 mins**
Tetrominoes and pentominoes (individual)
Pupils should attempt to find all the possible distinct arrangements of four, then five, squares. A useful hint is to think of letter shapes when looking for new arrangements.

Differentiation
Low Attainers – Square tiles of paper or card could be helpful.
High Attainers – Could proceed to hexominoes if time allows, but must predict the number first.

Plenary **5 mins**
Check the results of the investigation.

Lesson 5

Introduction **5 mins**
Make sure the pupils understand what is meant by a diagonal of a quadrilateral.

Activities **30 mins**
Diagonals (individual)
Give out Copymaster 54. They are led into an investigation by the copymaster.

Differentiation
Low Attainers – Should only be expected to tabulate the results.
High Attainers – Should be expected to express the rule logically.

Plenary **5 mins**
Check the results of the investigation.

Theme 8 Measuring capacity

Objectives
- To know and use the relationships between metric units of capacity
- To carry out estimations of capacity using suitable units
- To convert between metric units of capacity and their imperial equivalents
- To read capacity scales and solve problems involving capacity

Vocabulary
capacity, volume, millilitre, centilitre, litre, cubic centimetre, scale, division, convert

Resources
Copymasters 55 and 56, calculators, graph paper, measuring jugs/cylinders, containers, large bowl of water

Homework Copymaster 28

Mental maths starters 1, 3

Assessment
At the end of this theme is the pupil able to:
- Measure or estimate the capacity of a container;
- Convert between capacity units, metric and imperial;
- Solve problems involving capacity?

Lesson 1

Introduction **10 mins**
Revise the connections between the metric units of capacity. Ask questions like 'How many centilitres are there in a litre?', expecting the pupils to respond '100' together verbally.
Go over how to convert units, *e.g. when converting to a smaller unit, there are more of them, so multiply by the correct power of ten.* Ask questions like 'How do I change millilitres into litres?', expecting the pupils to reply 'divide by 1000'.

Activities **25 mins**
Conversion chains (whole class)
Work round the class like this: a pupil starts by calling out a measurement. The next few pupils give as many different equivalents as possible, using related units. If a pupil thinks all the equivalents have been given, but you know there are more, prompt him/her. An example might be: *'3 cl', '30 ml', (prompt: litres…) '0.03 l'.*
Estimation (whole class)
Brainstorm a number of objects used to hold liquids (teaspoon, bucket, tank etc.). By reasoning and comparison with known measurements, estimate the capacity of each object.
You may also wish to discuss the fact that 1 cm^2 = 1 ml. This may help with some of the estimations.

Differentiation
Low Attainers – Omit the cubic/capacity link.
High Attainers – Ask them to calculate the capacity of some cuboidal containers.

Plenary **5 mins**
Review the facts from the lesson. Ask various pupils to give examples of containers that match given measurements, *e.g. '2 l', 'large milk carton'.*

Lesson 2

Introduction **10 mins**
Brainstorm any imperial units of capacity that the pupils are aware of. Find out if anyone knows the relationships between fluid ounces, pints and gallons. Use the fact that 1 litre = 1.75 pints to make a table of equivalents. Pupils should use their calculators and round to an appropriate degree of accuracy.

Activities **25 mins**
Practice (individual)
Find the list of estimates made in Lesson 1. Pupils should convert these to suitable imperial units using the table of equivalents.
Conversion graphs (individual)
Pupils will need graph paper. They should make two conversion graphs:
1 Up to 20 litres to gallons
2 Up to 8 pints to cl

Differentiation
Low Attainers – Ensure they work to an appropriate degree of accuracy, and only attempt the first conversion graph.
High Attainers – Could also look at making a ml/fl oz conversion graph.

Plenary **5 mins**
Check the 'Practice' answers. Ask various pupils to use their graphs to carry out unit conversions.

Lesson 3

Introduction **10 mins**
Draw 4 copies of the same scale with major divisions marked 0, 1, 2, 3. Subdivide the four scales into 2, 4, 5 and 10 minor divisions respectively *(e.g. a mark every 0.5, 0.25, 0.2, 0.1)*. Discuss the differences between the scales, how relatively easy they are to use, the difficulty of interpolation (particularly on the 0.25 scale) etc.

Activities **25 mins**
Practice (individual)
Give out Copymaster 55. The pupils have to identify readings on various scales, indicated by arrows. They also have to mark new readings onto the scales.
Measuring capacity (pairs)
If you have some jugs or measuring cylinders, pairs of pupils, in turn, could find the capacity of two or three different objects *(e.g. cup, kettle, spoon etc.)* while the class activity is proceeding. A large bowl of water for 'storage' would be useful.

Differentiation
Low Attainers – Help might be needed in identifying on which scale each new measurement belongs.
High Attainers – Could convert their measurements to appropriate imperial units.

Plenary **5 mins**
Mark the copymaster and give out the correct capacities for the objects being measured.

Lesson 4

Introduction **10 mins**
Using the relationship 1 inch = 2.5 cm, work through how to produce a conversion scale for up to 12 inches to centimetres. This will be a single line (horizontal or vertical) calibrated in inches on one side, centimetres on the other. Draw the centimetre scale first, then use this to mark out the inch scale.

Activities **25 mins**
Conversion scales (pairs)
Pupils should use their equivalence table to help them produce conversion scales for:
1 Up to 20 litres to gallons (as found by petrol pumps)
2 Up to 8 pints to cl
3 Up to 20 fl oz to ml (as found on a measuring jug)

Differentiation
Low Attainers – Omit questions **2** and/or **3** as necessary.
High Attainers – Could pick a metric/imperial unit pair for another type of quantity *(e.g. length, mass)* and produce a conversion scale for it.

Plenary **5 mins**
Ask various pupils to do some conversions using their scales.

Lesson 5

Introduction **5 mins**
Review the relationships between units of capacity. Discuss the use of the correct unit and appropriate accuracy for the solution to a given problem.

Activities **25 mins**
Practice (individual)
Give out Copymaster 56. This contains various questions related to capacity and volume.
Fish tank (pairs)
How big would a fish tank holding 400 litres have to be? Remember that 1 cm^2 = 1 ml.

Differentiation
Low Attainers – Omit Fish tank.
High Attainers – Could try to find an optimal solution to Fish tank, e.g. *one which would use the least glass.*

Plenary **5 mins**
Mark the copymaster. Ask pupils to give possible solutions to 'Fish tank' and check them.

Theme 9 Addition and subtraction

Objectives
- To use mental methods of addition and subtraction fluently
- To perform accurate pencil-and-paper additions and subtractions
- To apply the correct methods in a problem-solving context

Vocabulary
add, subtract, sum, difference, plus, minus, digit, decimal, percentage

Resources
Copymasters 57 and 58, dice, plastic coins (or scrap paper to make them), calculators

Homework Copymaster 29

Mental maths starters 2, 8

Assessment
At the end of this theme is the pupil able to:
- Recall and use mental methods of addition and subtraction;
- Carry out pencil and paper calculations accurately;
- Analyse and solve problems involving addition and subtraction?

Lesson 1

Introduction **10 mins**
Discuss with the pupils some of the strategies for adding and subtracting numbers such as 9, 19, 29, 99 etc. Also look at 8, 18, 28 and even 7, 17 etc.

Activities **25 mins**
Quick fire (whole class)
Work round the class as follows: give a starting number and a number to add or subtract. Pupils call out the answers in turn, as you supply further instructions. An example might begin: *'35 + 14', '= 49', '– 29', '= 20', '+ 98', '= 118' etc.*
Work round the class as follows: call out a number to each pupil in turn. He or she has to respond with the difference between 100 and the number you called. Use decimals if you wish.

Dice darts (pairs)
Pupils need a pair of dice between them. Starting at 301 or 501 and working down, each 'dart' scores the product of the numbers on the two dice. Each 'visit to the oche' consists of three throws. These are added together mentally by the opponent and then the score is subtracted from the player's total. It is, of course, in the player's interest to check that the calculations are correct.

Differentiation
Low Attainers – Start at 301, or lower if desired.
High Attainers – Could use three dice per dart.

Plenary **5 mins**
Find the highest and lowest scores for three 'darts', and the smallest and largest number of darts that were needed to win.

Lesson 2

Introduction **10 mins**
Review the various written methods for carrying out addition and subtraction.

Activities **25 mins**
Practice (individual)
Write a number of addition and subtraction questions on the board for the pupils to carry out. Mark these after a suitable length of time.
Sums and differences (individual)
Pupils should choose two four-digit numbers each. They should then proceed as follows: find the sum and difference of their two numbers. Find the sum and difference of these new numbers. Find the sum and difference of these etc. A pattern should emerge.

Differentiation
Low Attainers – Start Sums and differences with two- or three-digit numbers.
High Attainers – Experiment with decimals: try to formulate an explanation of the results of the investigation.

Plenary **5 mins**
Discuss the results of the investigation. Pupils could check the 'doubling rule' using their calculators.

Lesson 3

Introduction **10 mins**
Review the concept of money represented by numbers with two decimal places. Write down some 'wrong' examples of money notation *(e.g. 256p, £2.8, £0.355)* and discuss what is wrong with them.

Activities **25 mins**
Practice (individual)
Give out Copymaster 57. This contains various money questions concentrating on addition and subtraction.
Prime kitty (pairs)
Each pupil needs some plastic coins (pieces of paper with the amounts written on them would do) as follows: 3 × 1p, 3 × 2p, 2 × 5p, 2 × 10p, 2 × 20p, 1 × 50p. Pupils play alternately, adding to the 'kitty' as they go. Players score a point if they lay a coin that makes the kitty contain a prime number of pence. Pupils may wish to make a list of prime numbers before they begin, or you could write the list out on the board.

Differentiation
Low Attainers – Could choose a different scoring criterion for the game, such as multiples of 3 or 10 etc.
High Attainers – Also issue a £1 denomination.

Plenary **5 mins**
Mark the copymaster. Find the highest and lowest scores in the game.

Lesson 4

Introduction **10 mins**
Review methods for calculating a percentage of a quantity.
Discuss the meaning of percentage increases and decreases and associated terminology: discount, interest etc.

Activities **25 mins**
Practice (individual)
Give out Copymaster 57. Give the pupils these instructions.
'The people in question 1 all got a pay rise of 4%. Work out their new salaries.'
'The music shop had a sale. They took 30% off all the prices. Work out the sale price of each type of disc.'
Trial and improvement (individual/pairs)
Give the pupils two amounts of money, where one is not more than twice the other *(e.g. £78.52 and £103.06)*. The pupils must experiment with their calculators to find (a) the percentage increase if the smaller amount increases to the larger; (b) the percentage decrease if the larger amount decreases to the smaller.
Pairs of pupils can then contribute an amount each and carry out the same exercise.

Differentiation
Low Attainers – Use amounts for Trial and improvement that are less than £20.
High Attainers – Remove the restriction that one quantity may not be more than twice the other.

Plenary **5 mins**
Mark the 'Practice' activity and the given 'Trial and improvement' example. Find the biggest and smallest percentage increases and decreases in the class.

Lesson 5

Introduction **5 mins**
Discuss the pitfalls when solving problems involving mixed-unit measures, i.e. the need to convert to the same type of unit first.

Activities **30 mins**
Practice (individual)
Give out Copymaster 58. This contains various questions on measures, concentrating on addition and subtraction.

Differentiation
Low Attainers – You may need to give some assistance with reasoning.
High Attainers – Could invent their own set of capacities for question 3, then see if the instructions can be followed.

Plenary **5 mins**
Mark the copymaster. Discuss the fact that there is always the same total amount of liquid in the last question.

Theme 10 Functions and formulae

Objectives
- To analyse factors and prime factors of numbers
- To analyse sequences, finding term-to-term and position-to-term formulae

Vocabulary
factor, prime, sequence, term, position, formula

Resources
Copymasters 59, 60 and 39, calculators, scrap paper

Homework Copymaster 30

Mental maths starters 10, 11

Assessment
At the end of this theme is the pupil able to:
- Find all the factors of a number;
- Decompose a number into prime factors;
- Analyse a sequence, finding a term-to-term and a position-to-term formula?

Lesson 1

Introduction **5 mins**
Review the definition of a **factor**. Illustrate with examples.

Activities **25 mins**
Factor chains (whole class)
Give the class a two-digit number. Work round the class as follows: one pupil gives a factor of the number, the next gives the co-factor with which it pairs. The next pair of pupils do the same with another pair of factors. This continues until all the factors have been found. Then begin with another number. This can lead to useful discussion of prime numbers and square numbers.
Factor lists (individual)
Ask various members of the class for two- and three-digit numbers. Write these on the board. The class exercise is to find all the factors of these numbers.

Differentiation
Low Attainers – Restrict the exercise to two-digit numbers.
High Attainers – Could include some four-digit numbers.

Plenary **5 mins**
Mark the 'Factor lists' exercise. Discuss why certain factors were missed by pupils and why some were included that should not have been.

Lesson 2

Introduction **10 mins**
Review the meaning of a **prime number**. Ask pupils to supply examples of prime numbers. Make sure the pupils understand that 1 is **not** a prime number.
Recall the exercise in which the prime factors of numbers were found (Spring Term, Theme 10, Lesson 3). Pick an example *(e.g. 120)* and show how it can be completely decomposed into prime numbers $(2 \times 2 \times 2 \times 3 \times 5)$. Work on some more examples with the pupils.

Activities **25 mins**
Prime factorisation (pairs)
The copymaster shows an example of prime factorisation. Pupils should work up through the counting numbers attempting to factorise each number in turn.
Practice (individual)
Give out Copymaster 39. In this, the pupils previously had to identify the prime numbers from a list and find prime factors of various numbers. They should now attempt a full decomposition of those numbers.

Differentiation
Low Attainers – Omit the Practice activity.
High Attainers – Could test a neighbour by constructing numbers that are the product of two larger primes *(e.g.* $667 = 23 \times 29$*)*.

Plenary **5 mins**
Mark the activities. Correct errors and try to find out why they occurred.

Lesson 3

Introduction **10 mins**

Write the first five terms of a sequence of numbers on the board whose common difference is a fixed whole number *(e.g. 3, 5, 7, 9, 11, ...)*. Work through finding the 10th term with the pupils, by extending the sequence. Make sure the pupils understand the terminology: sequence, term, position etc.
Work through finding the 20th term by adding 10 times the common difference. Find the 100th term.

Activities **25 mins**

Match patterns (individual)
Give out Copymaster 59. For each sequence, the pupils have to identify the common difference, continue the sequence to 10 terms and find the 20th and 100th terms through reasoning using the common difference. At your discretion, they could copy the patterns and draw the next one or two. Work through the first one with the pupils if you wish.
Inventing patterns (pairs)
Pupils can make up their own matchstick patterns to test each other.

Differentiation

Low Attainers/High Attainers – The copymaster is graded in difficulty. Pupils will set sequences for their partners commensurate with their abilities.

Plenary **5 mins**

Mark the copymaster. Check over any errors. 'Inventing patterns' should be self-marking, but ask if there were any problems.

Lesson 4

Introduction **15 mins**

Revise position-to-term sequences as follows: write the first five multiples of 4 on the board as a sequence. Write the position numbers (1, 2, 3, 4, 5, ...) above the terms. Demonstrate that because the terms count up 4 times as fast as the positions, multiplying the position by 4 gives the term. Illustrate this with a function machine diagram of the form *position* $\rightarrow \times 4 \rightarrow$ *term*. Write the sequence 2, 6, 10, 14, 18, ... on the board and label the positions. Demonstrate that $\times 4$ is still required to make the numbers count up fast enough, but that an additional -2 is needed as well to get the starting number right. This yields *position* $\rightarrow \times 4 \rightarrow -2 \rightarrow$ *term*.
Work through finding the 10th, 20th and 100th term by using the function machines on the position numbers. Try a few more examples, including some with negative differences.

Activities **20 mins**

Practice (individual)
Give out Copymaster 59. For each sequence, the pupils have to find the position-to-term rule, and calculate the 1000th term of each sequence.
Inventing sequences (pairs)
Pupils can make up their own sequences to test each other, as in Lesson 3. However, they should invent the **rule** first and generate the terms from that. Check that no-one is over-complicating the rules!

Differentiation

Low Attainers/High Attainers – The copymaster is graded in difficulty. Pupils will set sequences for their partners commensurate with their abilities.

Plenary **5 mins**

Mark the copymaster. Check over any errors. 'Inventing sequences' should be self-marking, but ask if there were any problems.

Lesson 5

Introduction

None: this is a 'puzzle' lesson!

Activities **30 mins**

Puzzles (individual/pairs)
Give out Copymaster 60. Pupils need calculators and scrap paper.

Plenary **10 mins**

Mark the copymaster and discuss the answers.

Doubling and halving

Fill in the missing numbers. The first one has been done for you.

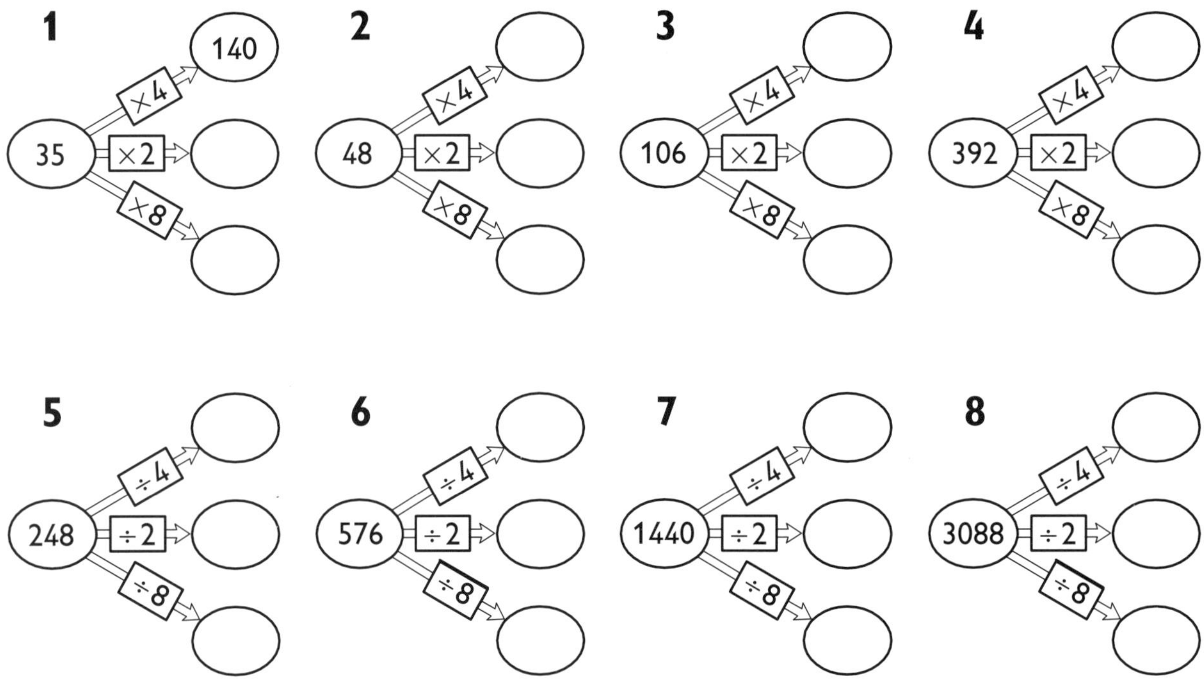

Join numbers connected by doubling or halving to find the picture. Use straight lines.

25 50 75
101 1 32 1024
26
300 56
102 11
8 128
50 632 79 25
16
125 33 728 91 64
24
631 44 83 4
40 256
500 29
104 90
5 6
316 158 364 182

Splitting up calculations

Work out the answers to move round the grid. You can make jottings as you work.

FINISH

START

42×5	21×50	$740 \div 5$	15×480
231×5	16×150	$3100 \div 50$	$5250 \div 50$
3525×5	23×75	59×25	250×250
507×50	$3175 \div 25$	61×15	12×500
25×25	$375 \div 25$	230×15	$615 \div 5$

Multiplying with grids

Use these grids to multiply the numbers.

1 28 × 5

×	20	8
5		

....

2 73 × 7

×	70	3
7		

....

3 436 × 3

×	400	30	6
3			

....

4 5219 × 8

×	5000	200	10	9
8				

....

....

Draw your own grids to answer these.

5 125 × 7

6 508 × 5

7 1296 × 4

8 8888 × 8

9 30 511 × 3

10 75 275 × 5

11 636 236 × 6

12 1 481 481 × 9

Catalogue

Mrs Semple is buying things for the school computer room. This is a page from the catalogue.

UNBEATABLY LOW WHOLESALE PRICES!

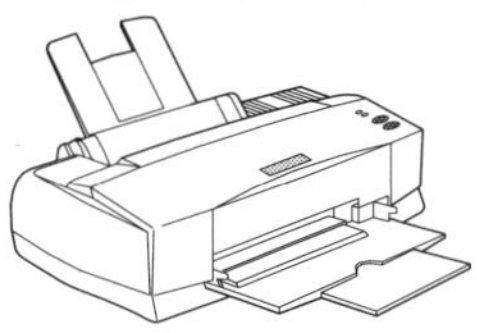

Inkjet printer
£108.95

Mouse mat
£2.51

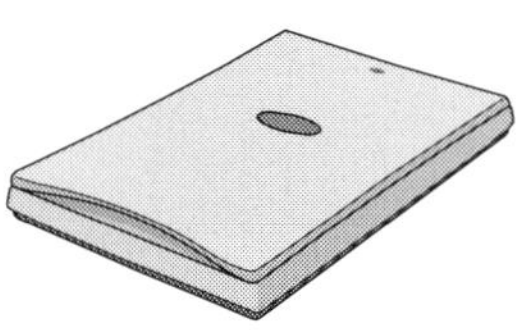

Flatbed scanner
£125.95

SALE !

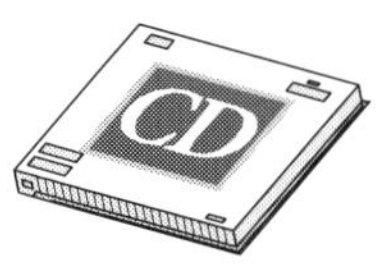

Software CDs
£9.72

A4 paper
(pack of 250 sheets)
£10.40

Floppy disks
(box of 10)
£1.90

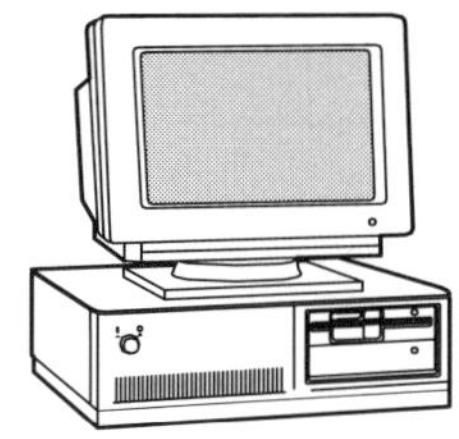

Multimedia PC
£899.95

Ink cartridges
£12.55

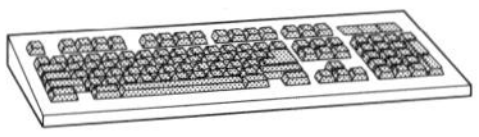

Replacement keyboard
£36.46

Complete Mrs Semple's order form.

Item	Number required	Cost of one item	Item total
Multimedia PC	*2*		
Replacement keyboard	*3*		
Software CDs	*9*		
Inkjet printer	*2*		
Ink cartridges	*4*		
A4 paper (pack of 250 sheets)	*5*		
Mouse mat	*7*		
Floppy disks (box of 10)	*6*		
		Order Total	

Fraction diagrams

A fraction of each diagram has been shaded. Write the numerator and denominator in the correct places. The first one has been done for you.

1 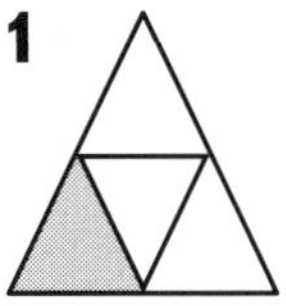 $\frac{1}{4}$

2 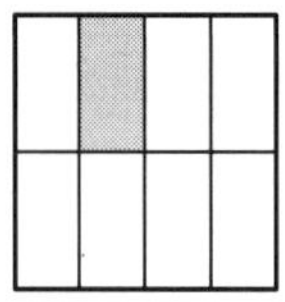 —

3 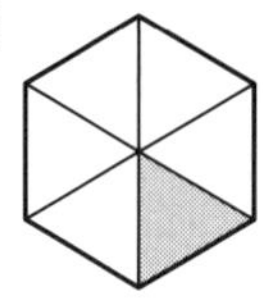 —

4 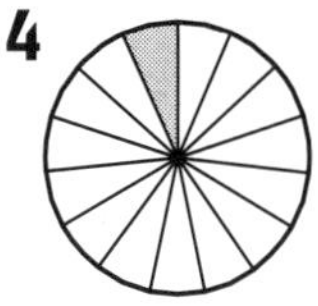 —

5 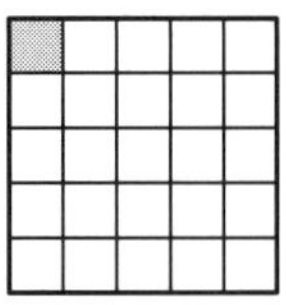 —

6 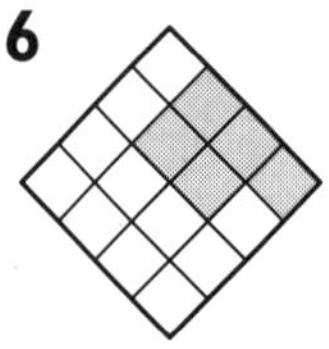 —

7  —

8 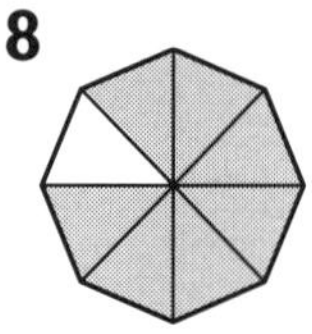 —

9 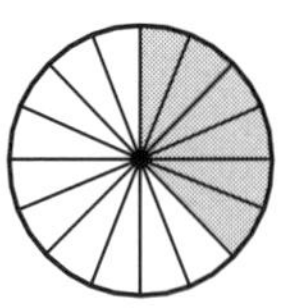 —

10  —

11  —

12 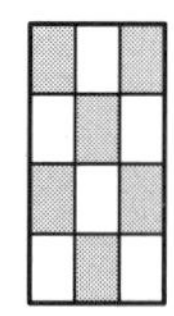 —

13 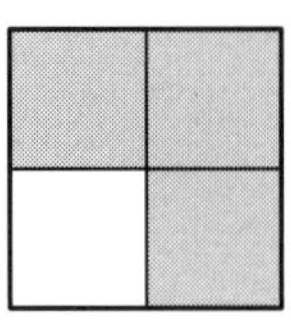 —

14 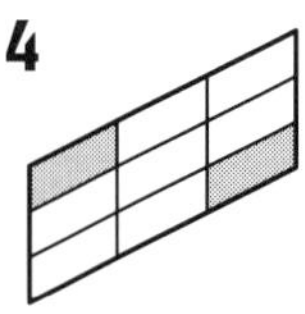 —

15 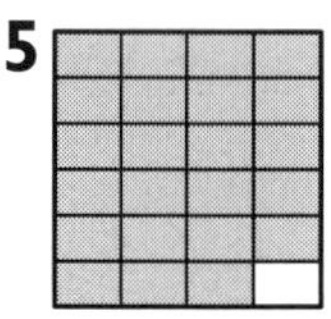 —

16  —

17 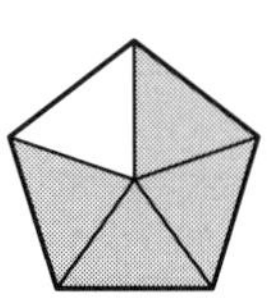 —

18 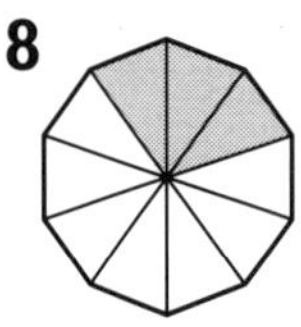 —

19 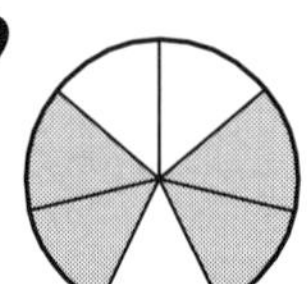 —

20 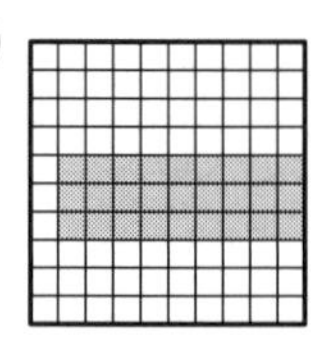 —

21 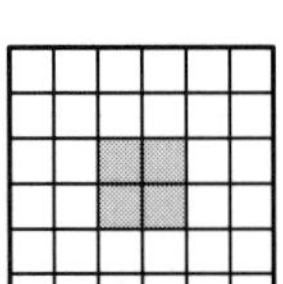 —

22 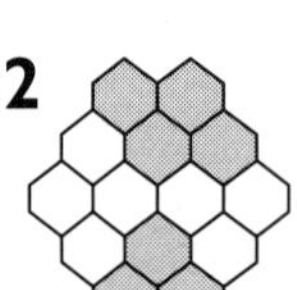 —

23 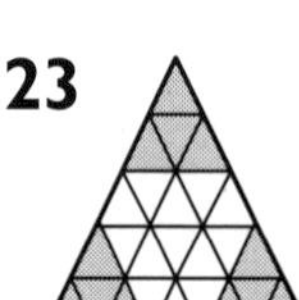 —

24 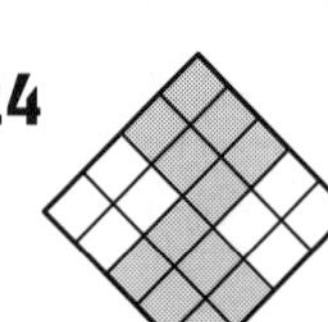 —

Converting units

1		mm =	12 cm =	m =	km
2		5 ml =	cl =	l	
3		g =	1.5 kg =	t	
4	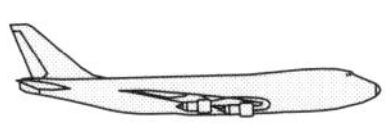	mm =	cm =	35 m =	km
5	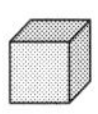	1 mm =	cm =	m =	km
6		g =	kg =	4 t	
7		ml =	cl =	14 l	
8	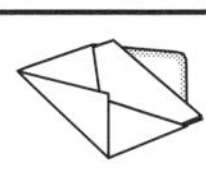	g =	0.01 kg =	t	
9		ml =	70 cl =	l	
10	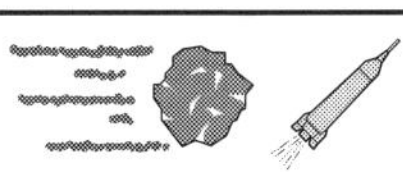	mm =	cm =	m =	12 km
11		g =	30 kg =	t	
12		mm =	250 cm =	m =	km
13	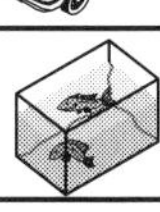	ml =	5000 cl =	l	
14	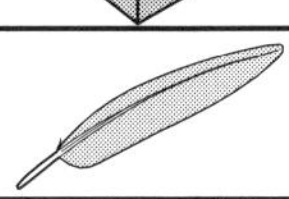	1 g =	kg =	t	
15		ml =	cl =	0.2 l	
16		g =	kg =	0.002 t	
17	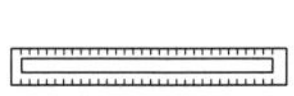	300 mm =	cm =	m =	km
18		454 ml =	cl =	l	
19		g =	25 500 kg =	t	
20	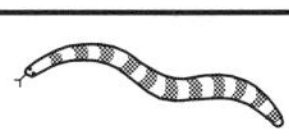	mm =	cm =	m =	0.003 km

Matching ratios

1

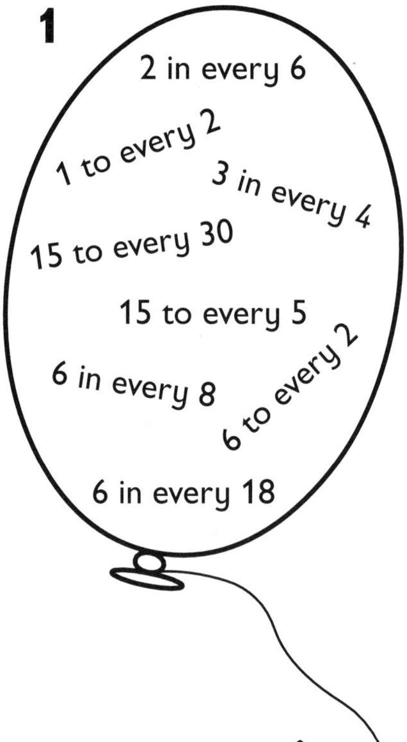

2

3

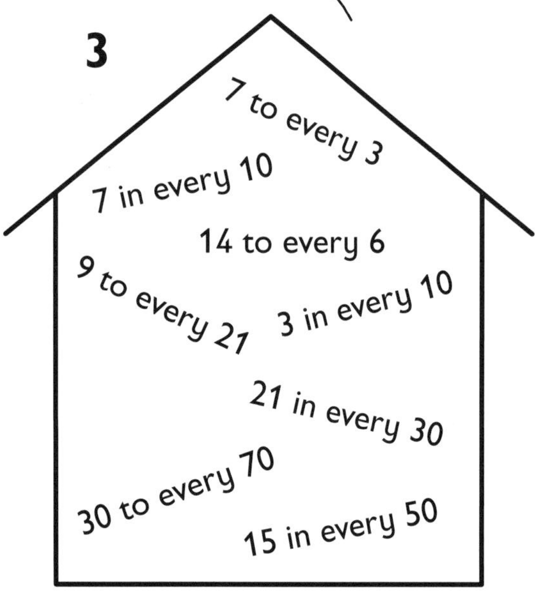

4

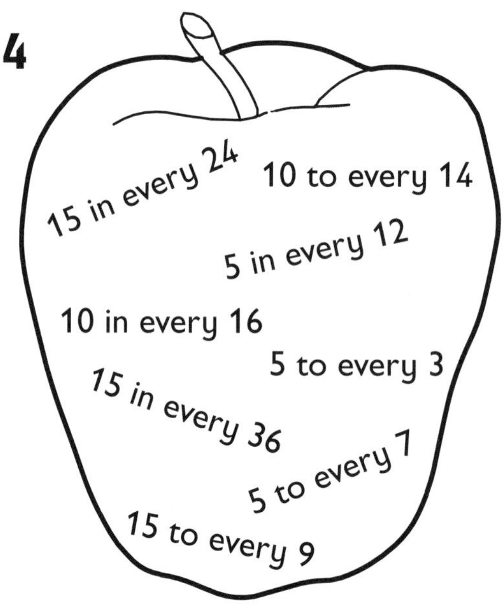

5

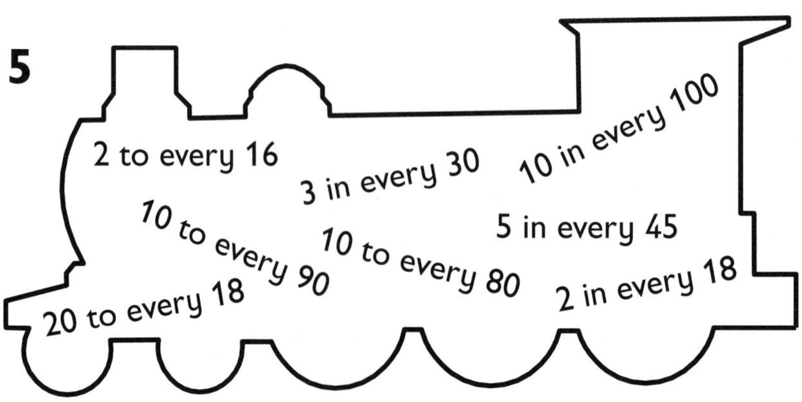

Ratio problems

1 Write a new list of ingredients to prepare this meal for
(a) 6 people
(b) 10 people.

2 1 in every 12 eggs in a supermarket is broken. The shelves hold 900 boxes. Each box contains half a dozen eggs.
(a) How many eggs are there?
(b) How many are broken?
(c) How many are intact (not broken)?

3 When Harry plays darts, he misses the board 3 times to every 5 times he hits it. One evening, he throws 120 times.
(a) How many times does he hit the board?
(b) How many times does he miss?
Another evening, he misses the board 36 times.
(c) How many throws does he have?
(d) How many times does he hit the board?

4 Sally draws this pattern of squares: 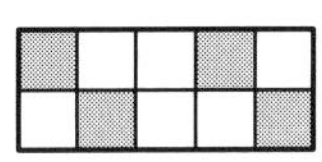
She repeats the pattern until she has completed a grid with 200 squares in it.
(a) How many squares has she coloured?
(b) How many squares does she leave blank?

Another time, she draws this pattern: 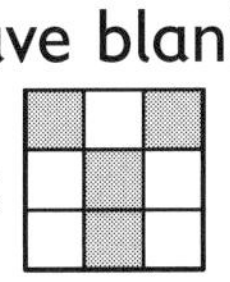

She repeats this pattern until she has **coloured** 200 squares.
(c) How many squares are in her grid?
(d) How many squares does she leave blank?

5 Talvin is clearing a site ready to build on it. He knows that with 2 dump trucks, he can clear the site in 15 days.
(a) His boss tells him that he can get an extra truck. How long will it take to clear the site now?
(b) Talvin would really like to clear the site in just 6 days. How many trucks would he need to do this?

Personal details

Name	
Height (cm)	
Mass (kg)	
House number (0 if just a name)	
Shoe size	
Number of siblings (brothers and sisters)	
Eye colour	
Hair colour	
Favourite breakfast	

Name	
Height (cm)	
Mass (kg)	
House number (0 if just a name)	
Shoe size	
Number of siblings (brothers and sisters)	
Eye colour	
Hair colour	
Favourite breakfast	

Facts and figures

	Height (cm)	Mass (kg)	House number	Shoe size	Number of siblings	Eye colour	Hair colour	Favourite breakfast	
1									
2									
3									
4									
5									
6									
7									
8									
9									
10									
11									
12									
13									
14									
15									
16									
17									
18									
19									
20									
21									
22									
23									
24									
25									
26									
27									
28									
29									
30									

Plotting quadrilaterals

For each question, you need to draw a coordinate grid with *x*- and *y*-axes from 0 to 10. Plot and join the points in the order given, then write the name of the quadrilateral inside it.

1 (2, 4) → (9, 4) → (9, 7) → (2, 7) and back to (2, 4).
2 (8, 0) → (2, 7) → (2, 10) → (8, 3) and back to (8, 0).
3 (4, 2) → (7, 1) → (9, 7) → (3, 5) and back to (4, 2).
4 (2, 7) → (6, 8) → (6, 1) → (2, 4) and back to (2, 7).
5 (4, 4) → (8, 1) → (8, 6) → (4, 9) and back to (4, 4).
6 (5, 9) → (10, 8) → (3, 1) → (2, 6) and back to (5, 9).
7 (0, 6) → (6, 7) → (7, 1) → (1, 0) and back to (0, 6).
8 (1, 3) → (4, 5) → (7, 3) → (4, 8) and back to (1, 3).
9 (8, 2) → (4, 10) → (2, 9) → (6, 1) and back to (8, 2).
10 (1, 8) → (4, 2) → (8, 0) → (5, 6) and back to (1, 8).

1 (2, 4) → (9, 4) → (9, 7) → (2, 7) and back to (2, 4).
2 (8, 0) → (2, 7) → (2, 10) → (8, 3) and back to (8, 0).
3 (4, 2) → (7, 1) → (9, 7) → (3, 5) and back to (4, 2).
4 (2, 7) → (6, 8) → (6, 1) → (2, 4) and back to (2, 7).
5 (4, 4) → (8, 1) → (8, 6) → (4, 9) and back to (4, 4).
6 (5, 9) → (10, 8) → (3, 1) → (2, 6) and back to (5, 9).
7 (0, 6) → (6, 7) → (7, 1) → (1, 0) and back to (0, 6).
8 (1, 3) → (4, 5) → (7, 3) → (4, 8) and back to (1, 3).
9 (8, 2) → (4, 10) → (2, 9) → (6, 1) and back to (8, 2).
10 (1, 8) → (4, 2) → (8, 0) → (5, 6) and back to (1, 8).

1 (2, 4) → (9, 4) → (9, 7) → (2, 7) and back to (2, 4).
2 (8, 0) → (2, 7) → (2, 10) → (8, 3) and back to (8, 0).
3 (4, 2) → (7, 1) → (9, 7) → (3, 5) and back to (4, 2).
4 (2, 7) → (6, 8) → (6, 1) → (2, 4) and back to (2, 7).
5 (4, 4) → (8, 1) → (8, 6) → (4, 9) and back to (4, 4).
6 (5, 9) → (10, 8) → (3, 1) → (2, 6) and back to (5, 9).
7 (0, 6) → (6, 7) → (7, 1) → (1, 0) and back to (0, 6).
8 (1, 3) → (4, 5) → (7, 3) → (4, 8) and back to (1, 3).
9 (8, 2) → (4, 10) → (2, 9) → (6, 1) and back to (8, 2).
10 (1, 8) → (4, 2) → (8, 0) → (5, 6) and back to (1, 8).

Tangrams

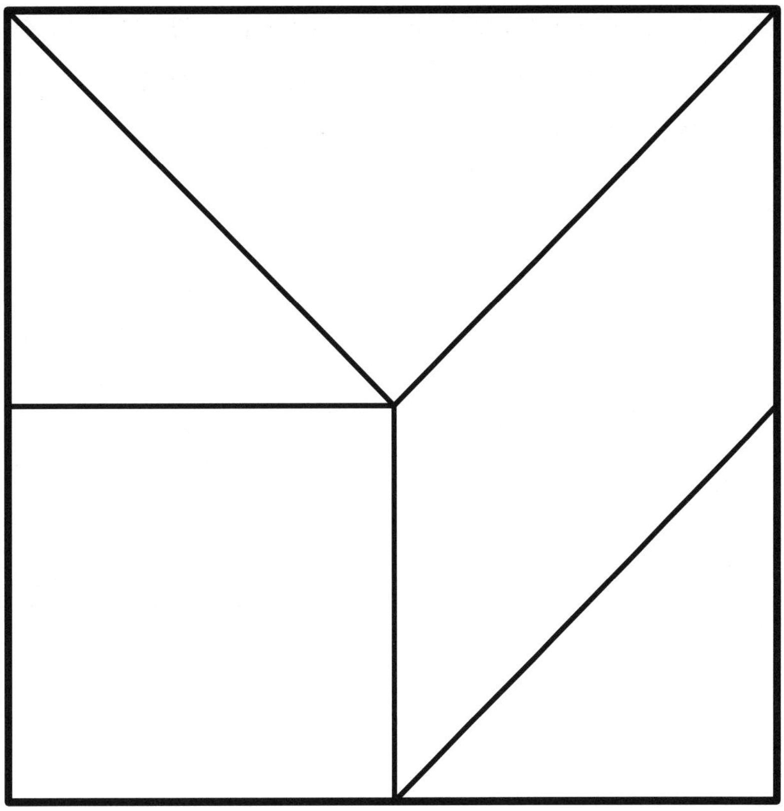

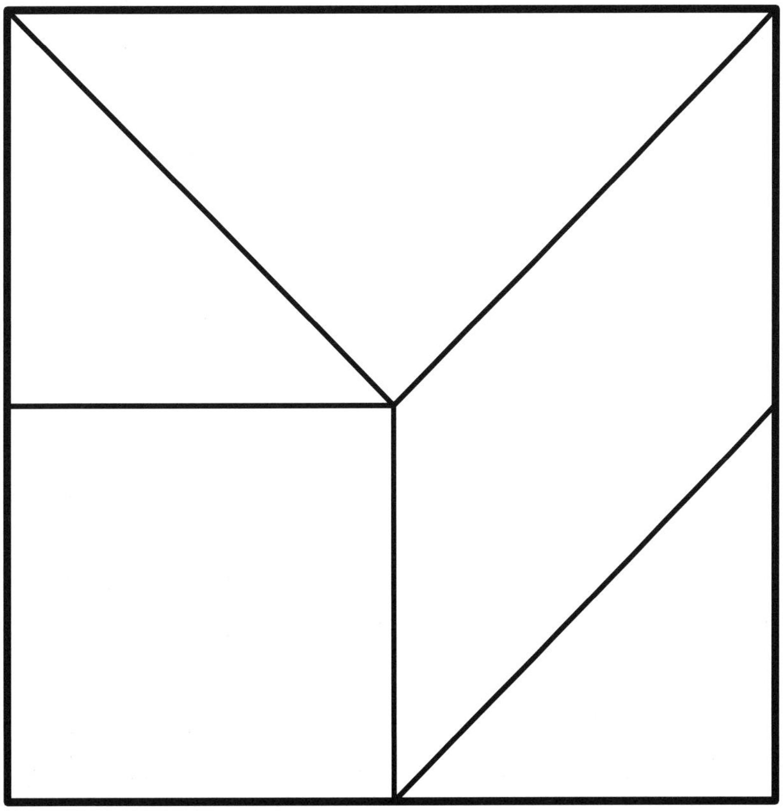

Perimeters of rectangles

Find the perimeter of each object.

1 14 cm

21 cm

2 8.5 cm

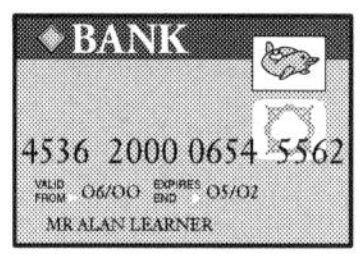

5.3 cm

3 45 cm

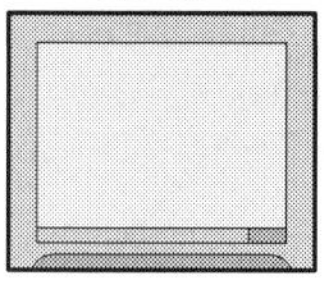

36 cm

4

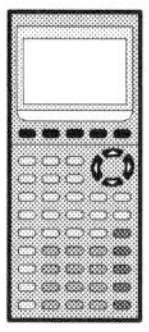

12 cm

6 cm

5 5 m

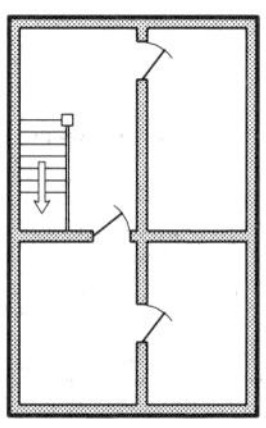

11 m

6 220 m

340 m

7 14 cm

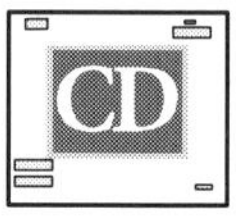

12.5 cm

8

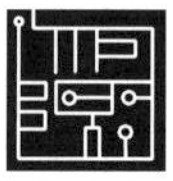

8 mm

8 mm

9 1.1 m

55 cm

10 2 cm

23 mm

Work out the missing measurements.

11 12 cm

?

Perimeter = 30 cm

13 ?

500 m

Perimeter = 4 km

12 2.5 cm

?

Perimeter = 13.5 m

14 7 mm

?

Perimeter = 28 mm

Perimeters of shapes

Work out the perimeter of each shape.

1

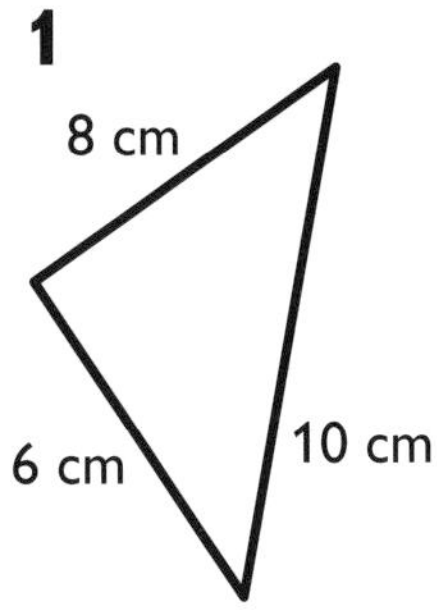

2

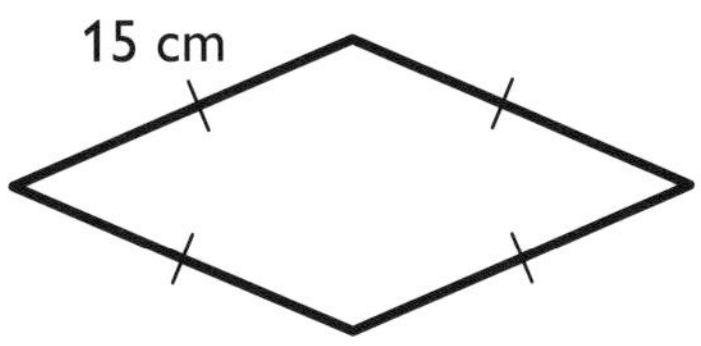

3

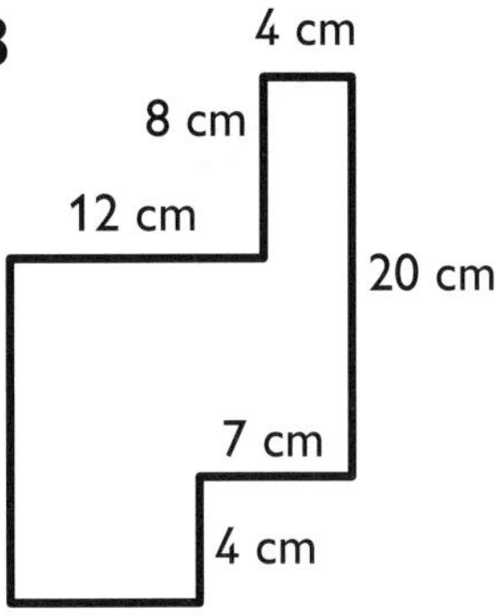

4

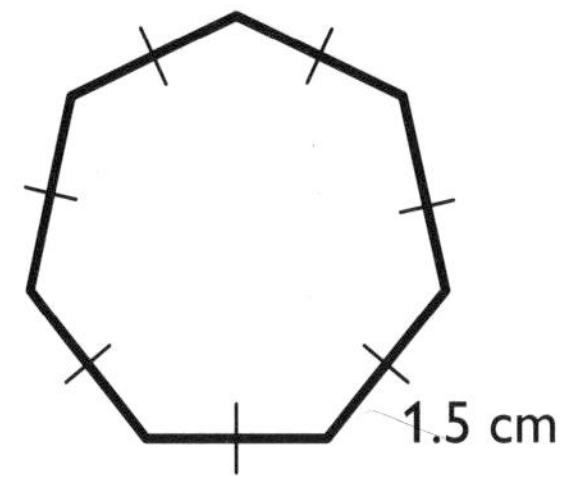

5

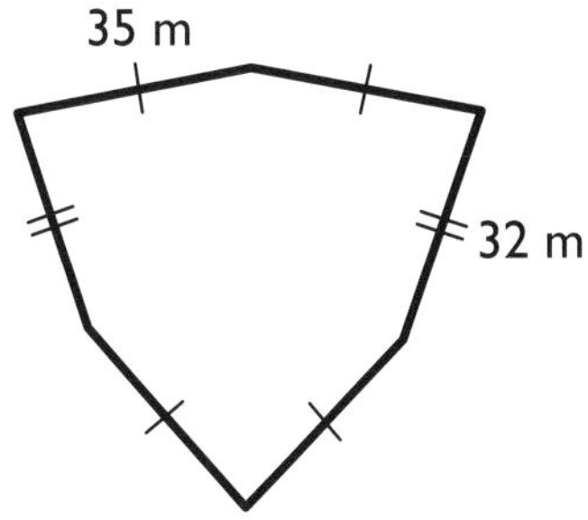

6

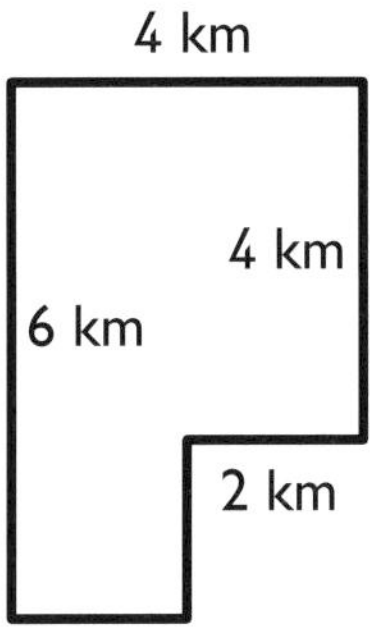

7

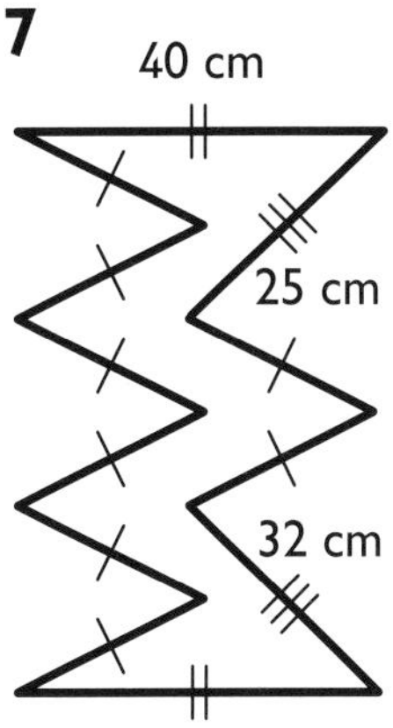

8

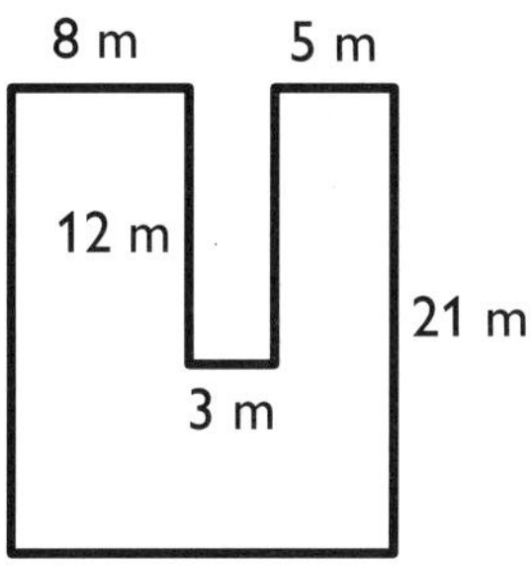

9

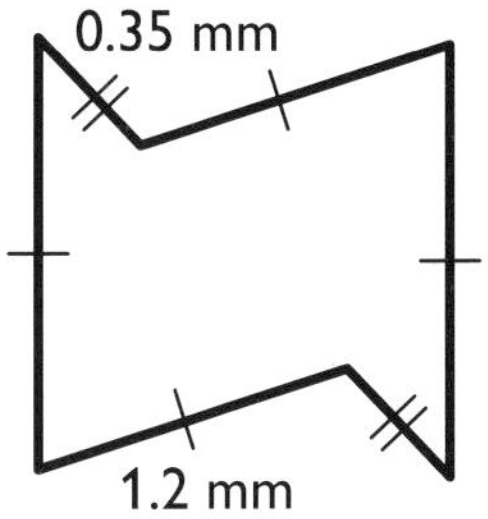

10

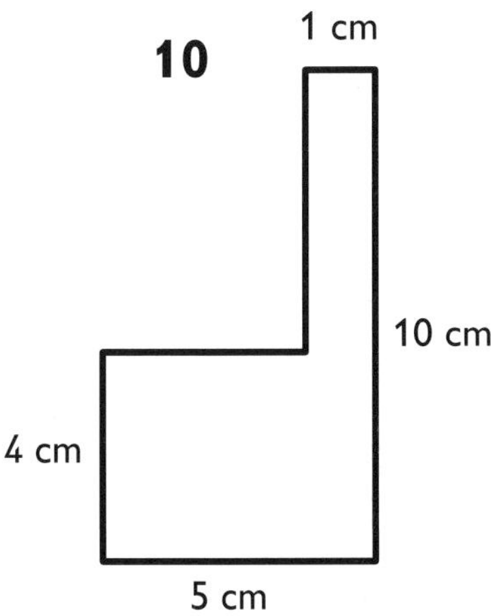

11

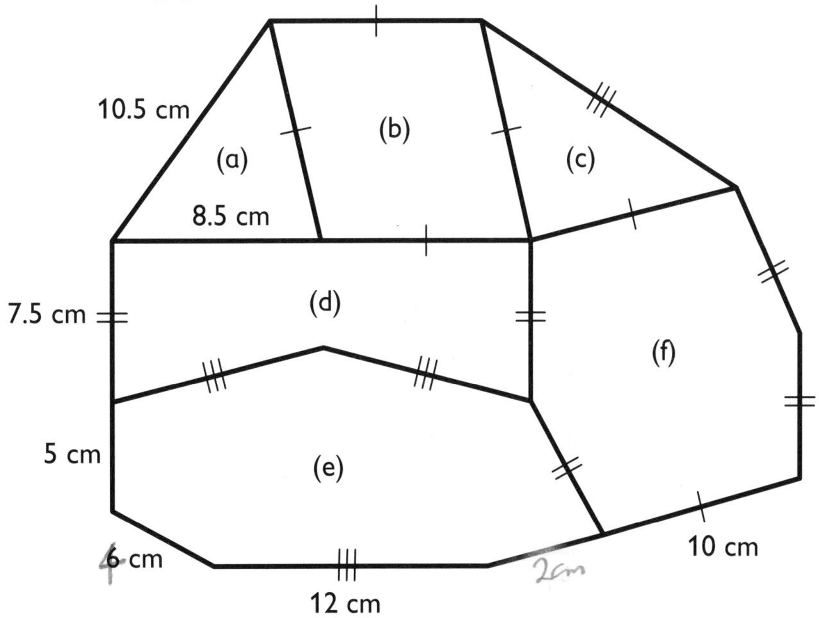

Time zones

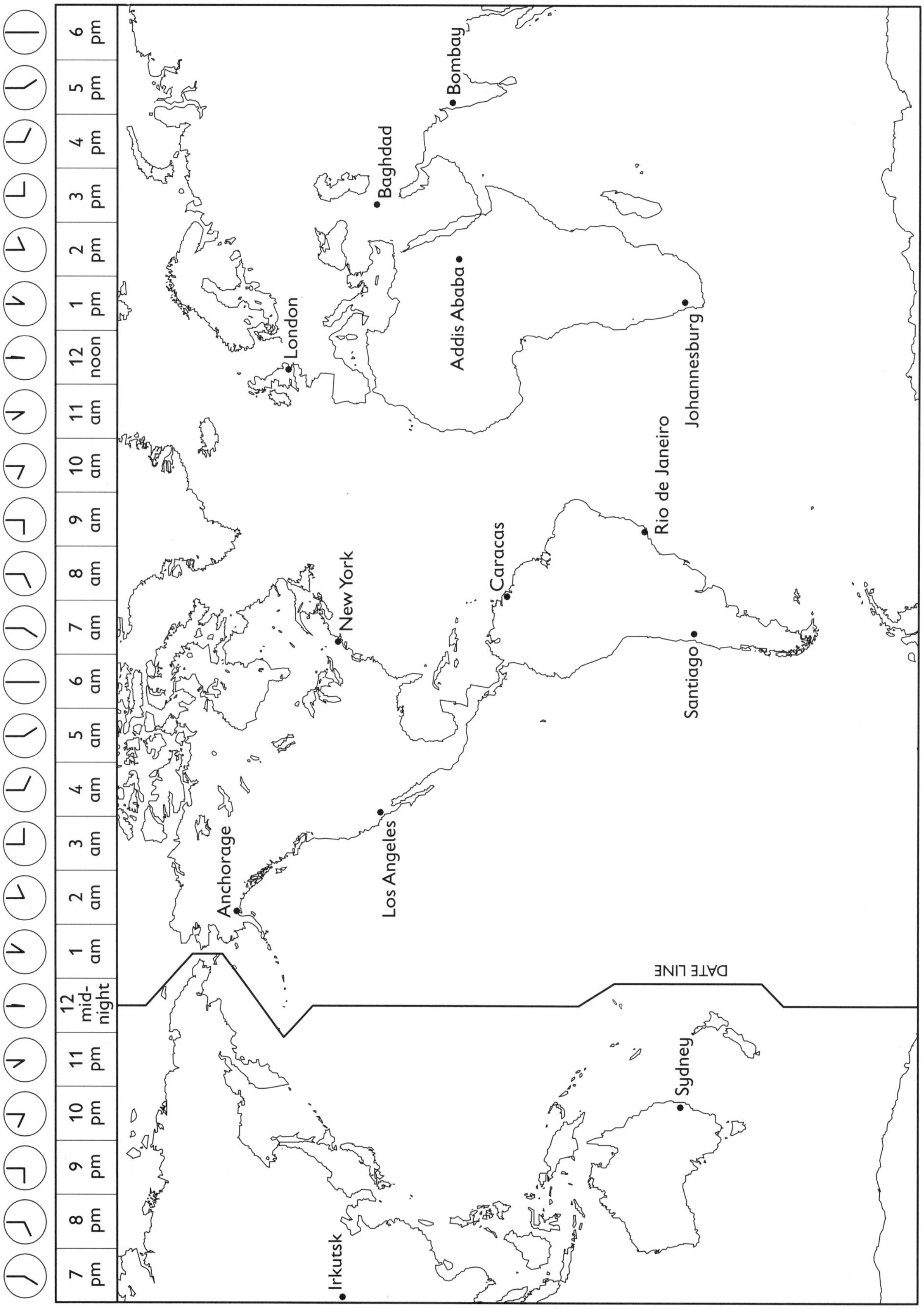
6 pm
5 pm
4 pm
3 pm
2 pm
1 pm
12 noon
11 am
10 am
9 am
8 am
7 am
6 am
5 am
4 am
3 am
2 am
1 am
12 mid-night
11 pm
10 pm
9 pm
8 pm
7 pm
Bombay
Baghdad
Addis Ababa
London
Johannesburg
Rio de Janeiro
Caracas
New York
Santiago
Anchorage
Los Angeles
DATE LINE
Sydney
Irkutsk

Timetables

	Register (20 min)	Lesson 1 (0910)	Lesson 2 (1010)	Break (15 min)	Lesson 3 (1125)	Lunch (1 hour)	Register (5 mins)	Lesson 4 (1330)	Lesson 5 (1430)
MON		SCIENCE	ENGLISH		PE	Football practice		MATHS	FRENCH
TUE		FRENCH	ART		ENGLISH	Band practice		TECH	MUSIC
WED		MATHS	TECH		SCIENCE			ICT	DRAMA
THU		TECH	SCIENCE		FRENCH	French club		PSE	ENGLISH
FRI		MATHS	ART		PE			ICT	MUSIC

North-West England to The Midlands and East Anglia

Saturdays

	🍴	🍴		🍴	🍴	🍴			
Liverpool Lime Street	1352	1452	1552	1652	1752	1852	1952	2052	—
Warrington Central	1418	1518	1618	1718	1818	1918	2018	2118	—
Manchester Piccadilly	1443	1543	1643	1743	1843	1943	2043	2145	2228
Stockport	1453	1553	1653	1753	1853	1953	2053	2155	2238
Sheffield	1540	1638	1747	1840	1940	2038	2140	2238	2340
Chesterfield	1554	1654	1801	1854	1954	2053	2154	2302	0002
Nottingham	1625	1733	1840	1926	2041	2130	2229	2344	0042
Grantham	—	1813	—	—	2112	—	—	—	—
Peterborough	—	1852	2001	—	2143	—	—	—	—
Ely	—	1925	2033	—	2231	—	—	—	—
Thetford	—	1952	2100	—	2251	—	—	—	—
Norwich	—	2026	2129	—	2326	—	—	—	—

NOTES: 🍴 food trolley service

LINCOLN–SWANPOOL–BIRCHWOOD *Service 99*

Monday to Saturday only

	S	NS					S
LINCOLN City Bus Station	**0715**	**0745**		**:45**		**1745**	**1815**
The Junction	**—**	**0755**	then	**:55**		**1755**	**—**
Swanpool Almond Avenue	**0730**	**0800**	at	**:00**		**1800**	**1830**
Birchwood The Wildlife Inn	**0732**	**0802**	these	**:02**		**1802**	**1832**
Birchwood The Neighbourhood Centre	**0740**	**0810**	minutes	**:10**	until	**1810**	**1840**
Birchwood The Wildlife Inn	**0742**	**0812**	past	**:12**		**1812**	**1842**
Swanpool Almond Avenue	**0745**	**0815**	each	**:15**		**1815**	**1845**
The Junction	**0750**	**0820**	hour	**:20**		**1820**	**1850**
LINCOLN City Bus Station	**0800**	**0830**		**:30**		**1830**	**1900**

NOTES
S – Saturday only
NS – Not Saturday

World facts

United Kingdom

Area: 244 100 km^2

Population: 57 240 000

Highest mountain:
Ben Nevis, 1344 m

Greece

Area: 131 990 km^2

Population: 10 140 000

Highest mountain:
Mount Olympus, 2917 m

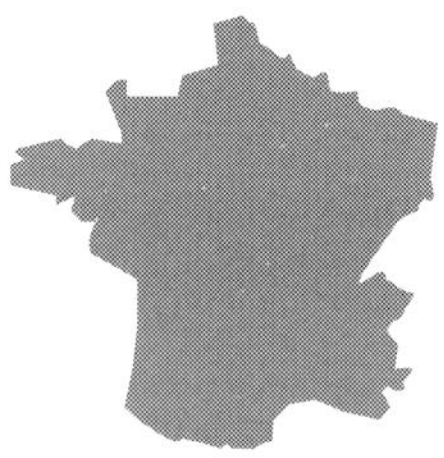

France

Area: 551 500 km^2

Population: 56 180 000

Highest mountain:
Mont Blanc, 4807 m

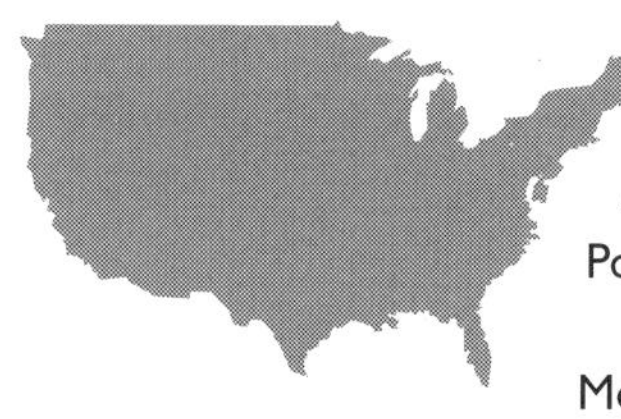

USA

Area: 9 372 614 km^2

Population: 249 630 000

Highest mountain:
Mount McKinley, 6194 m

Switzerland

Area: 41 293 km^2

Population: 6 700 000

Highest mountain:
Dufour, 4630 m

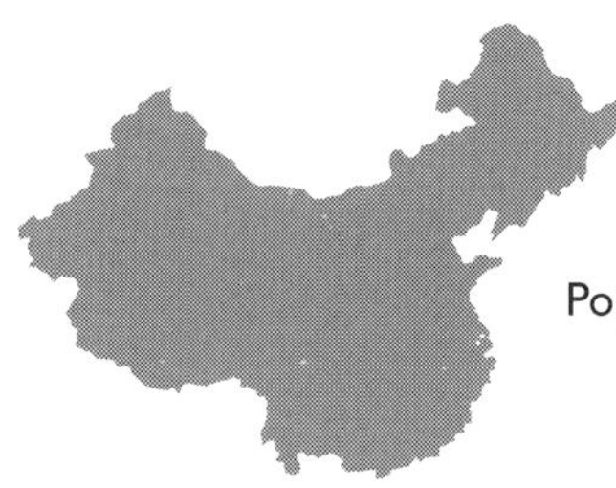

China

Area: 9 596 961 km^2

Population: 1 114 000 000

Highest mountain:
K2, 8611 m

Germany

Area: 356 910 km^2

Population: 79 070 000

Highest mountain:
Zugspitze, 2962 m

Nepal

Area: 140 797 km^2

Population: 18 000 000

Highest mountain:
Everest, 8848 m

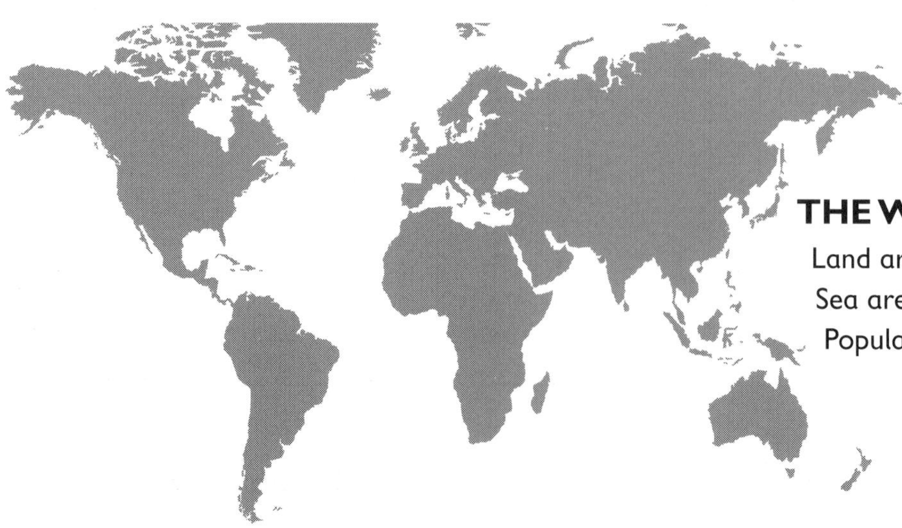

THE WHOLE WORLD

Land area: 148 326 000 km^2

Sea area: 361 740 000 km^2

Population: 6 158 000 000

Bank statements

Statement of Account — Megabank Limited

MR. N. E. BODDY ACCOUNT NO 12345678 — THE HIGH STREET

Date	Details		Debits	Credits	Balance
1 JUN	BROUGHT FORWARD FROM MAY				300.24
		CHEQUE NO 000123	31.50		
6 JUN		CASH MACHINE WITHDRAWAL	20.00		
	$$	W H SMITH	8.95		
7 JUN	$$	TOXACO FUEL SERVS	27.18		
10 JUN		BANK GIRO CREDIT		14.30	
13 JUN	DD	MORTGAGES DIRECT	198.55		
19 JUN	$$	SHIRTS R US	24.99		
		CHEQUE NO 000124	21.75		
20 JUN	DD	POWERGEN PLC	86.04		
22 JUN	DD	THE NEWSBOX	12.60		
	$$	SPINADISC LTD	14.95		
23 JUN		SALARY PAYMENT		647.08	
27 JUN		TRANSFER (SAVINGS ACCOUNT)	100.00		
30 JUN	$$	SAFEBURY'S FOODSTORE	54.62		

$$ = SWITCH TRANSACTION DD = DIRECT DEBIT ** = ACCOUNT OVERDRAWN

Statement of Account — BST Bank

MS. LENDA POUND ACCOUNT NO 98765432 — MAIN STREET

Date	Details		Debits	Credits	Balance
1 FEB	BROUGHT FORWARD FROM JAN				45.17
2 FEB		SALARY PAYMENT			475.73
	$$	MARRISON'S FOODSTORE			377.54
4 FEB		CASH MACHINE WITHDRAWAL			357.54
5 FEB	DD	RENTAFLAT PROPERTY SERVICES			146.59
8 FEB		BANK CHARGES			138.09
12 FEB		CHEQUE CREDIT			183.09
14 FEB		CASH MACHINE WITHDRAWAL			143.09
18 FEB	$$	GAPS			91.11
23 FEB	$$	EXTRAFLORA			76.79
27 FEB		CASH MACHINE WITHDRAWAL			46.79
28 FEB	DD	SUPER GAS			**18.21

$$ = SWITCH TRANSACTION DD = DIRECT DEBIT ** = ACCOUNT OVERDRAWN

Sequences

1.	3	5	7	9	11
2.	3	6	9	12	15
3.	1	6	11	16	21
4.	8	18	28	38	48
5.	5	6	7	8	9
6.	7	5	3	1	−1
7.	25	20	15	10	5
8.	25	24	23	22	21
9.	0	6	12	18	24
10.	−3	9	21	33	45
11.	0.5	7.5	14.5	21.5	28.5
12.	2	2.5	3	3.5	4
13.	4	3.5	3	2.5	2
14.	1.5	4	6.5	9	11.5
15.	3	3.1	3.2	3.3	3.4
16.	3	2.8	2.6	2.4	2.2
17.	3	4.3	5.6	6.9	8.2
18.	15	12.2	9.4	6.6	3.8
19.	−18	82	182	282	382
20.	−2	−52	−102	−152	−202

1.	2	5	8	11	14
2.	4	14	24	34	44
3.	12	11	10	9	8
4.	30	25	20	15	10
5.	0	0.5	1	1.5	2
6.	−1	−0.8	−0.6	−0.4	−0.2
7.	1	0.9	0.8	0.7	0.6
8.	8	7.4	6.8	6.2	5.6
9.	10	0.04	0.08	0.12	0.16
10.	−3	−3.25	−3.5	−3.75	−4
11.	1.5	3	4.5	6	7.5
12.	−11	−8.8	−6.6	−4.4	−2.2
13.	−11	0	11	22	33
14.	1200	1188	1176	1164	1152
15.	58.9	55.8	52.7	49.6	46.5
16.	0.8	1.81	2.82	3.83	4.84
17.	−1000	−900	−800	−700	−600
18.	512	472	432	392	352
19.	8.62	18.63	28.64	38.65	48.66
20.	−11.1	20.65	52.4	84.15	115.9

MathHopper's staircases

This is MathHopper. He likes to jump up staircases.

He can jump one stair or two stairs. He's not strong enough to jump three.

This is MathHopper's staircase number 4. You can see two different ways he can get to the top.

1 + 2 + 1

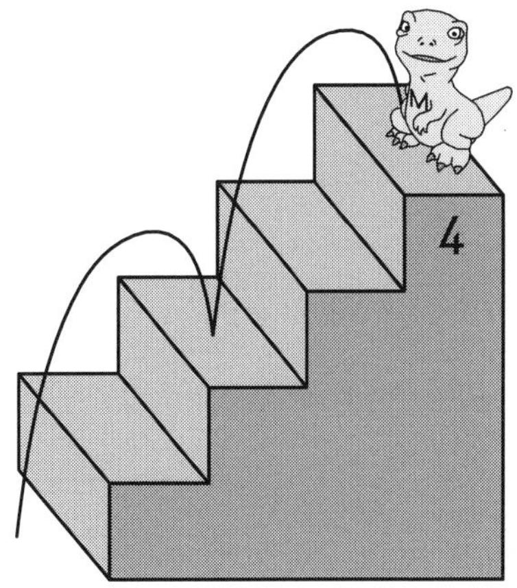

2 + 2

There are more ways he can get to the top of staircase number 4. Can you find them all? How many are there?

MathHopper has lots of different staircases. Your job is to work out how many different ways he can get up each staircase. There's a rule to find. How many ways are there for MathHopper to get to the top of staircase number 20?

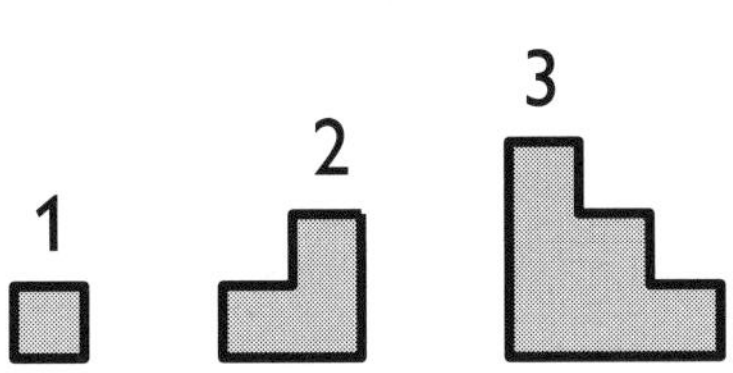

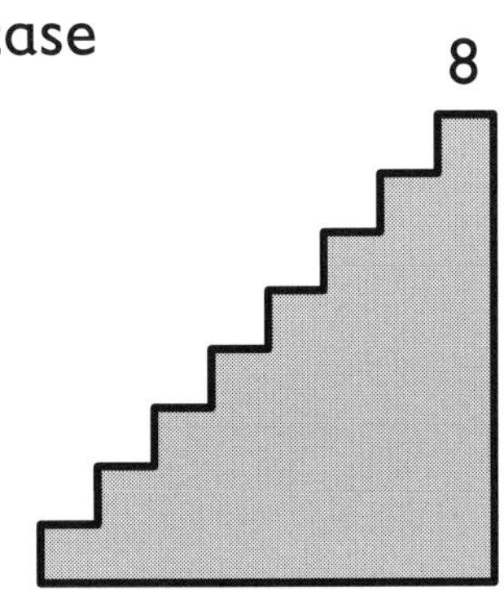

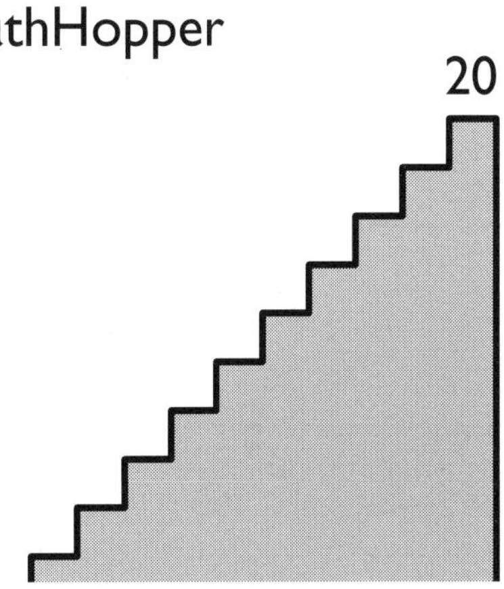

Number lines

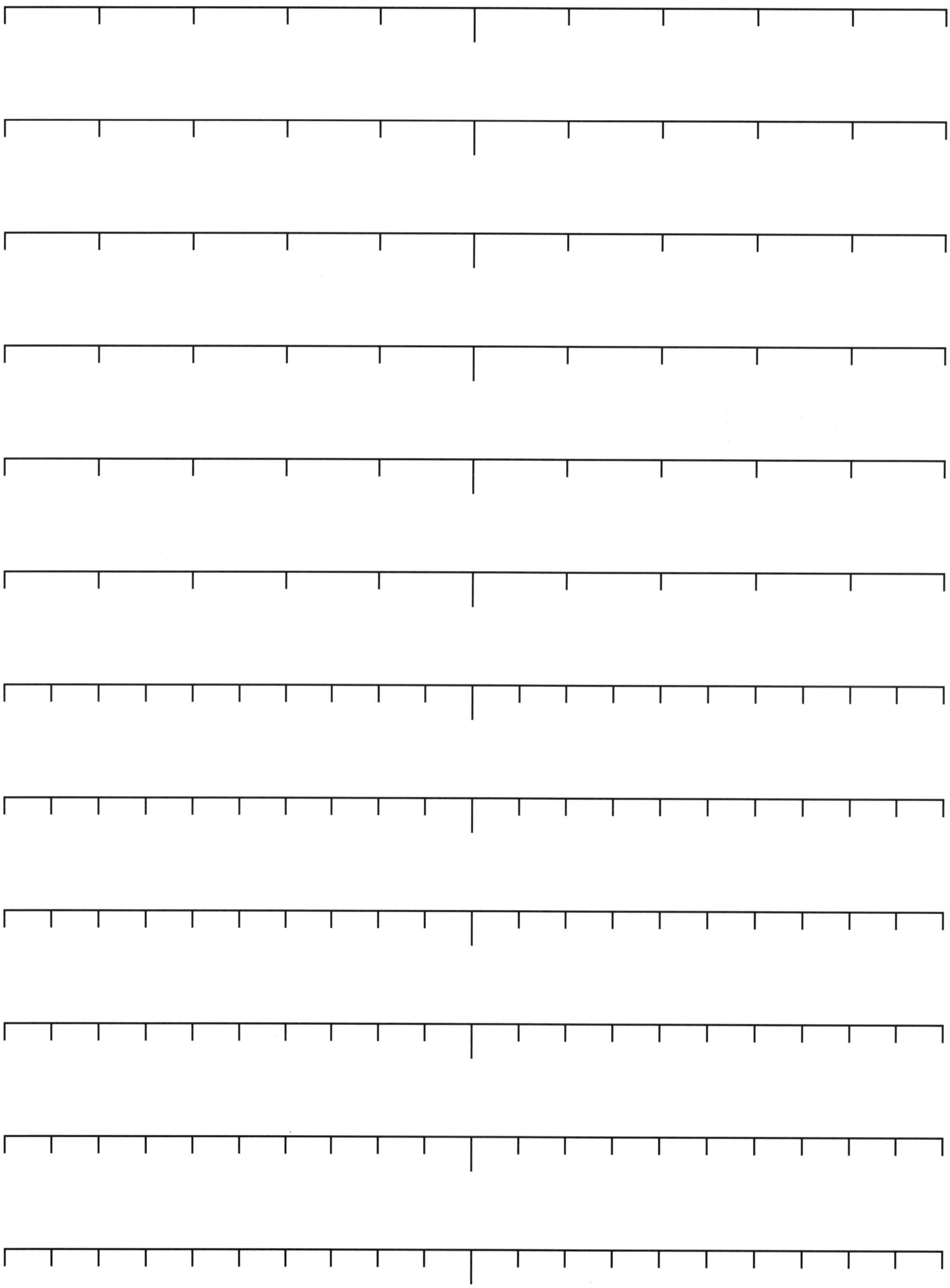

Coordinate grid

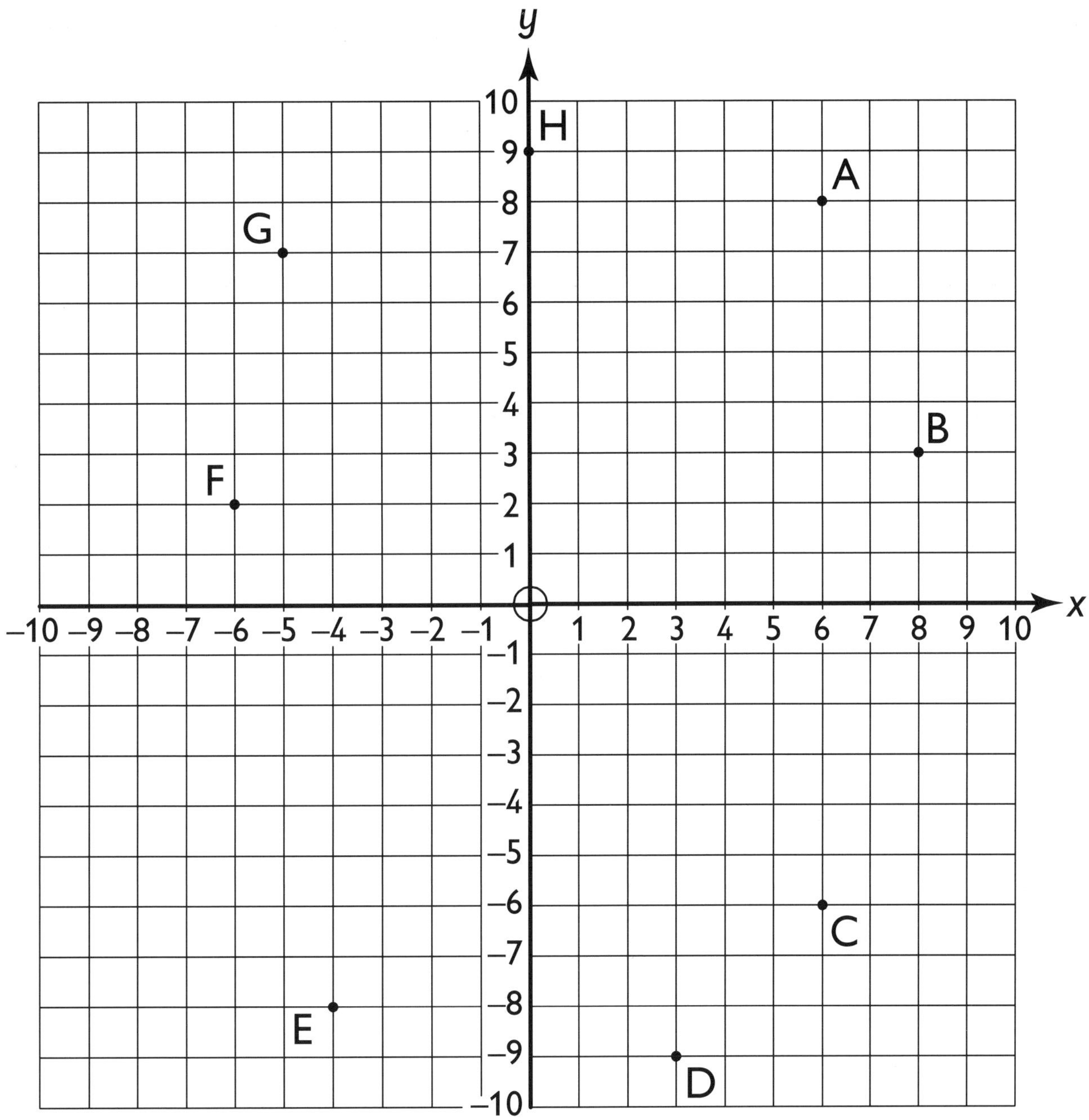

1 Write down the coordinates of all the points marked with letters.

2 Join A to B, B to C, C to D etc. Then join H back to A.

3 For each part, plot the coordinates, then join the points in order to make a joined-up shape. What shape have you drawn?

(a) (1, 6) (4, 6) (4, 4) (1, 4)

(b) (−3, 4) (−4, 5) (−3, 6) (−2, 5)

(c) (1, 2) (2, 0) (1, −1) (−2, −1) (−3, 1) (−2, 2)

(d) (5, −2) (2, −6) (−3, −6) (−4, −2)

Chain multiplication

Remember that to multiply by 6, you can multiply by 2 and 3.

251 → × 2 → 502 → × 3 → 1506

251 → × 3 → 753 → × 2 → 1506

251 → × 6 → 1506

Work out how to multiply by these numbers in the same way.

→ × 12 →

→ × 15 →

→ × 35 →

→ × 16 →

→ × 49 →

→ × 21 →

→ × 48 →

→ × 80 →

→ × 56 →

→ × 60 →

→ × 63 →

→ × 72 →

Use **86, 3027** and **1.45** as starting numbers to test your ideas.

Chain division

In each question, the answer to part **(a)** is a whole number.

1	762	÷ 6	(a)	÷ 4	(b)
2	324	÷ 4	(a)	÷ 5	(b)
3	1044	÷ 3	(a)	÷ 5	(b)
4	189	÷ 7	(a)	÷ 2	(b)
5	2544	÷ 8	(a)	÷ 7	(b)
6	3798	÷ 9	(a)	÷ 6	(b)
7	46	÷ 2	(a)	÷ 5	(b)
8	156	÷ 4	(a)	÷ 3	(b)
9	3444	÷ 7	(a)	÷ 7	(b)
10	2190	÷ 3	(a)	÷ 8	(b)
11	885	÷ 5	(a)	÷ 5	(b)
12	528	÷ 6	(a)	÷ 10	(b)

Copymaster 25a

Balance Sheet

Balance Sheet | *SHW Computers*

Date	Details	Income	Expenditure	Balance
01 Oct	Starting Balance			£1235.50
07 Oct	Shop sales, week 1	£3022.40		
08 Oct	Order: PCs and monitors		£2589.95	
08 Oct	Order: blank disks		£250.50	
14 Oct	Shop sales, week 2	£2480.85		
15 Oct	Order: business software		£399.62	
19 Oct	Order: games		£488.25	
21 Oct	Shop sales, week 3	£2261.53		
21 Oct	Order: Games console + Joypads		£855.32	
28 Oct	Pay for advertising		£45.50	
28 Oct	Shop sales, week 4	£2622.54		
29 Oct	Order paper supplies		£175.30	
31 Oct	Mail order sales, October	£595.20		

Copymaster 25b

Order form

Order Form | *Bulk Food Stores*

Item	Quantity	Item price	Item total
Large Tin Baked Beans (4 pack)	4	1.05	
Variety Pack Breakfast Cereals	12	1.98	
Sparkling Spring Water (6 pack)	10	1.32	
Biscuits for Cheese (giant tin)	8	4.98	
Rainbow Ice Lolly (10 pack)	6	2.12	
Cheese Selection Pack	5	5.68	
Potatoes (large bag)	7	1.51	
Pitta Bread (catering pack)	9	3.18	
Vegetable Soup (12 large tins)	3	3.35	
Coffee Whitener (jumbo tin)	2	4.29	
$1\frac{1}{2}$ kg Sugar	11	0.74	
		Grand Total	

Lottery winners

1. SIX LUCKY WINNERS SHARE £16,000!
2. £25,000? That'll do nicely, say four friends
3. A COOL THREE AND A HALF MILLION FOR 3 FRIDGE SALES STAFF
4. A slip in time saves nine… they're £600,000 better off!
5. "It won't change our lives," say 20-strong syndicate who won £550
6. THE MAGNIFICENT 7 LIFT 60 GRAND
7. Nearly, just nearly… Twins share £999 999.999!
8. MUSICAL OCTET READY TO BLOW £26,750

Funny money

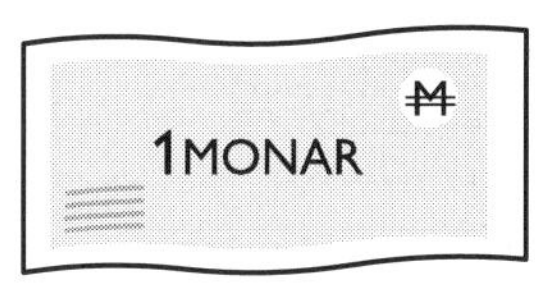

In the country of Nar the currency is the Monar (M̶). M̶1 is worth £1.27 in British money.

There are 100 centars in a Monar.

What is a centar (M̶0.01) worth in British money?

There are Narian coins worth M̶0.02, M̶0.05, M̶0.10, M̶0.25, and M̶0.50.

What are these worth in British money? 

What is £1 worth in Narian money? £5? £10?

If a CD cost £14.50 in Britain, what would you pay in Narian money?

What does a Narian motor car costing M̶5950 cost in Britain?

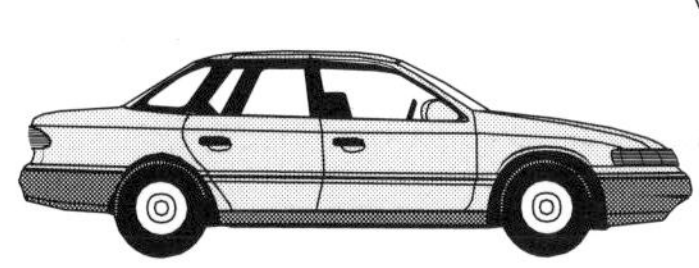

Fraction flags

Write the fractions on each flagpole in order, from smallest to largest.

1 $\frac{1}{4}$, $\frac{1}{3}$, $\frac{3}{8}$, $\frac{1}{6}$, $\frac{5}{12}$

2 $\frac{3}{4}$, $\frac{7}{8}$, $\frac{9}{10}$, $\frac{4}{5}$, $\frac{5}{8}$

3 $\frac{3}{8}$, $\frac{1}{2}$, $\frac{3}{4}$, $\frac{1}{4}$, $\frac{5}{8}$

4 $\frac{1}{10}$, $\frac{2}{5}$, $\frac{1}{2}$, $\frac{1}{5}$, $\frac{7}{10}$

5 $\frac{1}{3}$, $\frac{1}{2}$, $\frac{5}{6}$, $\frac{1}{6}$, $\frac{2}{3}$

6 $\frac{1}{10}$, $\frac{1}{8}$, $\frac{7}{40}$, $\frac{3}{20}$, $\frac{1}{4}$

7 $\frac{1}{6}$, $\frac{1}{8}$, $\frac{1}{4}$, $\frac{5}{12}$, $\frac{11}{24}$

8 $\frac{1}{2}$, $\frac{2}{3}$, $\frac{2}{5}$, $\frac{5}{6}$, $\frac{7}{10}$

9 $\frac{3}{7}$, $\frac{2}{5}$, $\frac{4}{7}$, $\frac{3}{5}$, $\frac{5}{7}$

10 $\frac{1}{25}$, $\frac{1}{12}$, $\frac{3}{25}$, $\frac{11}{75}$, $\frac{7}{60}$

11 $1\frac{1}{2}$, $\frac{9}{10}$, $1\frac{1}{4}$, $1\frac{1}{100}$, $\frac{89}{90}$

12 $\frac{10}{9}$, $\frac{7}{6}$, $\frac{19}{18}$, $\frac{28}{27}$, $\frac{4}{3}$

Conveyor belts

$\frac{3}{8}$ 0.42 $\frac{2}{5}$ 0.45 $\frac{11}{25}$

1 

0.1 $\frac{3}{20}$ $\frac{3}{25}$ 0.17 0.16

2 

0.51 $\frac{11}{20}$ 0.53 $\frac{1}{2}$ $\frac{14}{25}$

3 

0.42 $\frac{2}{5}$ $\frac{9}{25}$ 0.38 0.45

4 

$\frac{11}{30}$ $\frac{1}{3}$ $\frac{3}{5}$ $\frac{3}{10}$ $\frac{2}{5}$

5 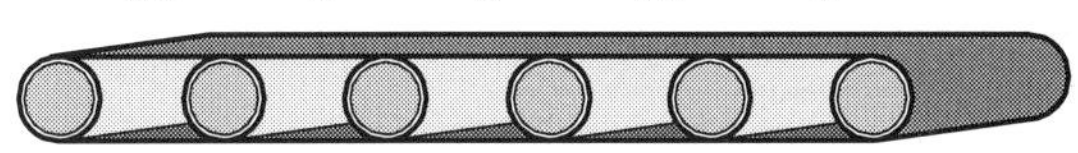

$\frac{5}{11}$ $\frac{7}{10}$ $\frac{9}{22}$ $\frac{1}{2}$ $\frac{23}{55}$

6 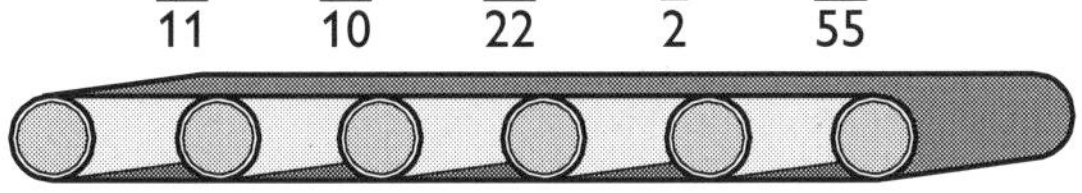

0.25 $\frac{1}{3}$ $\frac{1}{5}$ 0.4 $\frac{5}{12}$

7 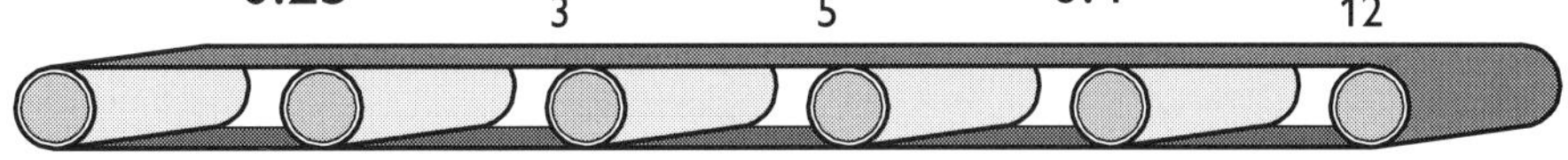

1.5 $1\frac{2}{5}$ 1.44 $1\frac{1}{4}$ 1.14

8 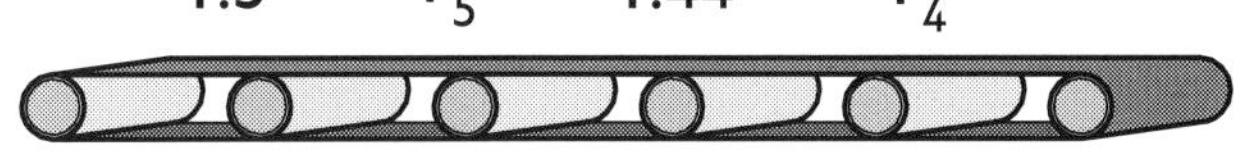

$\frac{21}{20}$ 1.1 $1\frac{1}{5}$ 1.15 $1\frac{3}{40}$

9 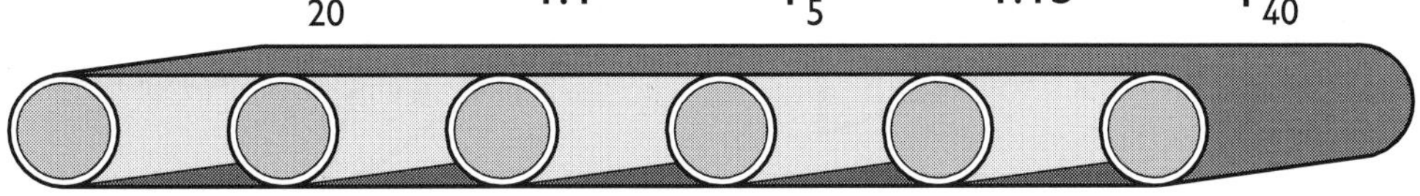

Triangles

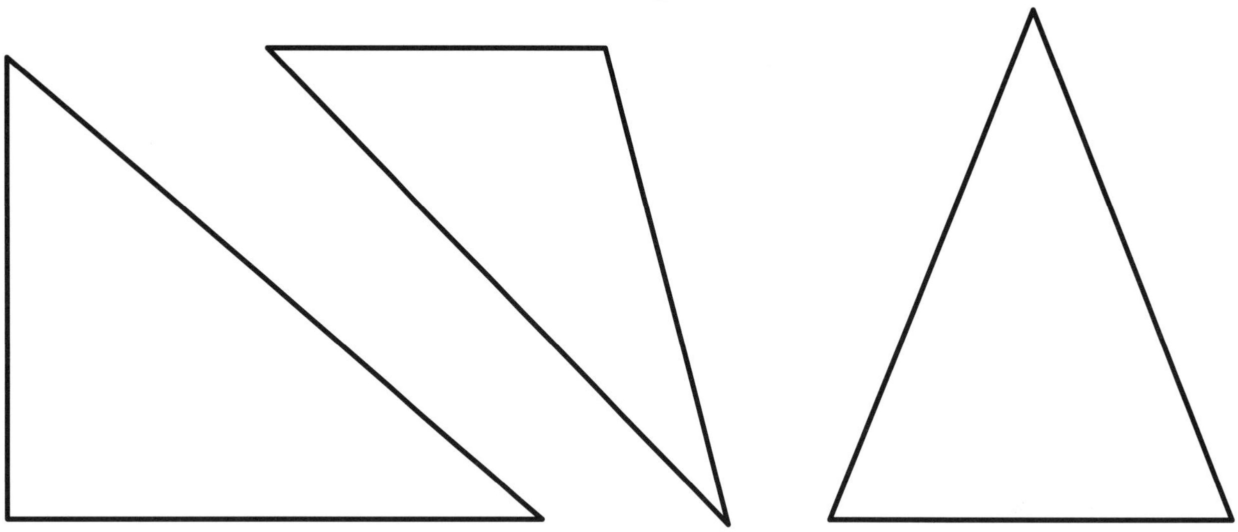

1

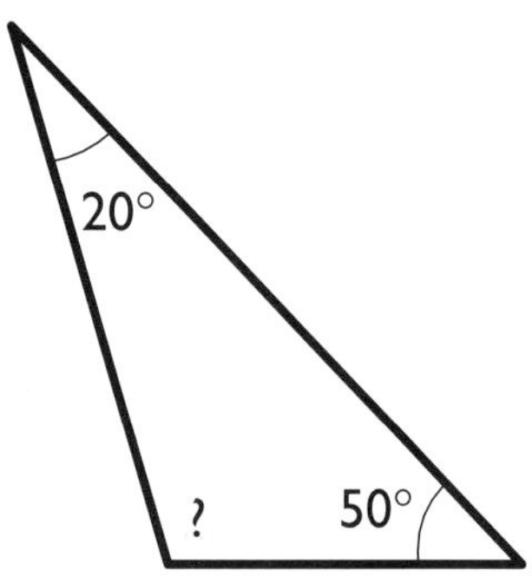

2

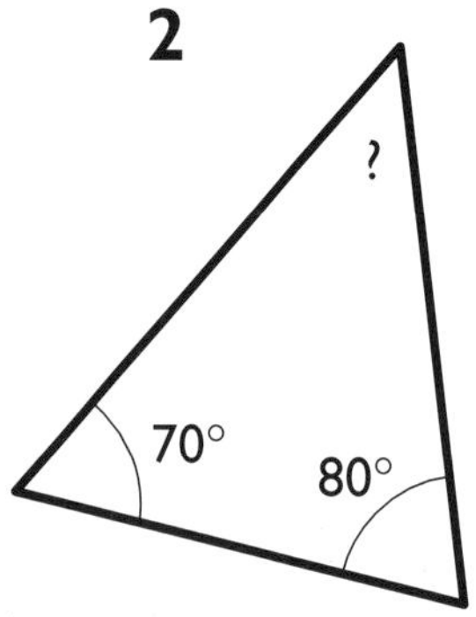

3

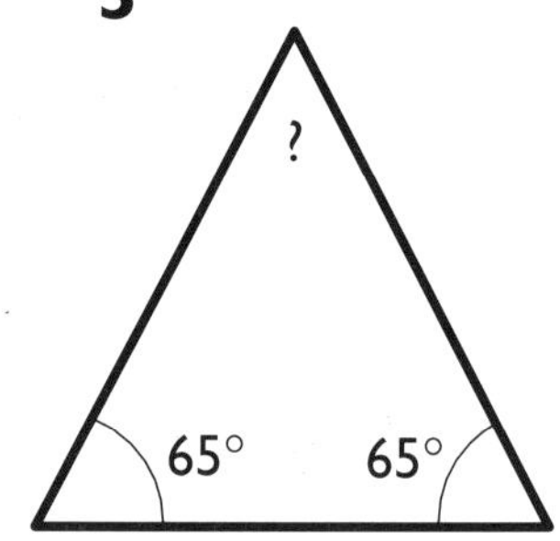

4

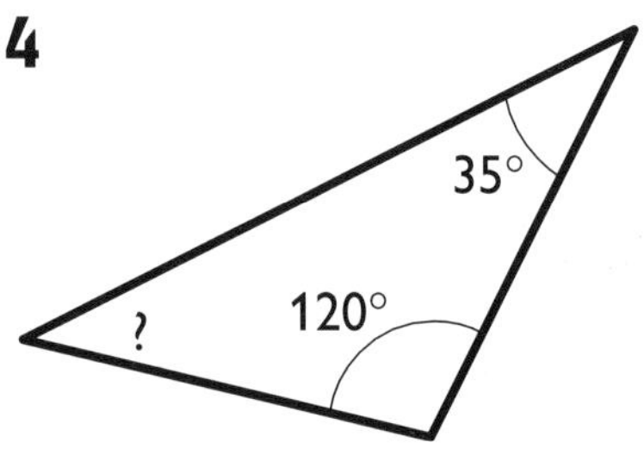

5

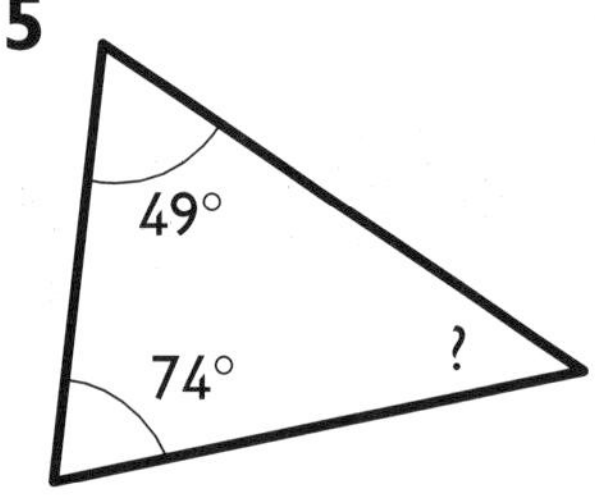

6

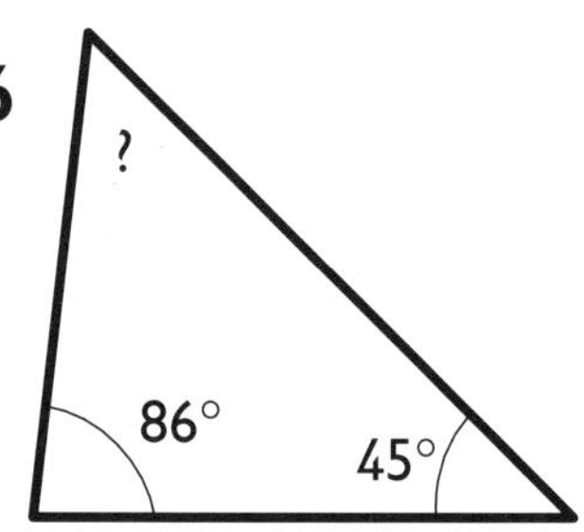

7

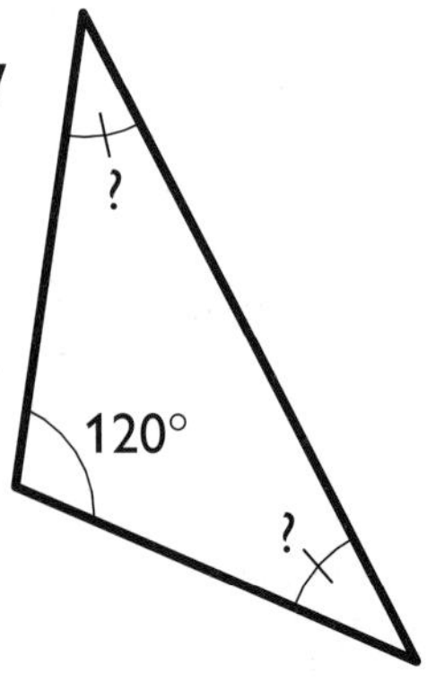

8

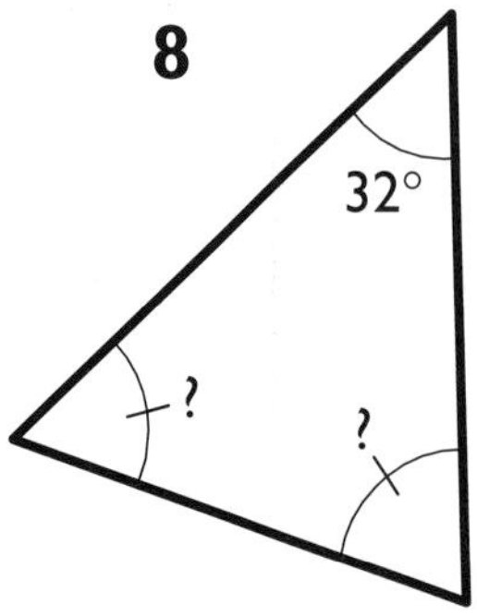

9

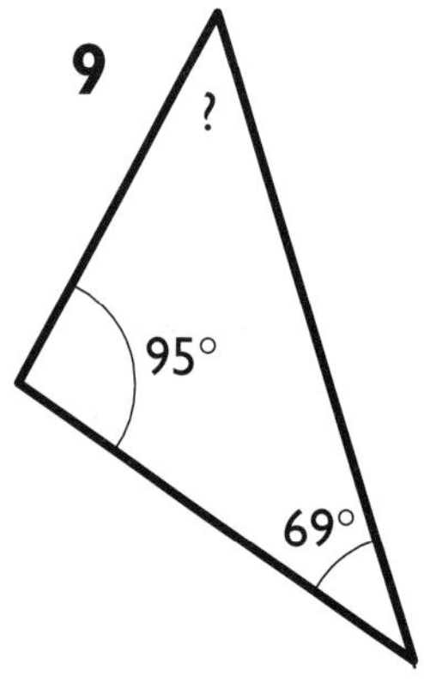

10

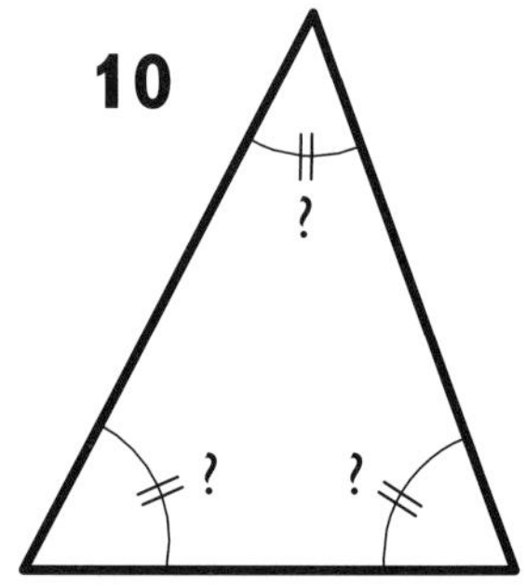

Rotation grids

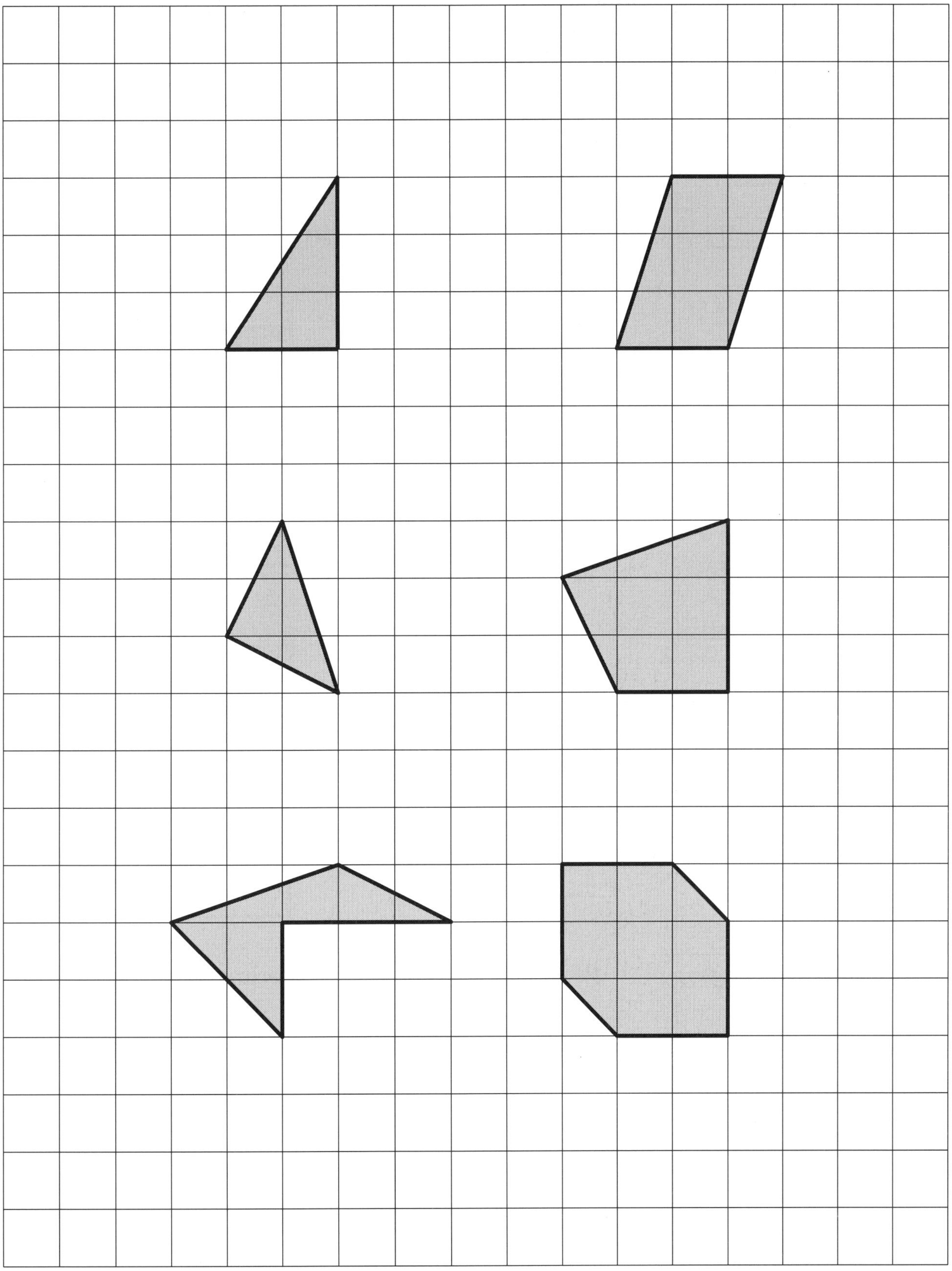

Lengths and widths

Work out the missing lengths and widths. Write them in the boxes.
Find the perimeter of each triangle.

1

10 cm

30 cm² [ ]

Perimeter = ______

2

5 cm

25 cm² [ ]

Perimeter = ______

3

1 cm

16 m² [ ]

Perimeter = ______

4

[ ]

60 cm² 5 cm

Perimeter = ______

5

24 mm

24 mm² [ ]

Perimeter = ______

6

10 cm

35 cm² [ ]

Perimeter = ______

7

16 m

80 m² [ ]

Perimeter = ______

8

[ ]

40 m² 2.5 m

Perimeter = ______

9

[ ]

2000 cm² 32 cm

Perimeter = ______

10

[ ]

10 cm² 5 mm

Perimeter = ______

11

4 cm

50 mm² [ ]

Perimeter = ______

12

[ ]

100 km² 100 m

Perimeter = ______

Triangles

Work out the area of each triangle.

1

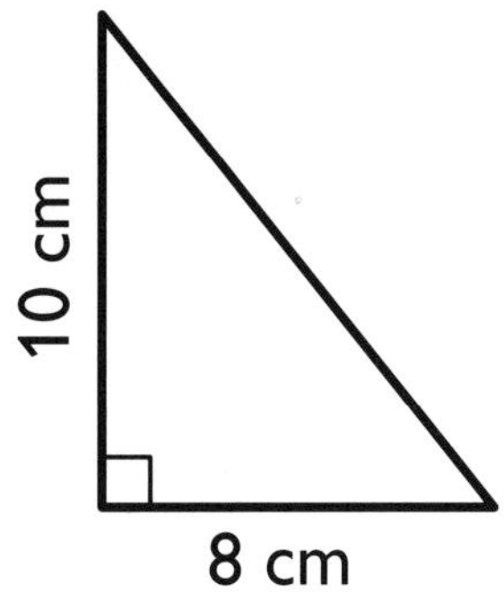

2

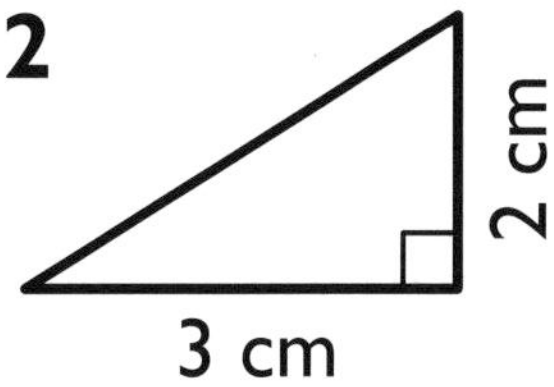

3

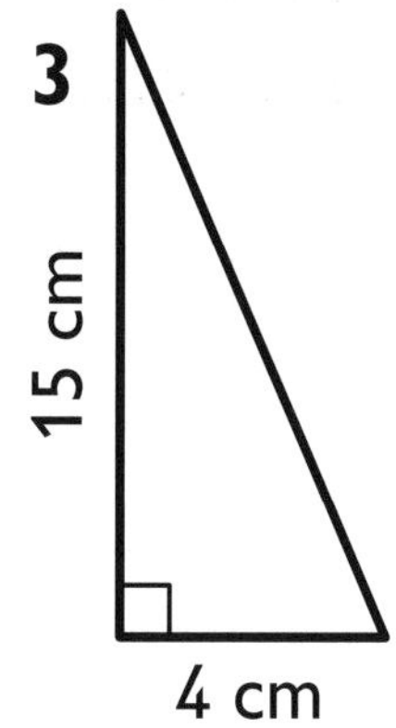

4

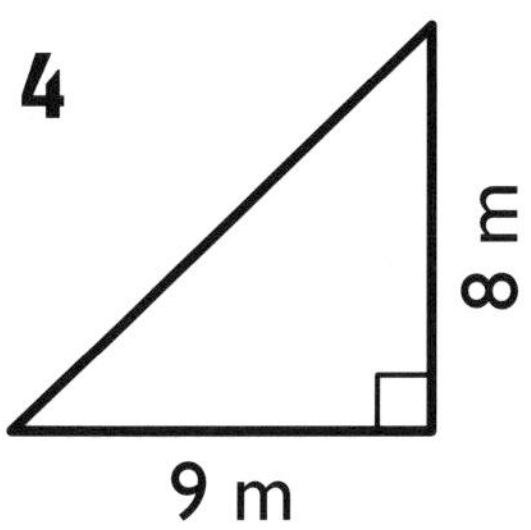

5

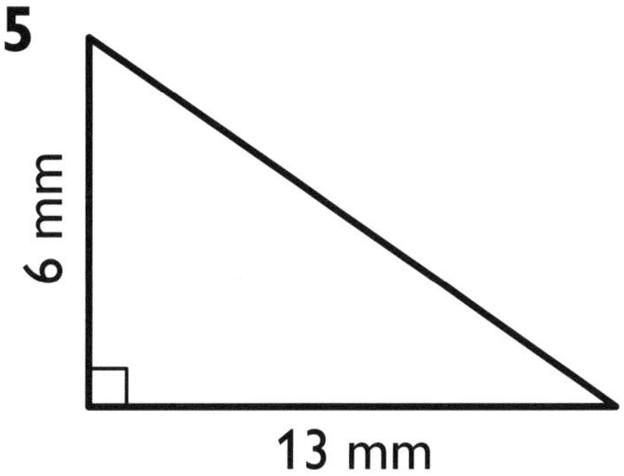

6

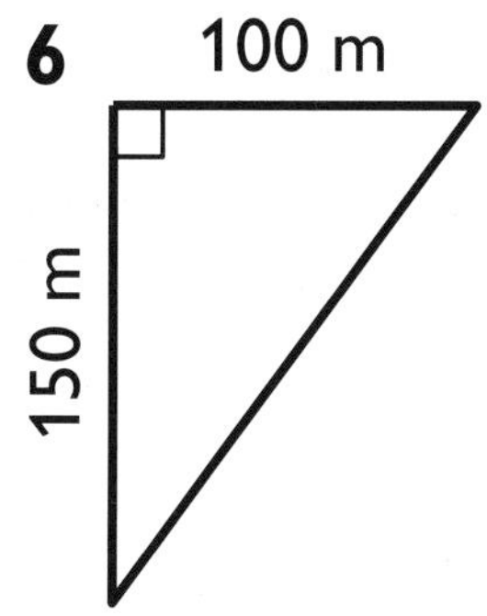

7

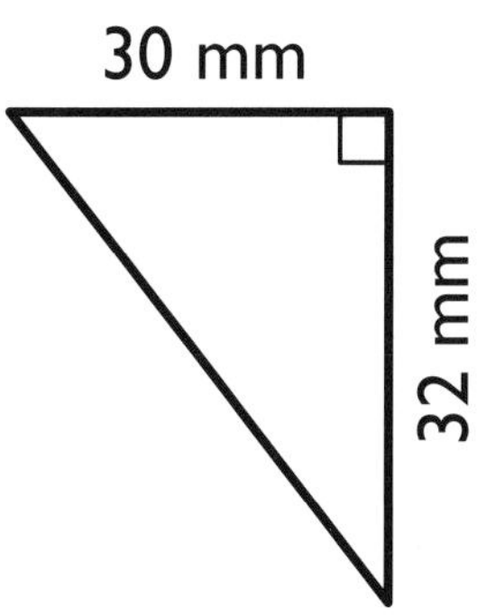

8

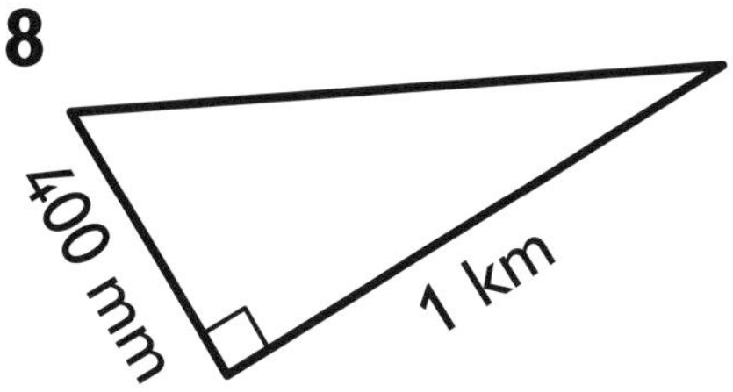

9

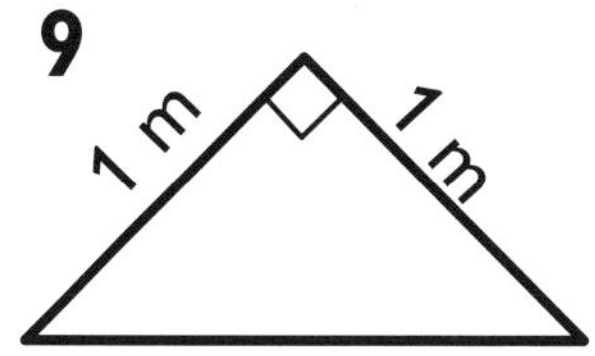

10

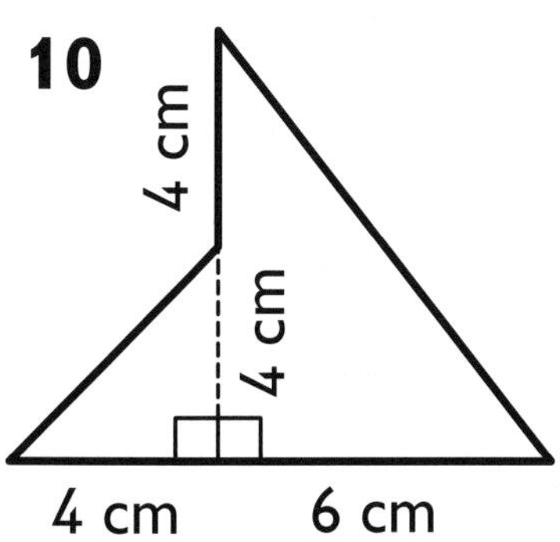

11

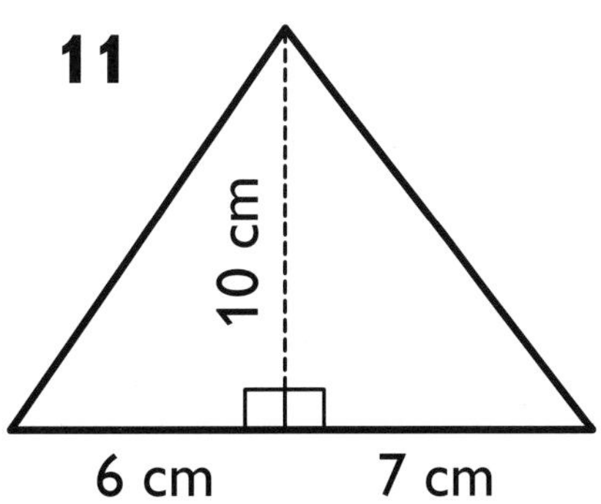

12

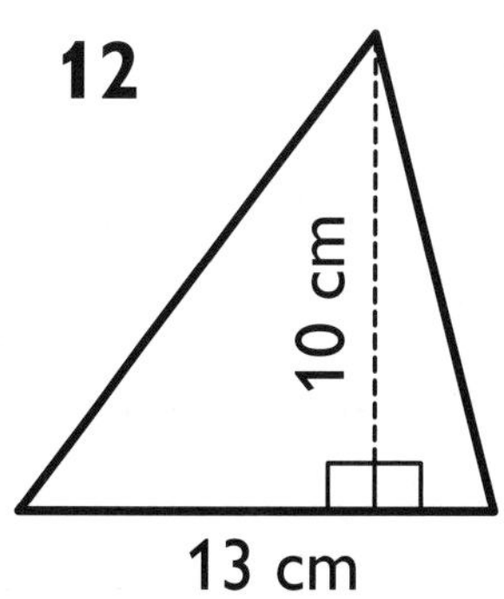

Food facts

Complete each table.

CORN FLAKES	per pack (750 g)	per 100 g	per serving (30 g)
Protein	60 g		
Carbohydrates	615 g		
Fat	6 g		
Fibre	22.5 g		
Energy	2775 kcal		

BAKED BEANS	per tin (415 g)	per 100 g	per serving (207 g)
Protein	19.505 g		
Carbohydrates	56.44 g		
Fat	0.83 g		
Fibre	15.355 g		
Energy	311.25 kcal		

ORANGE JUICE	per carton (1 l)	per 100 ml	per serving (250 ml)
Protein	7 g		
Carbohydrates	90 g		
Fat	0 g		
Fibre	5 g		
Energy	430 kcal		

STRAWBERRY JAM	per jar (454 g)	per 100 ml	per serving (18 g)
Protein	1.362 g		
Carbohydrates	59.02 g		
Fat	0.454 g		
Fibre	0.454 g		
Energy	1271.2 kcal		

For each item listed in the tables, write the four foods in order, with the one that contains the most first. For example, your first list would be about protein. Think about how you can compare the different foods. A litre of orange juice weighs 1 kg.

A delivery lorry is allowed to carry 1 tonne. How many packs, tins etc. of each type of food can it carry? Why will your answers not be quite right?

Units of mass

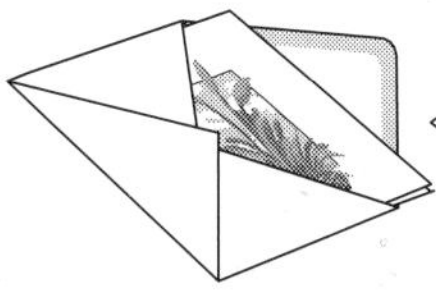

1 oz g

2 lb g

7 st kg

120 g oz

$1/2$ lb g

10 oz g

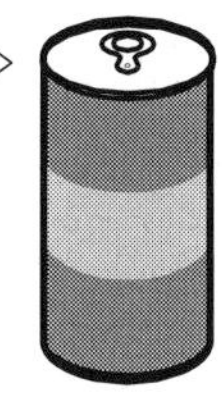

500 g lb

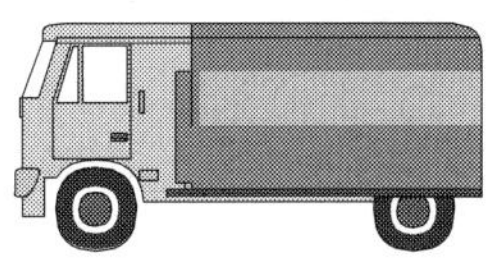

$1\,1/2$ tons kg

1 kg lb

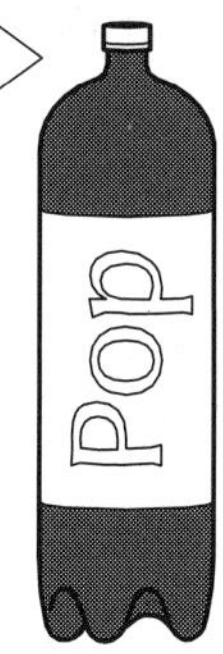

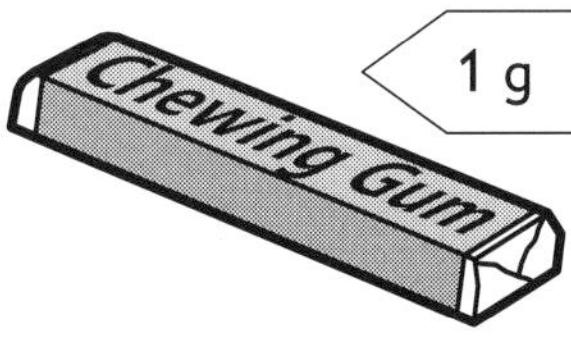

1 g oz

44 t tons

1 lb g

50 g oz

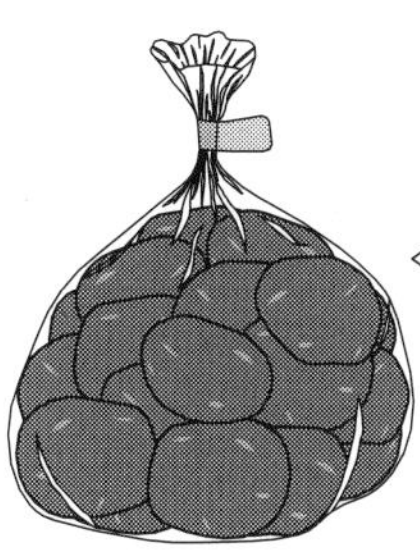

5 kg lb

5 g oz

4 oz g

12 lb kg

20 kg lb

55 kg lb

6 oz g

Adding and subtracting decimals

Add the numbers inside each balloon together.

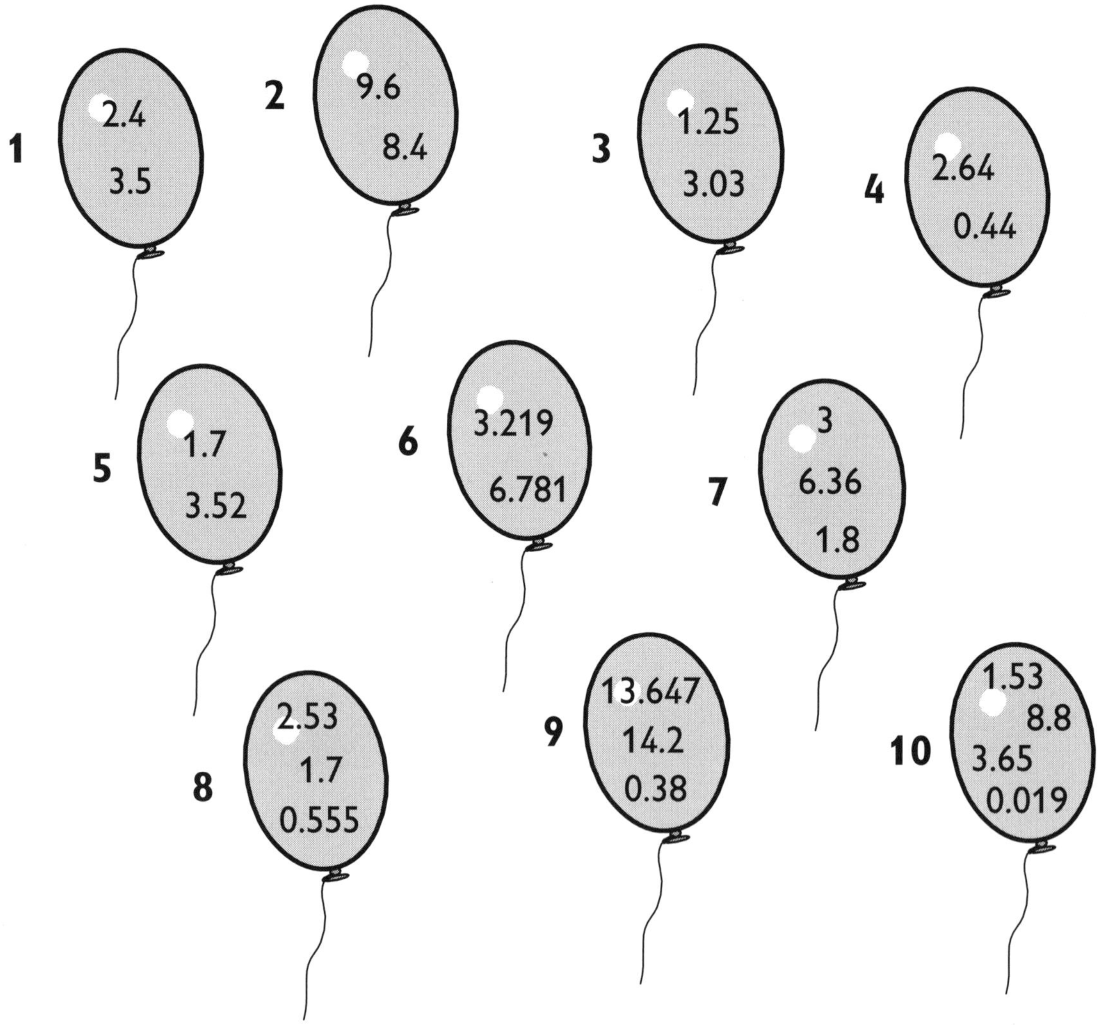

Find the difference between **every** number on the left-hand kite and **every** number on the right-hand kite.

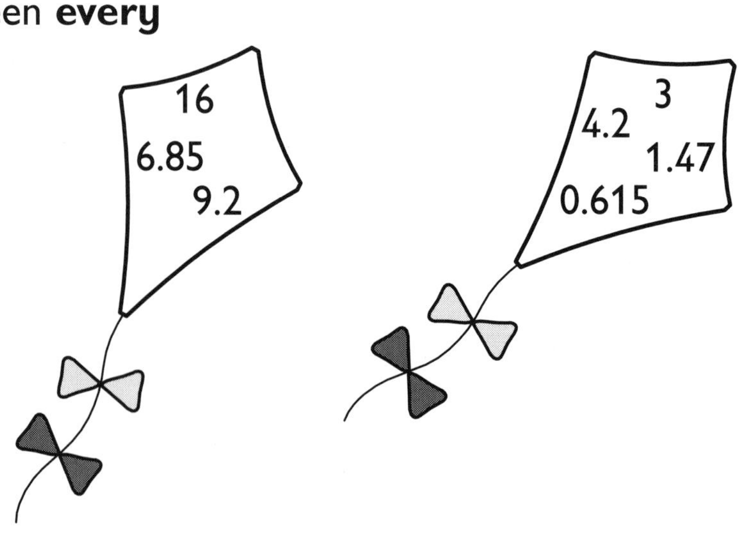

Place value calculations

Work out the numbers at the end of the arrows.

1 2.8
- × 1000 →
- × 100 →
- × 10 →
- ÷ 10 →
- ÷ 100 →

2 1.45
- × 1000 →
- × 100 →
- × 10 →
- ÷ 10 →
- ÷ 100 →

3 5.06
- × 1000 →
- × 100 →
- × 10 →
- ÷ 10 →
- ÷ 100 →

4 0.56
- × 1000 →
- × 100 →
- × 10 →
- ÷ 10 →
- ÷ 100 →

5 7
- × 100 →
- × 10 →
- ÷ 10 →
- ÷ 100 →
- ÷ 1000 →

6 1.002
- × 1000 →
- × 100 →
- × 10 →
- ÷ 10 →
- ÷ 100 →

7 14.56
- × 1000 →
- × 100 →
- × 10 →
- ÷ 10 →
- ÷ 100 →

8 305.3
- ÷ 10 →
- ÷ 100 →
- ÷ 1000 →
- ÷ 10 000 →
- ÷ 100 000 →

Multiply **every** number in the left-hand box by **every** number in the right-hand box.

1 Left box: 6, 0.6, 0.06 — Right box: 2, 200, 0.2

2 Left box: 4, 0.4, 0.04 — Right box: 4, 0.04, 0.04

3 Left box: 11, 0.11, 1.1 — Right box: 5, 0.5, 50

4 Left box: 12, 1.2, 0.12 — Right box: 8, 80, 0.8

5 Left box: 0.7, 0.07, 0.007 — Right box: 3, 0.3, 0.03

6 Left box: 15, 0.15, 1.5 — Right box: 15, 1.5, 0.015

Astronomical facts

Mercury is 58 million km from the Sun.

Venus is 108 million km from the Sun.

Earth is 149 million km from the Sun.

Mars is 228 million km from the Sun.

Jupiter is 779 million km from the Sun.

Saturn is 1.4 billion km from the Sun.

Uranus is 2.9 billion km from the Sun.

Neptune is 4.5 billion km from the Sun.

Pluto is 5.9 billion km from the Sun on average.

The comet cloud is 9.5 trillion km from the Sun.

Alpha Centauri, the nearest star, is 41 trillion km from the Sun.

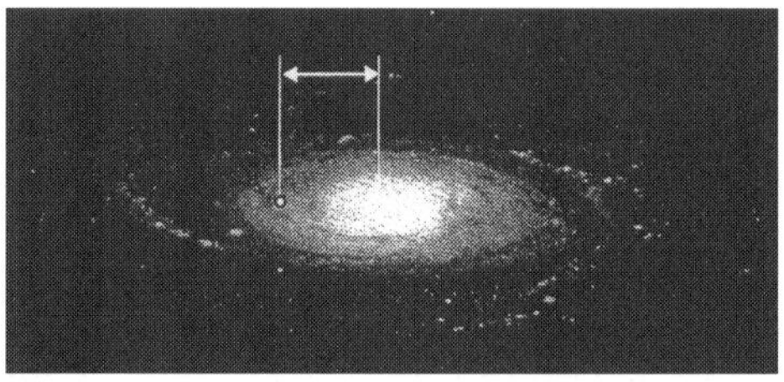

The centre of our galaxy is 285 300 000 000 000 000 km from the Sun.

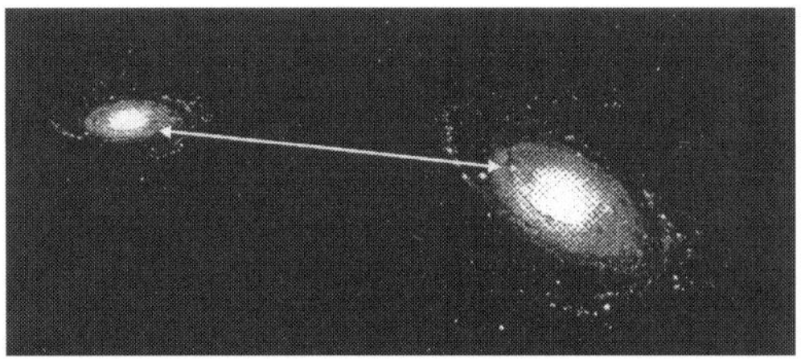

The Andromeda spiral galaxy is 1 902 000 000 000 000 000 km from the Sun.

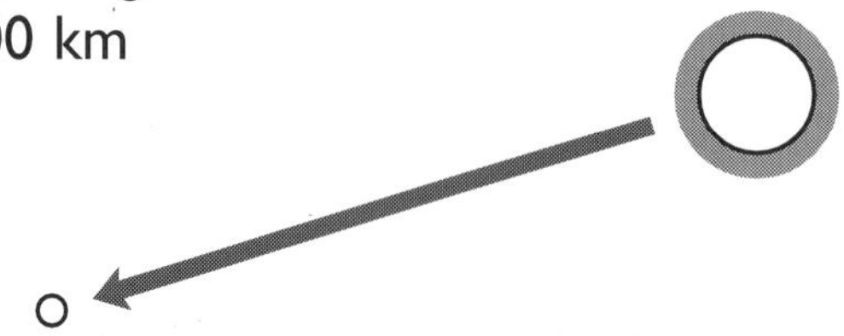

Light from the Sun takes 8 minutes to reach the Earth.

House and garden

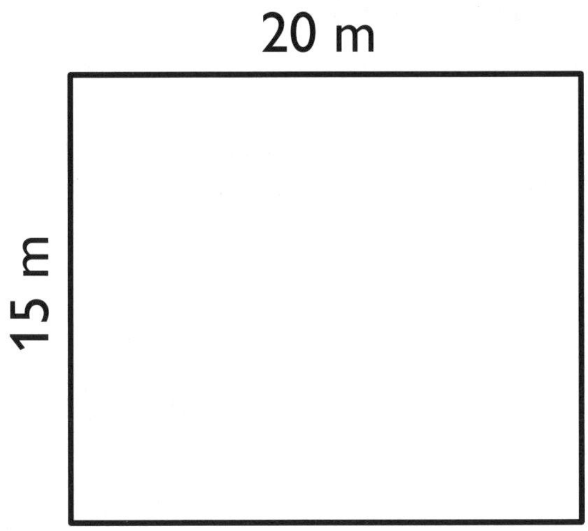

This is the plot of land for a house and garden.

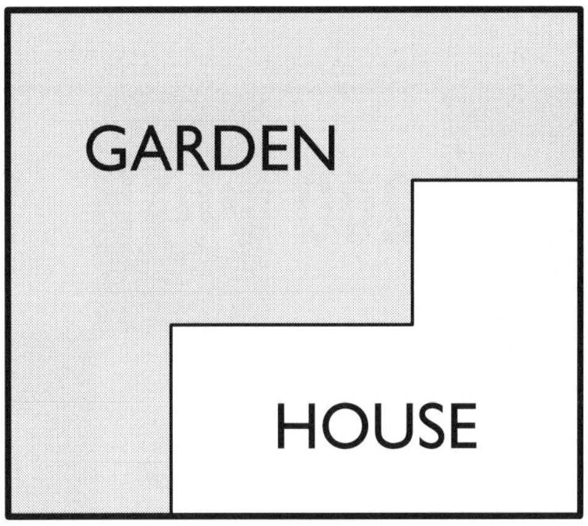

The house is to be L-shaped. The garden has to cover **twice** the area of the house.

Find as many different sets of measurements as possible for the house.

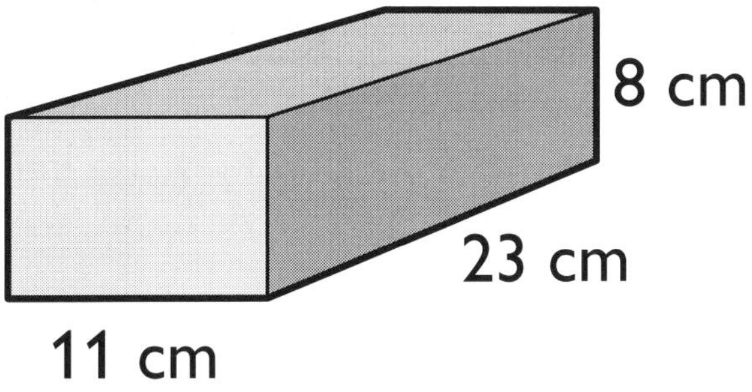

This house brick weighs 2.5 kg.

The mortar gaps between the bricks are 1 cm wide.

What does the house's brickwork weigh?

Prime numbers and prime factors

2	200	201	7	202	13	25	19
64	31	66	72	101	70	55	96
65	21	199	124	203	45	61	208
71	11	333	37	5	17	207	163
171	68	3	98	23	205	41	404
116	29	18	35	211	117	127	210

1 Find all the **prime** numbers in the grid.

2 Find the **prime factors** of all the other numbers.

Number puzzles

1 I thought of a number, doubled it, subtracted 10 and I got 52. What was my number?

2 If you add 10 to my number, then multiply the result by 3, you'll get 42. What was my number?

3 Multiply my number by 5, add 3 and you'll get 48. What was my number?

4 If you triple one-eighth of my number, you get 9.

5 If you take 4 away from my number, then divide the answer by 3, you'll get 11. What's my number?

6 Half of five times my number is 10.

7 I thought of a number, multiplied by 5, added 13, then divided the result by 7. I got 49. What was my number?

8 My two numbers work like this: if you multiply them together, you get 224. If you divide them, you get 14. What are they?

9 My two numbers work like this: if you add them together, you get 106. If you subtract them, you get 12. What are they?

10 The number I'm thinking of is 2 more than a multiple of 7 and 3 less than a multiple of 5. What is it?

11 If you divide this number by 8, the remainder is 2. If you divide it by 9, the remainder is 5. What is it?

12 My number is a square number. One-quarter of it is a triangular number. I can think of two answers to this puzzle! Can you?

Finding pairs

Multiply or divide **every** number in the first box by **every** number in the second box.

1 40, 4, 400 → × → 60, 6, 6000

2 2000, 20, 200 → × → 1100, 11, 110

3 800 000, 8000, 800 → ÷ → 2, 20, 200

4 56 000, 5 600 000, 5600 → ÷ → 70, 700, 7

5 8000, 80, 800 → × → 90, 9, 9000

6 270 000, 27 000, 27 000 000 → ÷ → 3000, 30, 300

Some of these have decimal answers.

7 36, 36 000, 360 → ÷ → 60, 40, 400

8 500, 5, 0.5 → × → 9, 0.9, 90

9 600, 6 → × → 5, 50 → × → 7000, 7

10 8, 80 → × → 6, 600 → ÷ → 40, 400

Clothes shop

Mr Teague is buying monthly stock for his clothes shop. Complete the order form.

Item	Number required	Wholesale price of one item	Item total
T-shirt	48	£13.50	
Pair of Socks	16	£2.60	
Polo Shirt	25	£12.48	
Coat	32	£65.00	
Suit	24	£149.99	
Sweatshirt	49	£25.12	
Shirt	99	£15.60	
Sweater	28	£31.35	
Skirt	44	£25.64	
Jacket	56	£45.86	
Leggings	71	£5.73	
Handkerchiefs	63	£1.28	
		Order Total	

This table shows a week's sales for each item. Work out what each one is sold for.

Item	Number sold	Selling price of one item	Total sales for this item
T-shirt	16		£302.40
Pair of Socks	5		£18.20
Polo Shirt	8		£139.76
Coat	10		£910.00
Suit	8		£1,679.92
Sweatshirt	16		£562.72
Shirt	33		£720.72
Sweater	9		£395.01
Skirt	14		£502.60
Jacket	18		£1,155.60
Leggings	23		£183.77
Handkerchiefs	21		£37.59

Density

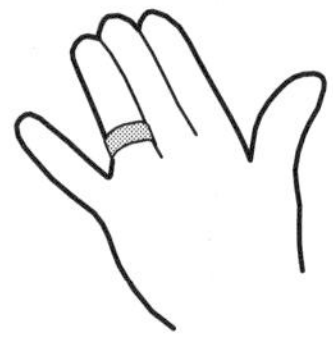

$\frac{1}{2}$ cm^3 of **silver** weighs 10.75 g.

8 cm^3 of **ice** weighs 7.36 g.

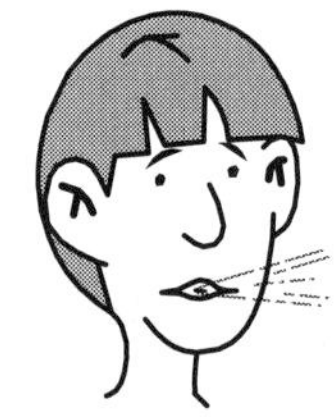

1 m^3 of **air** weighs 1.3 kg.

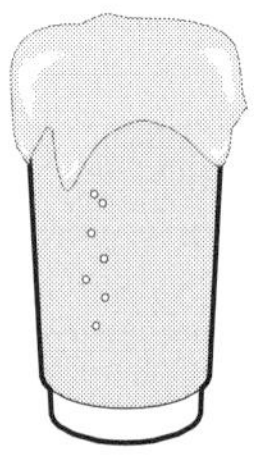

$\frac{1}{2}$ l of **beer** weighs 521 g.

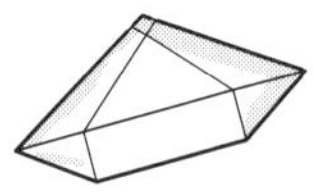

This **diamond** weighs 0.4 grams and its volume is 0.125 cm^3.

This cross made from **jet** weighs 5 g and its volume is 2 cm^3.

2 l of **milk** weighs 2.06 kg.

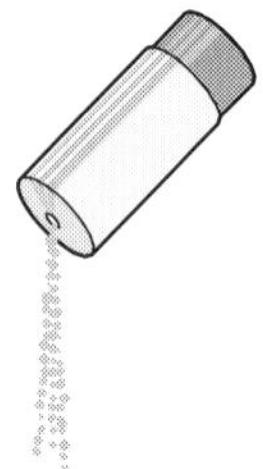

A single grain of **salt** is a 1 mm cube. 1 gram of salt contains 460 grains.

1 cubic kilometre of **sea water** weighs 1 025 000 tonnes.

A 5 ml teaspoonful of material from a **white dwarf** star weighs 5 tonnes!

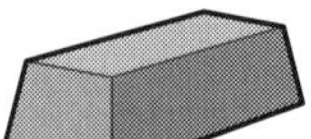

This 3000 cm^3 block of **osmium** metal weighs 67.8 kg.

10 litres of **helium** in this balloon weigh 1.664 g.

MegaPark

MegaPark charge for admission to their theme parks as follows. There is a 10% discount for bookings over £50.

ADULT TICKET	CHILD TICKET	FAMILY TICKET (2 adults + 2 children)
£5	£3.50	£15

These are the parking charges.

CAR	COACH
50 pence per hour or part of hour	£9 per day

Rides get cheaper if you buy more tickets.

Buy **1** ticket	Buy **2** tickets	Buy **3** tickets	Buy **4** tickets	Buy **5** tickets	Buy **6 or more** tickets
Adult £1	Adult 80p	Adult 70p	Adult 60p	Adult 50p	Adult 40p
Child 70p	Child 50p	Child 45p	Child 40p	Child 35p	Child 30p

Meals are a set price. Adults pay £4.50, children £2.50. There is a 5% discount for meal orders over £20.

---

1 Mr and Mrs Scott and their three children decide to visit MegaPark. They arrive at 11 am and stay until 4.30 pm. They have lunch while they are there. The children go on 4 rides each. Mr and Mrs Scott go on 2 of the rides as well. Work out the cost of their day.

2 Toni decides to have a day out at MegaPark. Her return bus fare is £4. She arrives at 10 am and stays until 2 pm. She takes a packed lunch with her and goes on 5 rides altogether. How much does her day out cost?

3 Miss Zahar takes her class of 26 children to MegaPark. She hires a coach for the day. This costs £80. She also books three ride tickets in advance for each child, and lunch for everyone. Three parent helpers also go on the trip.

(a) Work out the cost of the whole day out.

(b) The cost of the trip is divided up equally between all the people who went. How much should each person pay? Round the answer sensibly.

4 What would it cost *your* family to have a day out at MegaPark?

Ordering fractions

Change the fractions to decimals to find out which is bigger.

Write a < (less than) or > (greater than) sign between the fractions.

Example: $\frac{2}{3}$ [?] $\frac{7}{10}$

Working: $\frac{2}{3} = 0.6666\ldots$

$\frac{7}{10} = 0.7$

Answer: $\frac{2}{3} < \frac{7}{10}$

1 $\frac{1}{3}$ [?] $\frac{3}{10}$

2 $\frac{3}{8}$ [?] $\frac{7}{20}$

3 $\frac{2}{3}$ [?] $\frac{3}{4}$

4 $\frac{1}{5}$ [?] $\frac{3}{16}$

5 $\frac{4}{5}$ [?] $\frac{7}{9}$

6 $\frac{9}{14}$ [?] $\frac{7}{12}$

7 $\frac{7}{10}$ [?] $\frac{9}{13}$

8 $\frac{5}{8}$ [?] $\frac{31}{50}$

9 $\frac{17}{32}$ [?] $\frac{133}{250}$

10 $\frac{4}{7}$ [?] $\frac{21}{38}$

11 $\frac{131}{423}$ [?] $\frac{29}{95}$

12 $\frac{68}{69}$ [?] $\frac{205}{208}$

Change the fractions in each group to decimals, to help put them in order. Write the fractions in order of size, smallest to largest.

13

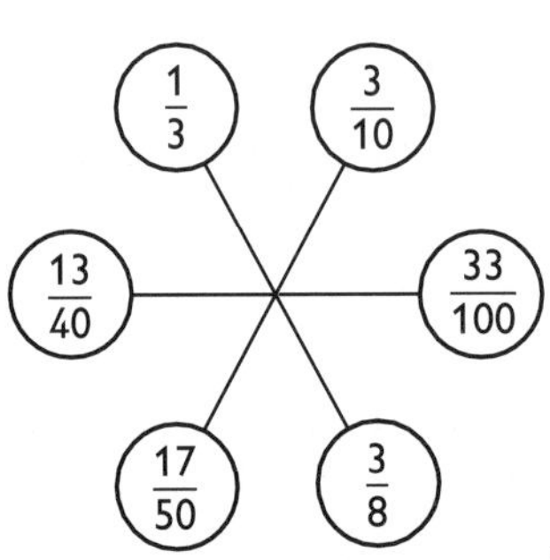

14

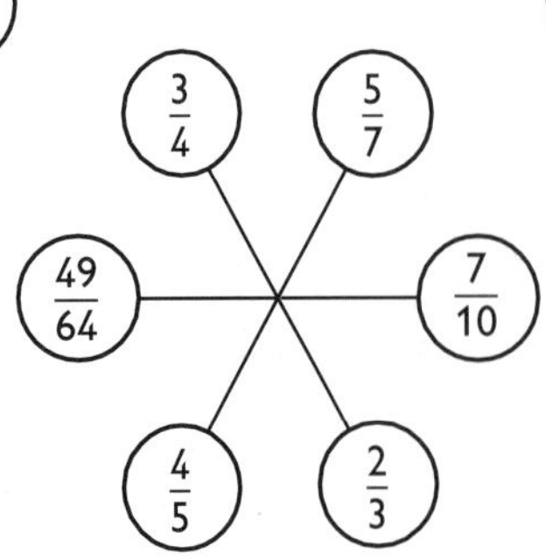

15

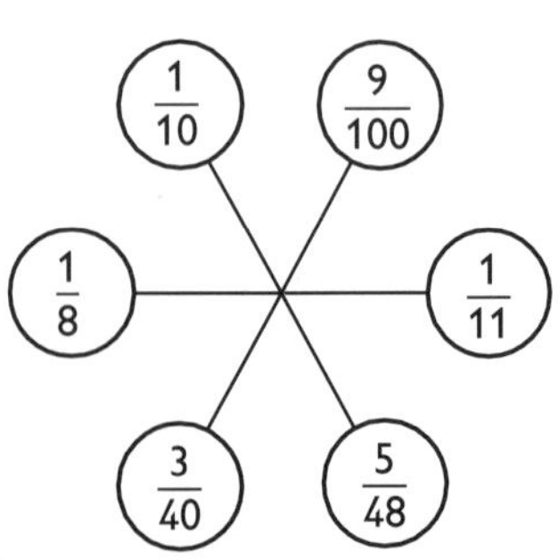

16

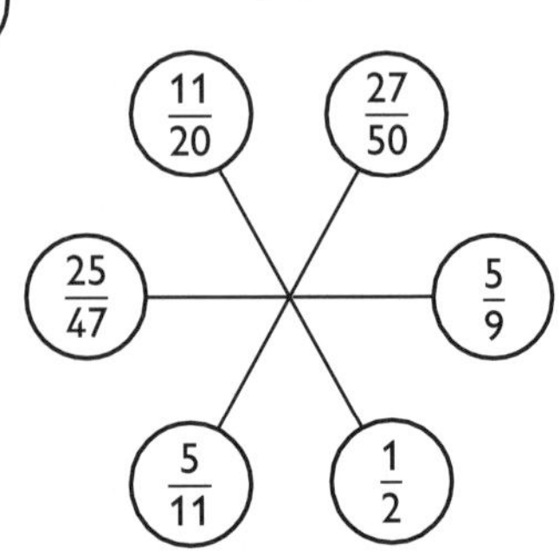

Calculating percentages

Work out these percentages.

1 20% of 300 kg
2 5% of £200
3 90% of 50 pence
4 25% of 44 tonnes
5 12% of 10 000 people
6 41% of 10 litres
7 16% of 5 km
8 98% of 40 m^2
9 44% of £12
10 $2\frac{1}{2}$% of 1000 homes

11 In a sale, 30% was taken off all items. Work out the amount taken off, and the new sale price. Round to the nearest penny if you have to.

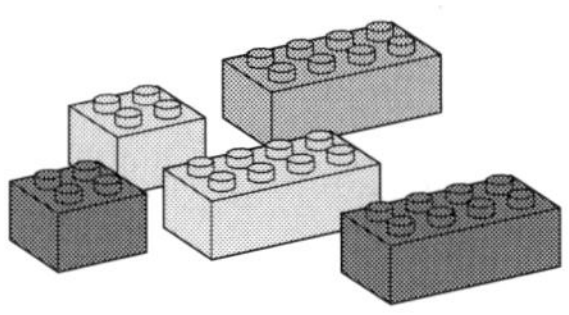
Construction set, £25

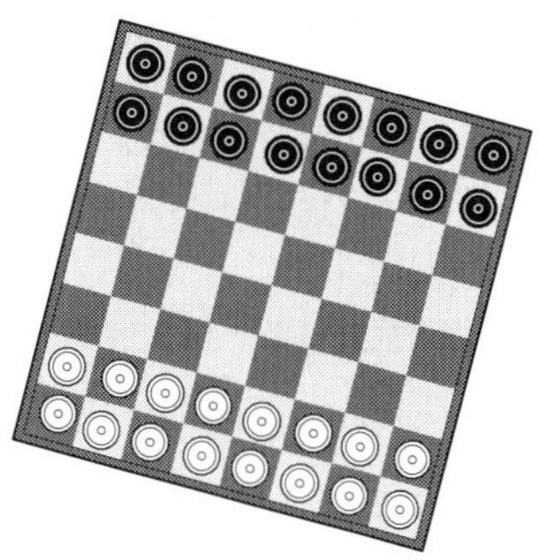
Board game, £10

Soft toy, £8.90

Computer game, £17.50

Dinosaur model, £5.25

12 All of these people got a 12% pay rise. Work out how much extra they earn, and their new pay.

Person	 Alex	 Ranjit	 Molly	 Dafydd	 Sky
Pay	£300/week	£580/month	£1250/month	£65/day	£15 500/year

Sharing

1 There are 100 counters in a box. There are 3 green counters to every 2 red ones.

(a) How many green counters are there?

(b) How many red counters are there?

2 A coin is weighted so that heads only comes up 5 times in every 12 flips.

(a) If the coin is flipped 60 times, how many heads do you expect?

(b) How many flips do you have to do to get 70 tails?

3 A shopkeeper finds that 2 out of every 20 biscuit bars are broken. The whole box contains 150 bars.

(a) How many bars are broken?

(b) How many bars are not broken?

4 Kirsty has two bank accounts. There is £300 in her current account and £1500 in her savings account.

(a) What is the ratio of the amounts in the two accounts?

She has £90 to put in the bank. She decides to divide it between her accounts in this ratio.

(b) How much does she put into each account?

(c) How much is in each account now?

5 Sanjeev's heart beats 6 times to every 8 beats of Allen's. In one minute, they have 126 heartbeats between them. How many heartbeats do they each have in a minute?

6 Mary has 2 classical CDs to every 6 pop CDs. She has 56 CDs altogether. How many of each type does she have?

7 £120 is divided between three children in the ratio of their ages. Andy is 8, Beatrice is 10 and Colin is 12. How much does each child receive?

8 Louis has 6 stickers to every 5 of Geri's. Marco has 4 stickers to every 3 of Geri's. They have 1060 stickers between them. How many does each have?

Gears

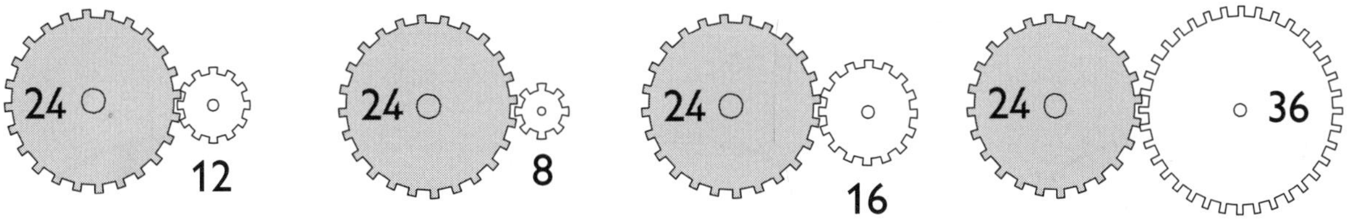
24
12
24
8
24
16
24
36

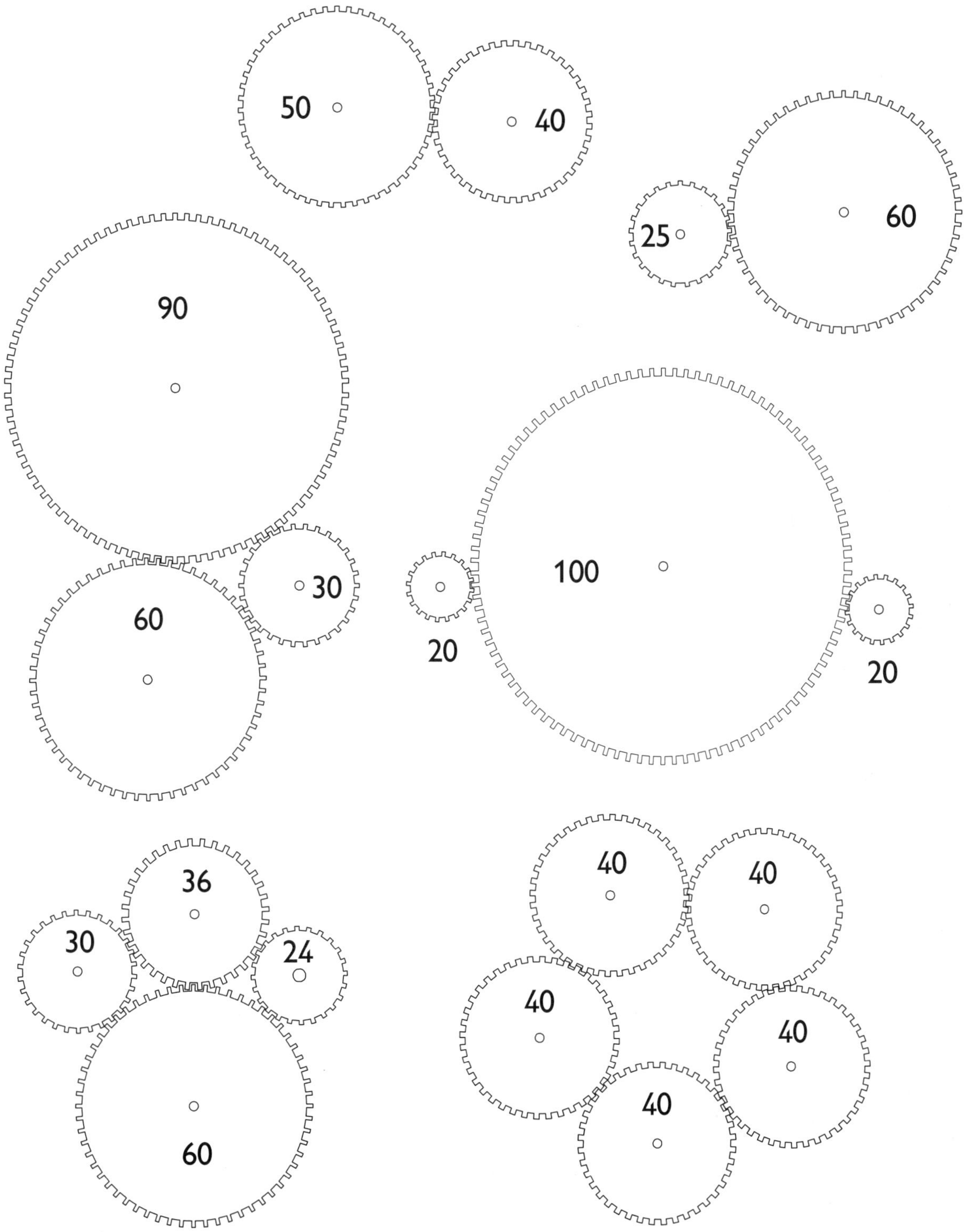
50
40
25
60
90
60
30
20
100
20
36
30
24
60
40
40
40
40
40

Pie charts I

eighths

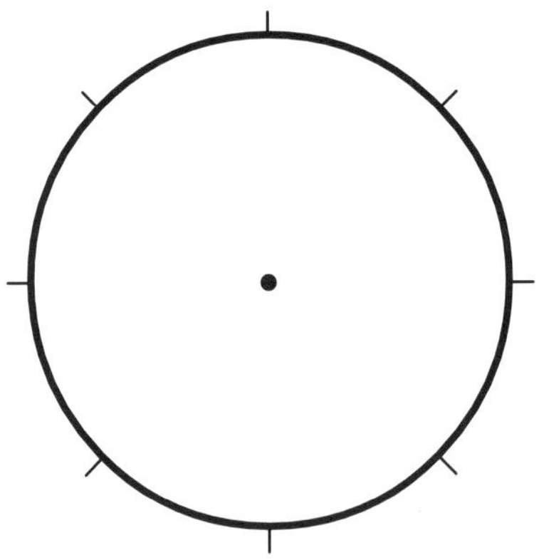

tenths

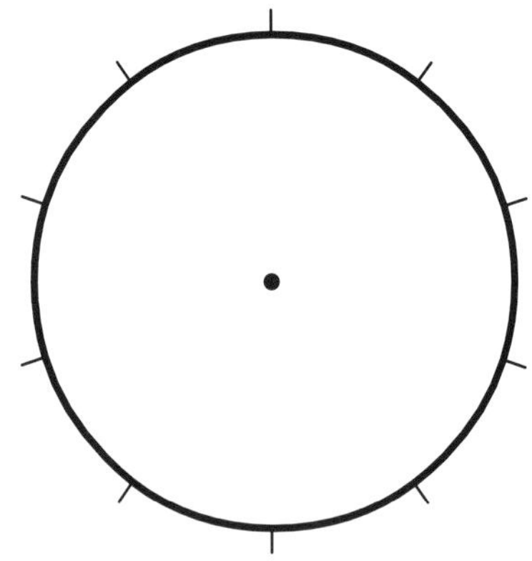

twelfths

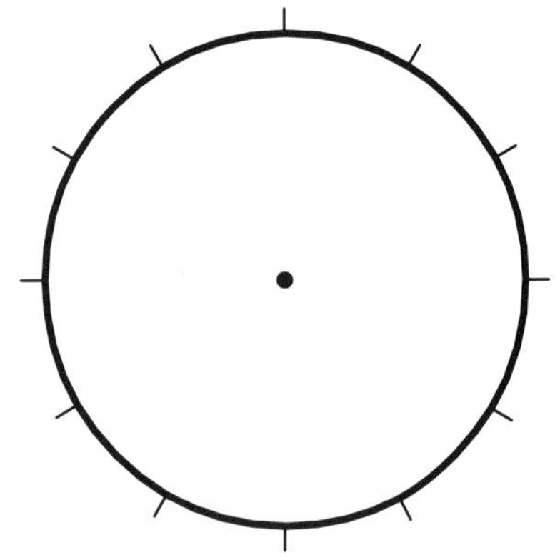

eighths

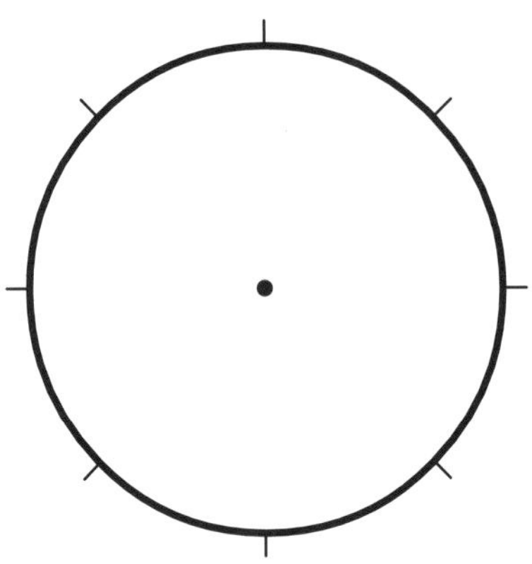

tenths

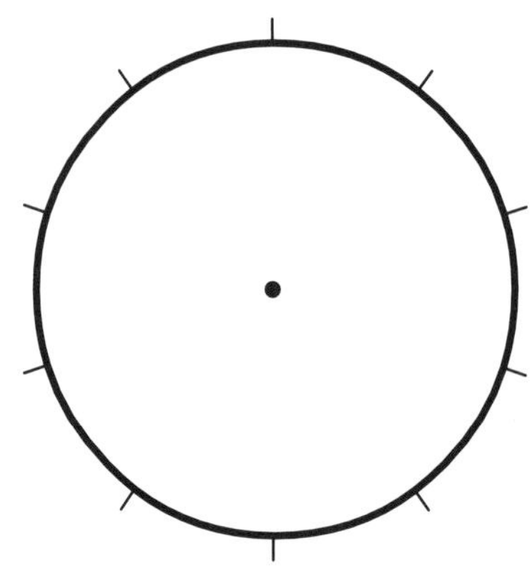

twelfths

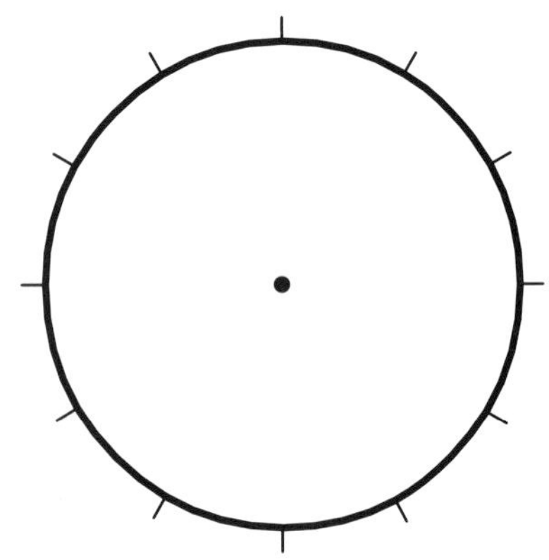

twentieths

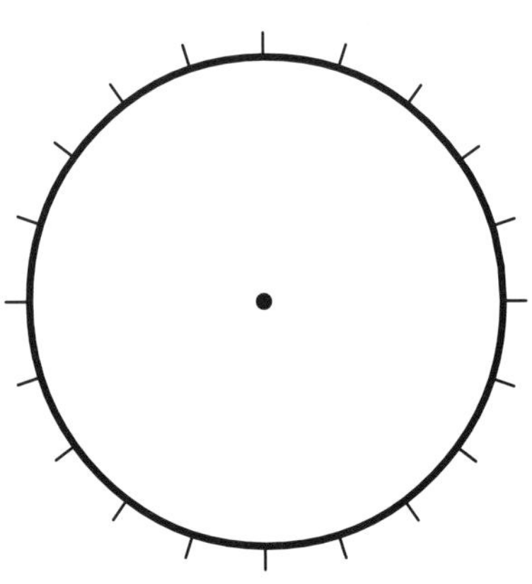

thirtieths

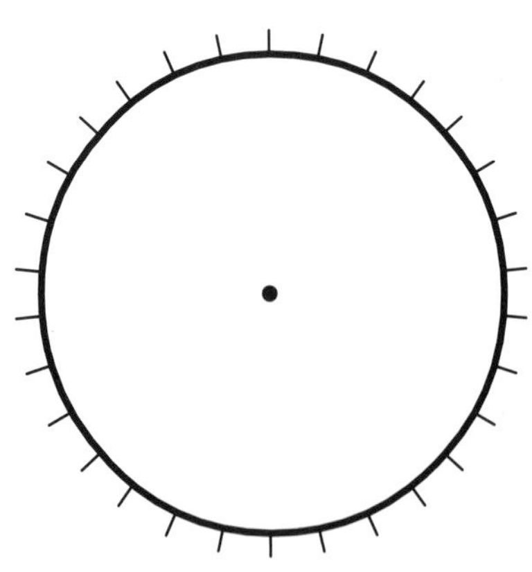

thirty-sixths

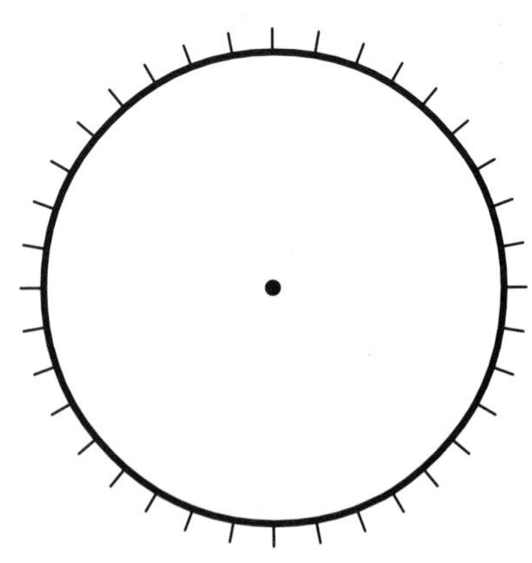

Pie charts II

Colours of 40 cows in a field

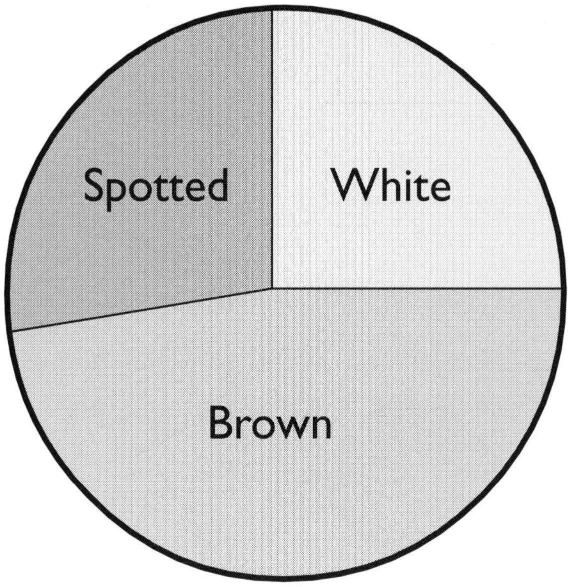

What 180 pupils have for breakfast

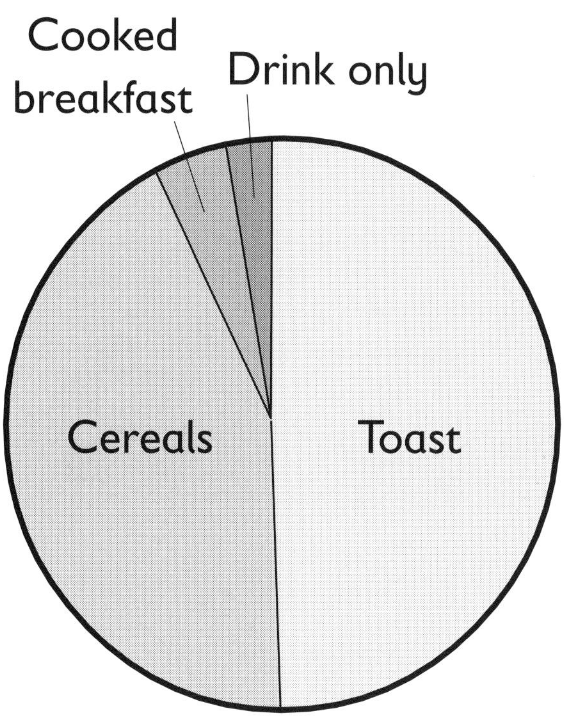

45 people's favourite entertainment

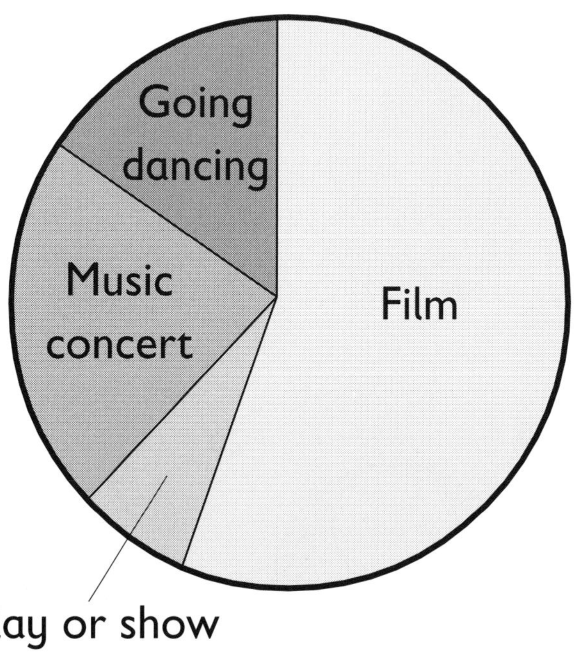

Lines of symmetry

If a shape has lines of symmetry, add them to the picture. Otherwise, write 'none'.

1
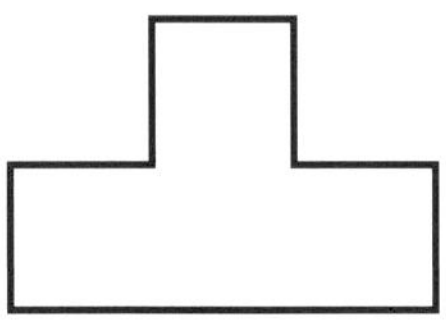

2
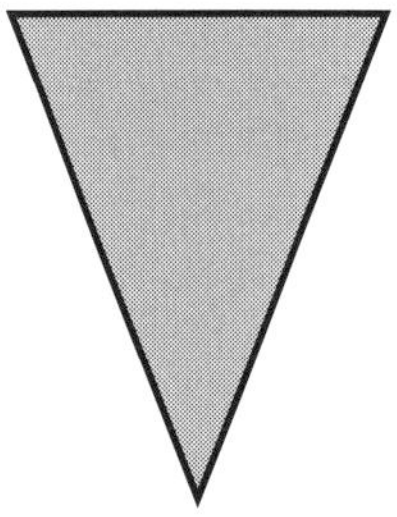

3

4

5
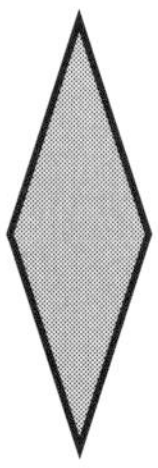

6
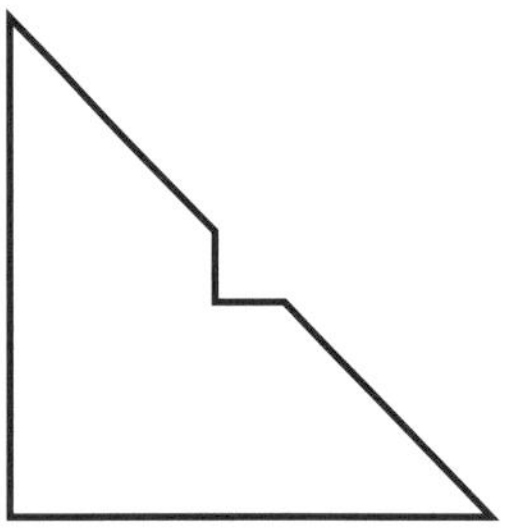

7
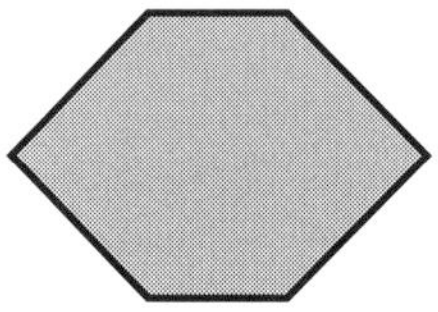

8

9
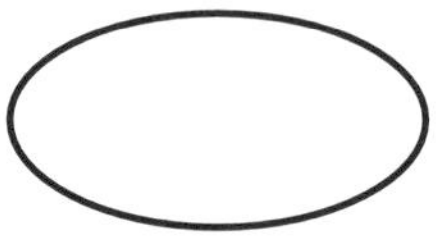

10
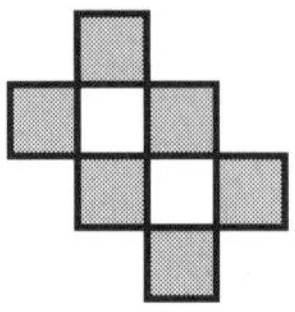

11
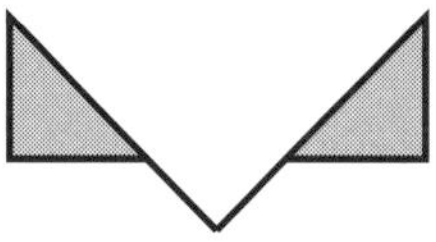

12
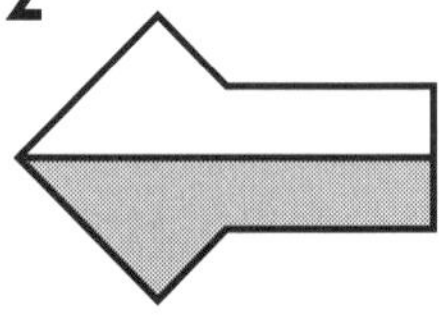

13
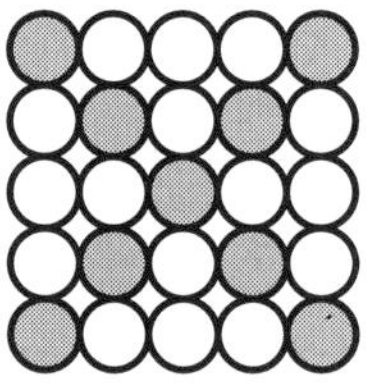

14
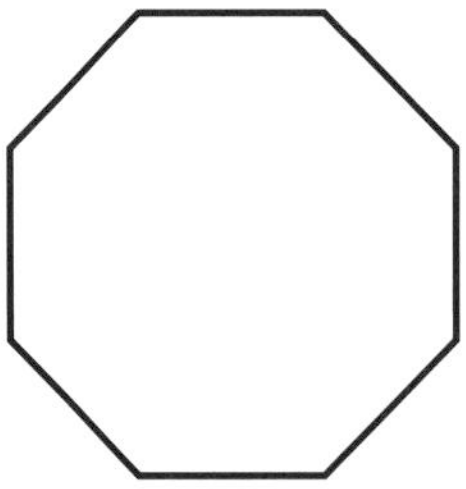

15
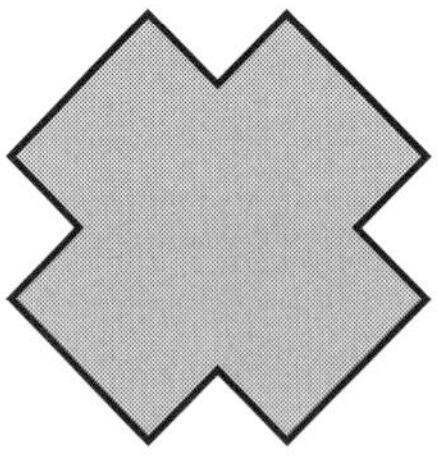

16
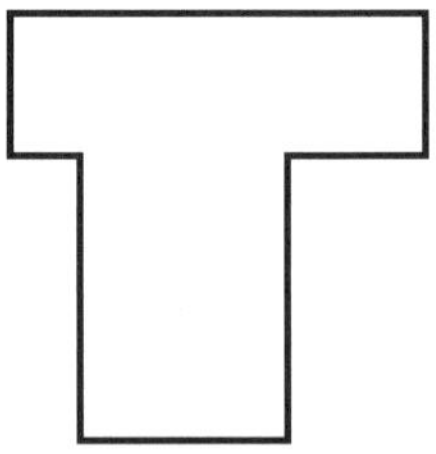

17

18

19
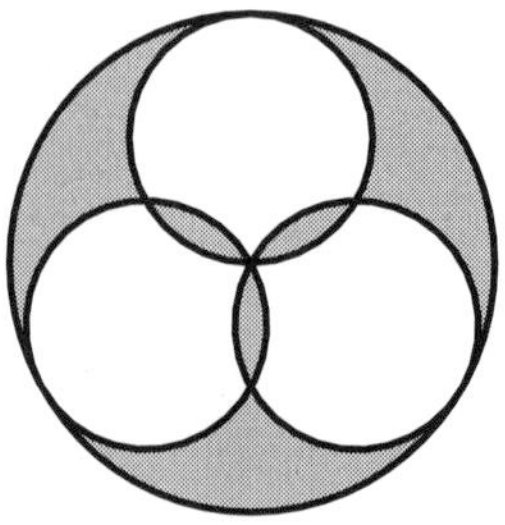

20
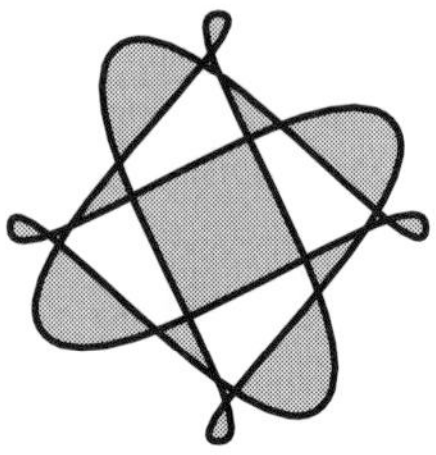

Rotational symmetry

If a shape has rotational symmetry, write down the order. Otherwise, write 'none'.

1

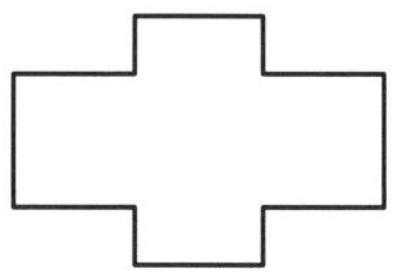

2

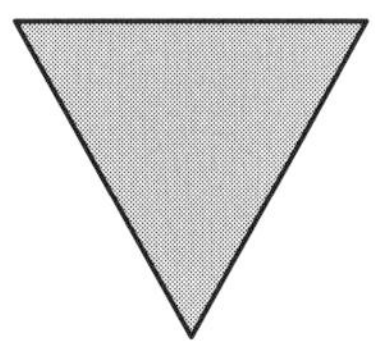

3

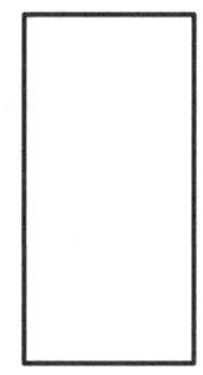

4

5

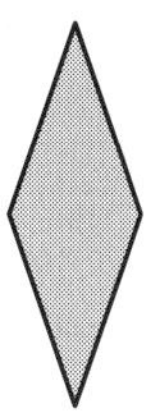

6

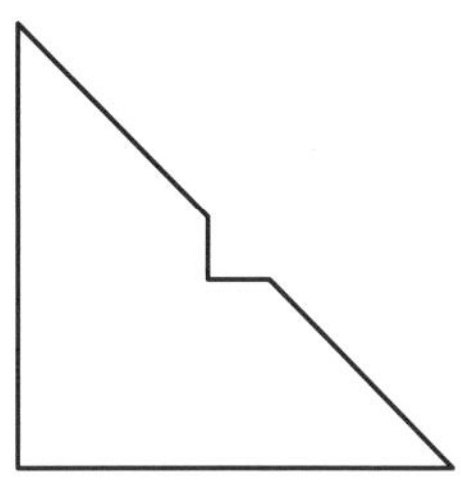

7

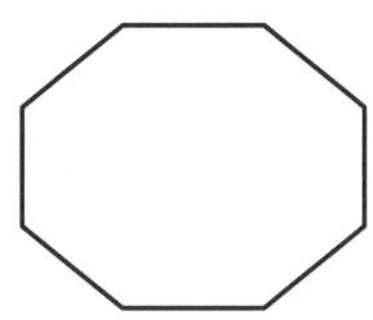

8

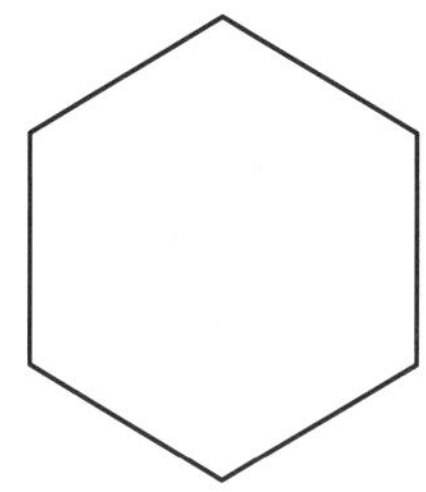

9

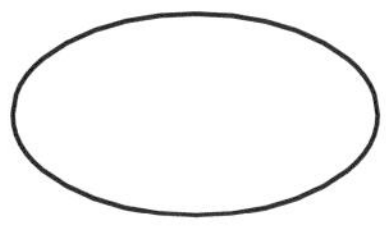

10

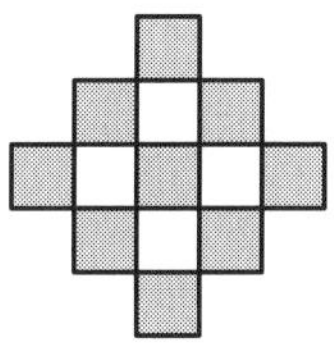

11

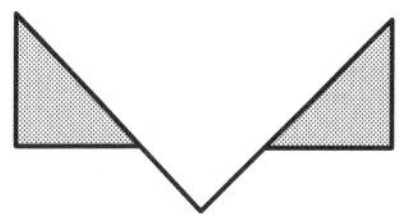

12

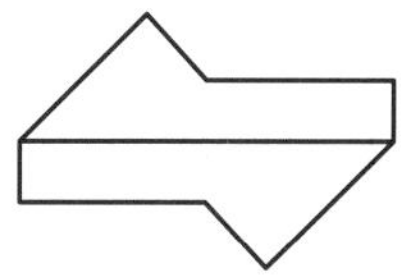

13

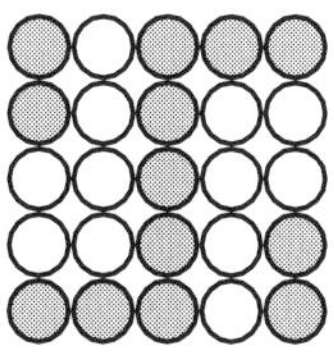

14

15

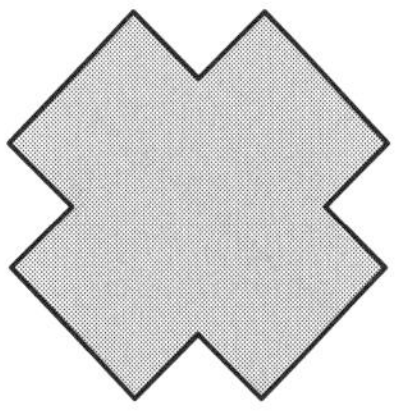

16

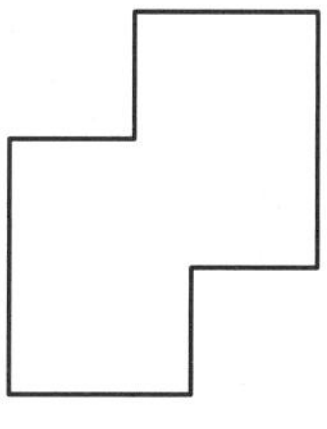

17

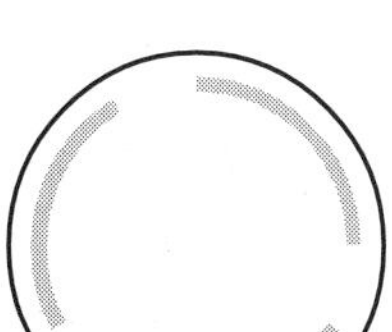

18

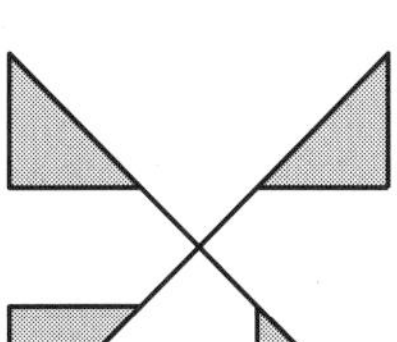

19

20

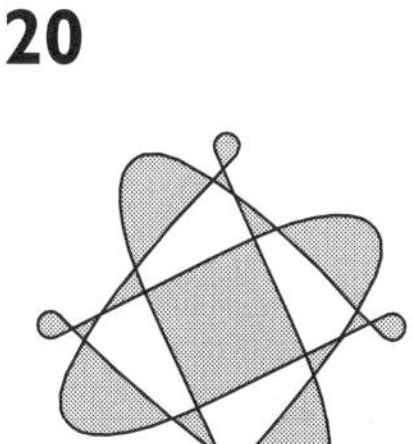

Angles in triangles

Find the angles marked **?**. If a diagram has more than one **?**, they stand for the same angle.

Careful! The diagrams are not to scale, so you can't measure the angles!

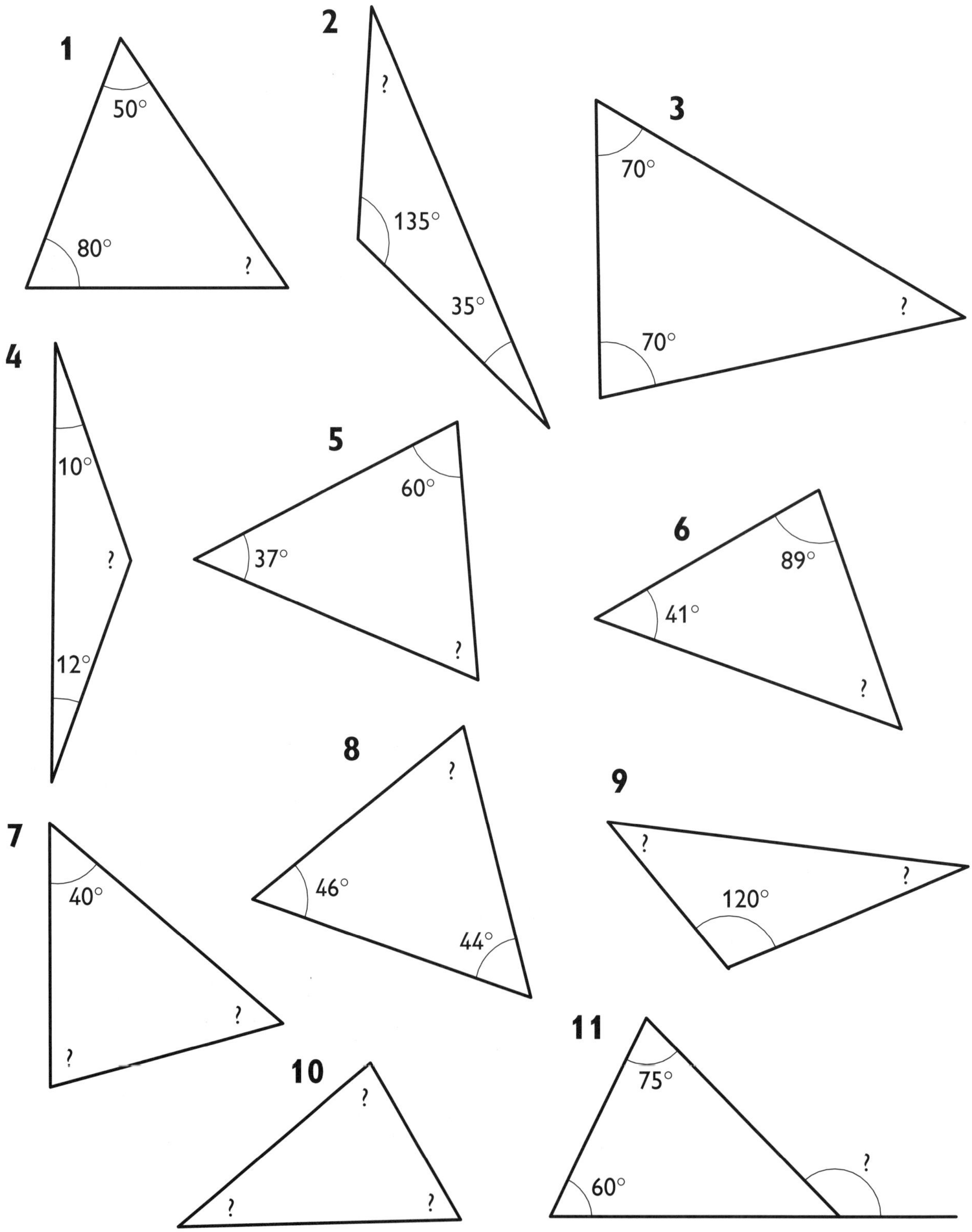

Diagonals

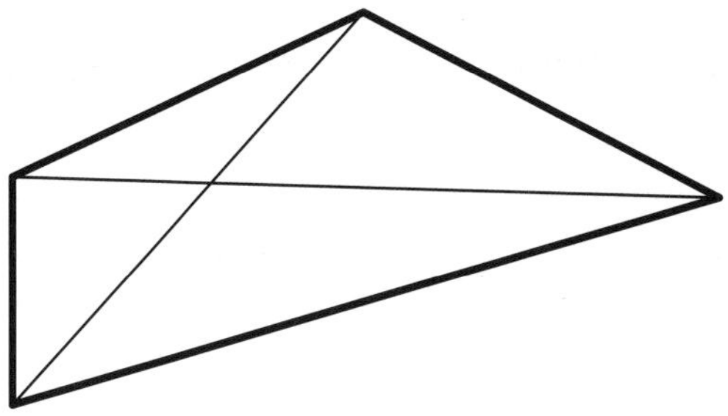

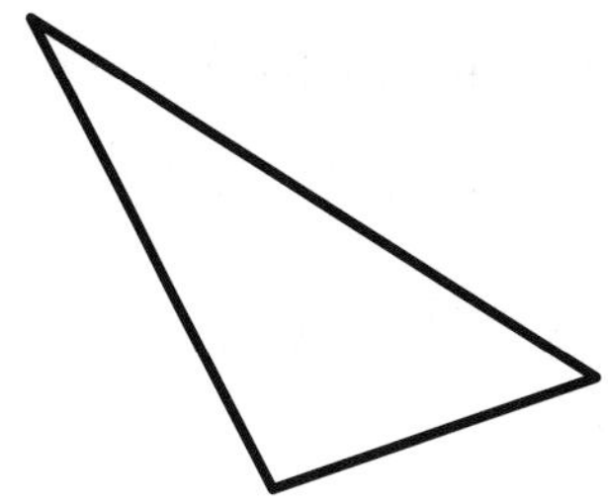

This quadrilateral has **2** diagonals.

Triangles don't have any diagonals.

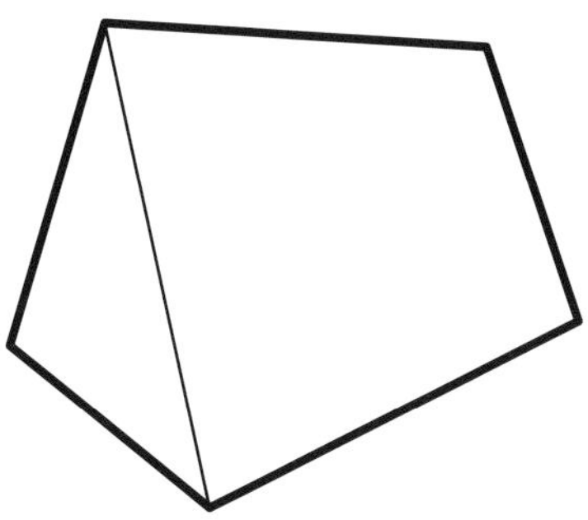

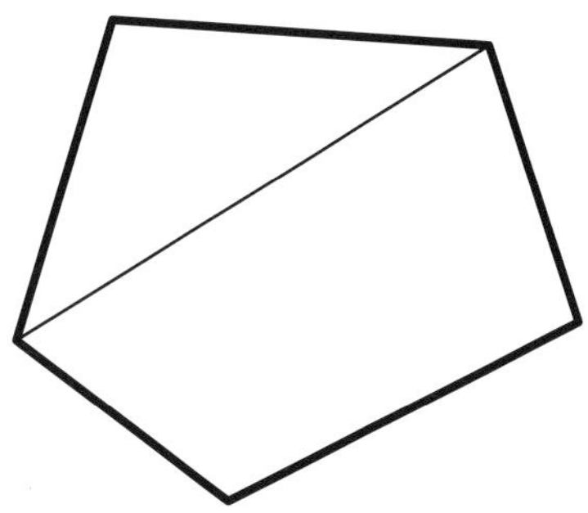

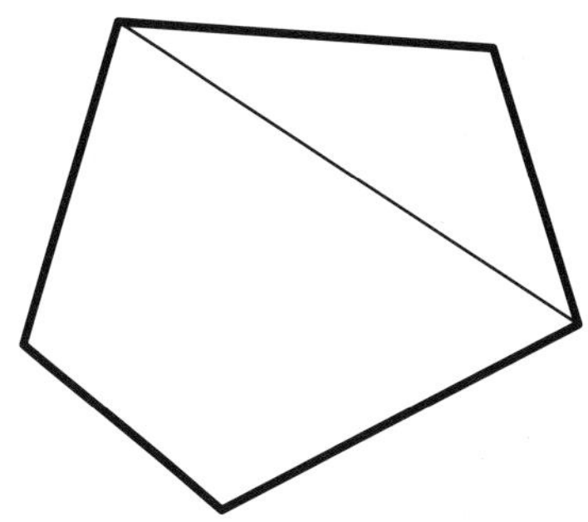

Here are some different diagonals of a pentagon.
How many diagonals does a pentagon have?

What about a hexagon? An octagon? Find a rule to help you.

How many diagonals does this dodecagon have?

Don't count! Calculate!

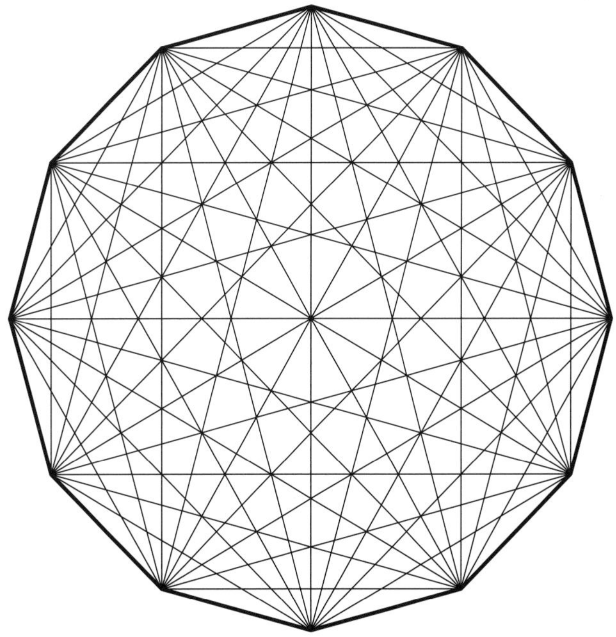

Reading scales

Write down the reading shown by each arrow.

1 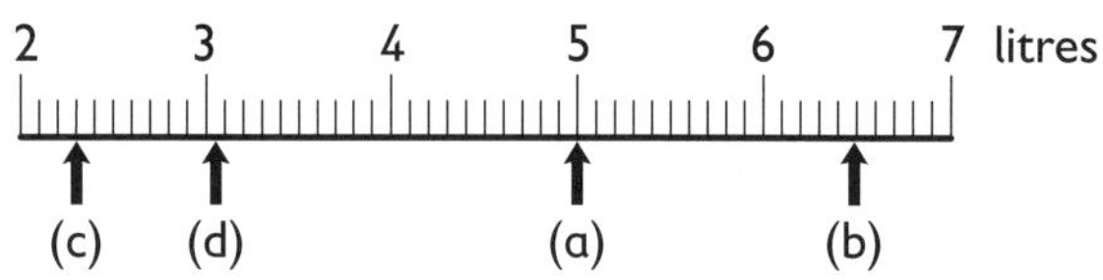

2 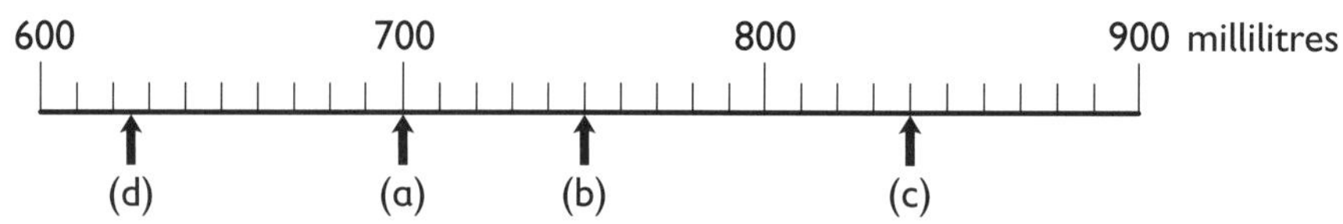

3 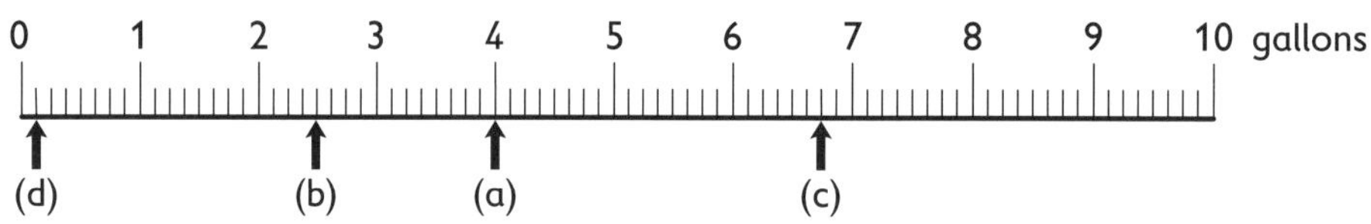

4 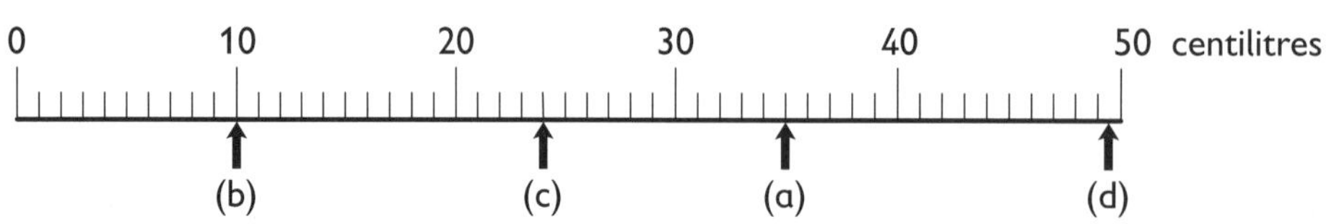

5 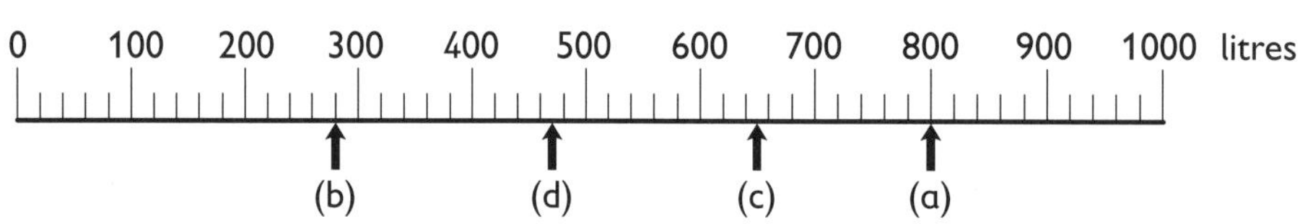

6 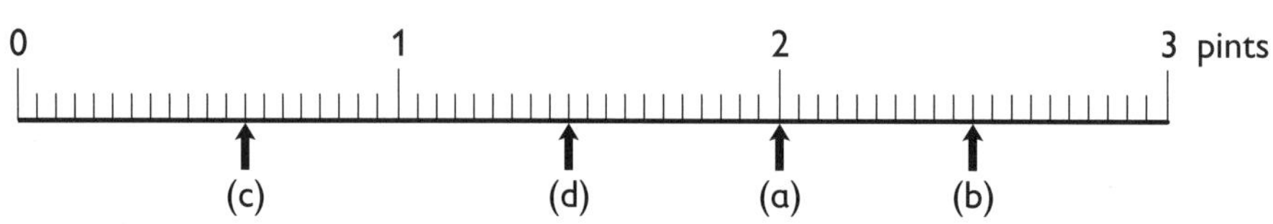

Mark each measurement on the correct scale.

3 l	680 ml	6 cl	40.5 cl	24 pints	350 l
$\frac{1}{4}$ pint	525 l	$1\frac{1}{2}$ gallons	875 ml	4.5 l	22 fl. oz.

Capacity problems

1 Amy makes the tea at her local fête. Each teacup holds 200 ml. Amy charges 30p a cup. At the end of the day she counts her money. She has taken £60.

(a) 10% of each cup is milk. How much milk is used in each teacup?

(b) How many cups of tea can she make with a litre carton of milk?

(c) How many cups of tea did she sell?

(d) How many litre cartons of milk did she use?

(e) A litre carton costs 60p. How much did she spend on milk altogether?

(f) What percentage of each cup is tea?

(g) How much tea did she make altogether?

(h) Her teapot holds 240 cl. How many times did she have to fill it?

(i) Every time she fills the teapot she uses 5 tea bags. How many tea bags did she use altogether?

(j) Tea bags cost 99p for a box of 40. How much does she spend on tea bags?

(k) Amy also used a bag of sugar costing 75p. How much profit did she make?

2 To answer this question, you need to know that 1 m^3 of space holds 1000 l of water.

(a) A swimming pool is 1 m deep, 40 m long and 20 m wide. What is the capacity of the swimming pool in cubic metres?

(b) What is the capacity in litres?

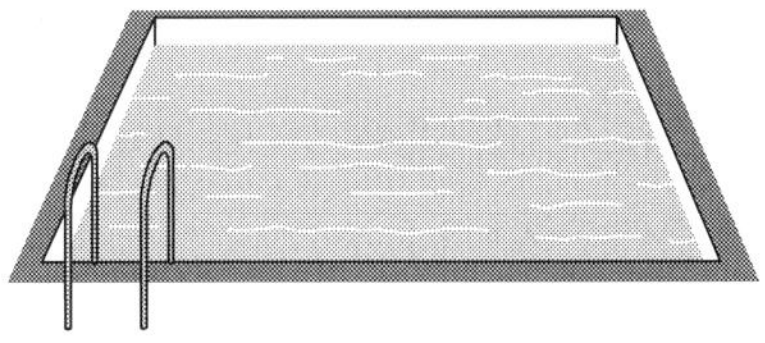

(c) When the pool is drained, water flows out at 5000 l per minute. How long does it take to drain the pool?

(d) When the pool is filled up again, water flows in at 80 l per second. How long does it take to fill the pool?

(e) How long does it take the water level to rise by 1 cm?

(f) One day, they forgot to shut the drain before they refilled the pool. What happened? Did the pool fill up eventually or not?

Money problems

1 These people all work for the same company. The amounts are their **salaries** – how much they earn in a year.

Cathy	**Mark**	**Ashok**	**Marisa**	**Dipa**
£12 560	£14 225	£12 243	£18 300	£25 648

(a) How much do they all earn between them?

(b) Which two salaries are closest together? What is the difference between them?

(c) Which two are furthest apart? What is the difference between them?

(d) Do Cathy and Mark between them earn more than Dipa?

2 These are the CD prices in a music shop.

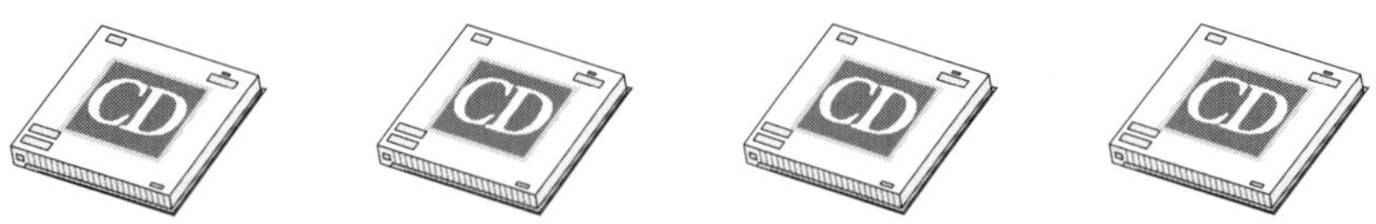

Full price:	Budget:	Special offer:	Bargain Bin:
£13.95	£6.99	£10.50	£3.25

Melanie buys 2 CDs. What could the total cost be?

3 This is what I found in my pocket.

(a) How much money is there?

(b) How much more do I need to make £10?

4 Marcus saves up money towards a computer. In six months, he saved these amounts.

March	April	May	June	July	August
£89.50	£75.77	£102.05	£66.80	£81	£96.65

(a) How much did he save altogether?

(b) What was the average (mean) amount each month?

(c) The computer costs £799. How much more does he need to save?

(d) If he carries on saving at the same average rate, when will he be able to buy his computer?

Addition and subtraction problems

1 Flowmaster make plastic pipes. They come in three sizes: Short (75 cm), Medium (1.6 m) and Long (3.35 m). The pipes can be joined together, and any extra cut off to make the right length. Work out how to combine the pipes to make the following lengths – write down which sizes are needed and how much has to be trimmed.

(a) 2 m **(b)** 3 m **(c)** 5 m **(d)** 10 m **(e)** 25 m

2 I have a pair of scale pans and three metal weights made of iron (130 g), brass (555 g) and lead (1.38 kg).

What different masses can I balance by combining these weights?

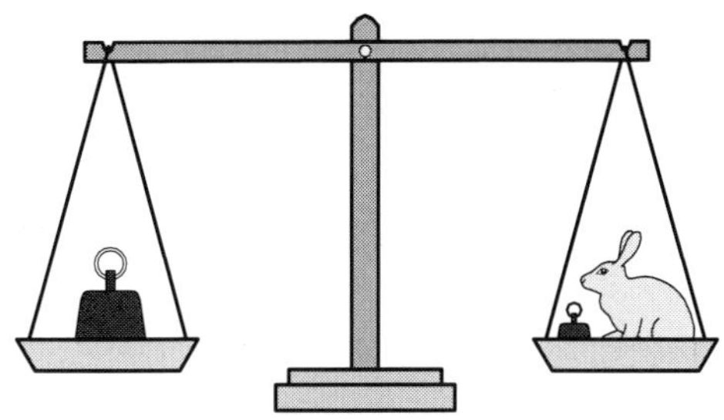

3 Four pans have the following capacities:

A: 450 ml B: 88 cl C: 1.25 l D: 2.04 l

Copy these table headings. Draw enough rows for parts **(a)**–**(j)**.

	Amount in A	**Amount in B**	**Amount in C**	**Amount in D**
(a)				
(b)				

In the table, write down the amount of water in each pan.

(a) Fill A and D.
(b) Pour as much from D into C as possible.
(c) Pour as much from C into B as possible.
(d) Empty D into C.
(e) Pour as much from A into C as possible.
(f) Empty A and B into D.
(g) Pour as much from C into A as possible.
(h) Empty C into B.
(i) Pour as much from A into B as possible.
(j) Pour as much from B into D as possible.

What should you do to make it look as if you had just done **(a)**?

Matchstick patterns

1
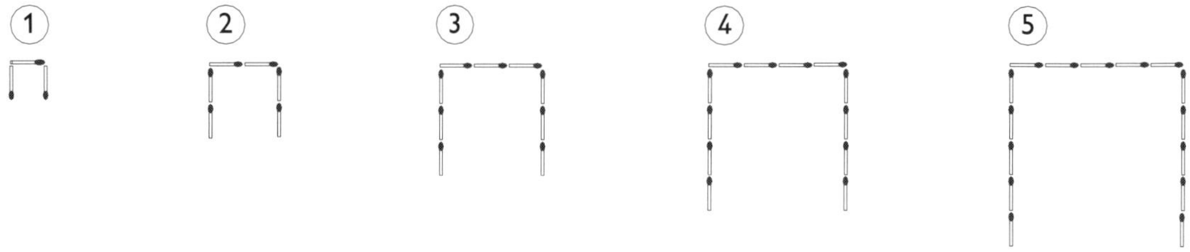

2
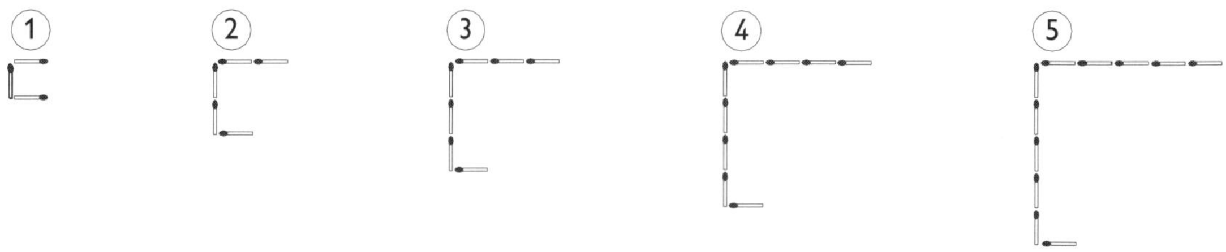

3
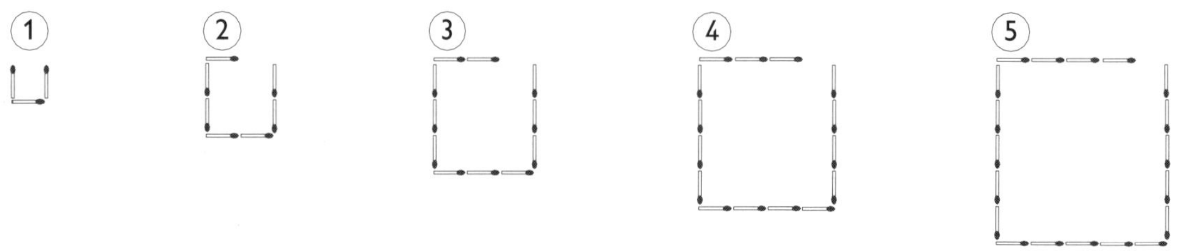

4
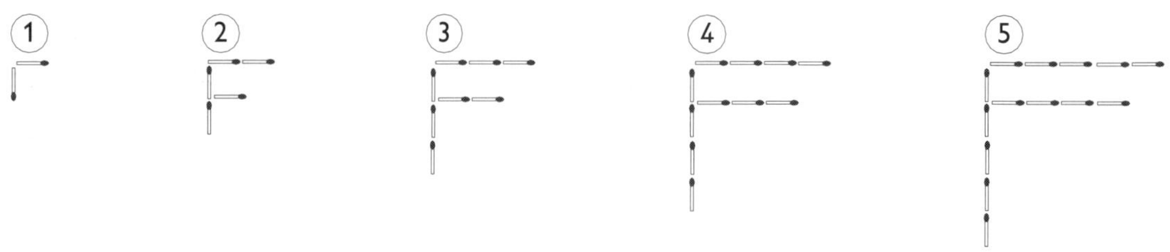

5
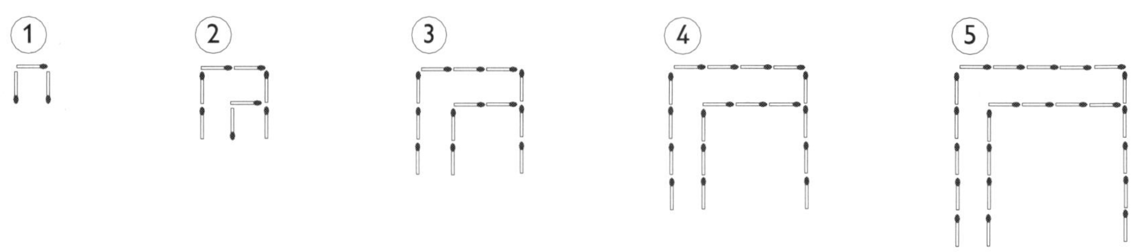

6
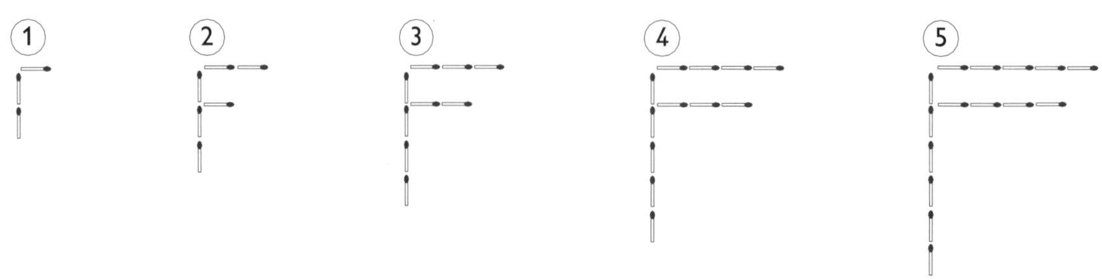

7
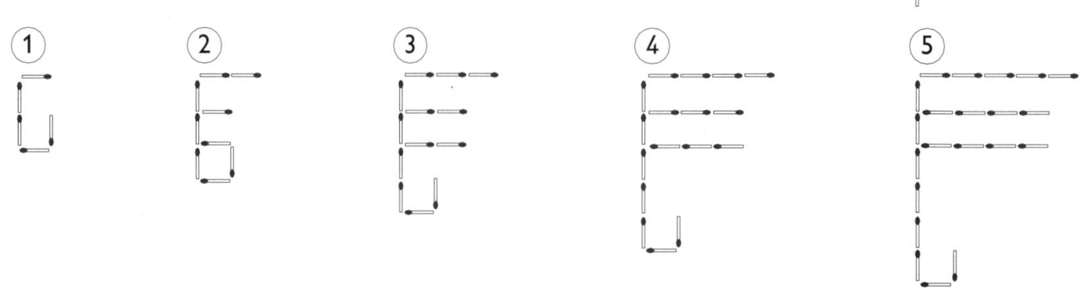

Mathematical puzzles

Find out how this triangle works.
Copy it and add on the next 3 rows.

1

1 1

1 2 1

1 3 3 1

1 4 6 4 1

Add up the numbers along each row.
What do you notice?

Look for other patterns in the triangle.
You may need to add more rows.

Use your calculator to add up these fractions:

$\frac{1}{2} + \frac{1}{4} + \frac{1}{8} + \frac{1}{16} + \frac{1}{32} + \frac{1}{64} + \ldots$

$\frac{1}{2} + \frac{1}{3} + \frac{1}{4} + \frac{1}{5} + \frac{1}{6} + \frac{1}{7} + \ldots$

What happens as you add more and more?

'In 1985 I put £1000 into a bank account. Every year, I earn 5% interest on whatever is in the account. One year I looked at the account and there was just over £2000 in it! What was the year?'

Find the next number in this sequence:
3, 3, 5, 4, 4, 3, 5, 5, 4, ?

How many squares are there in this diagram?

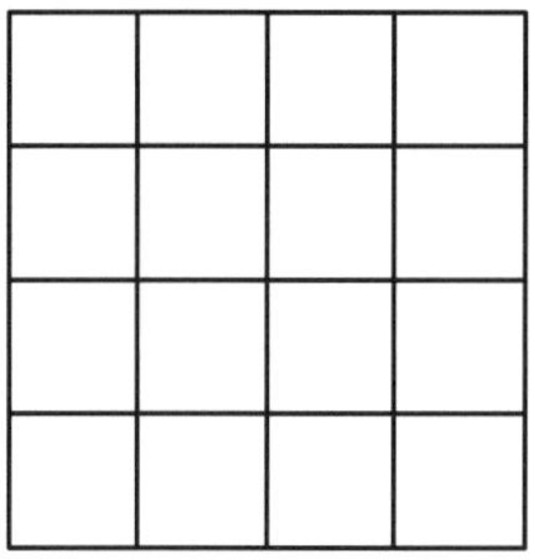

How many rectangles are there?

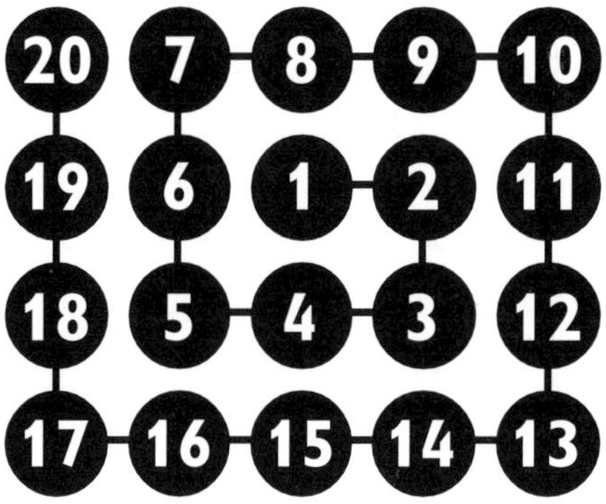

If you put 1p on the first circle, 2p on the second, 4p on the third, 8p on the fourth etc., how much money will there be altogether?

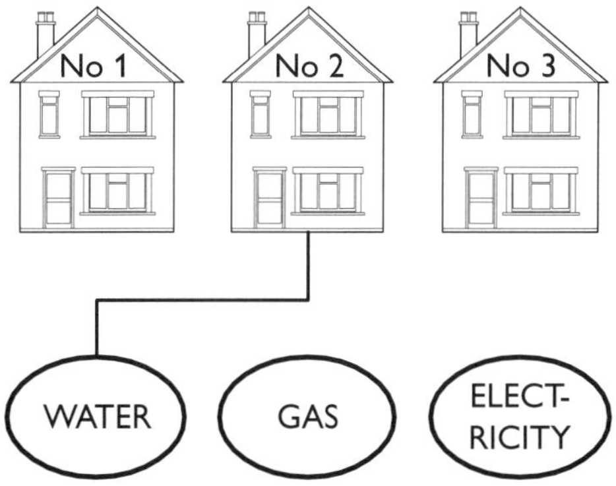

Can you connect all three supplies to all three houses without any lines crossing?

Homework 1

This week's work is about multiplying and dividing mentally.

1 Use doubling to fill in this multiplication square.

×	2	4	8	16
12				
32				
57				
105				

2 Use multiplication and division by 10 and 2 to answer these.

(a)	26×10	26×20	26×40	26×80
(b)	43×10	43×100	43×50	43×25
(c)	$15 \div 3$	$150 \div 3$	$150 \div 6$	$1500 \div 12$
(d)	$56 \div 7$	$560 \div 7$	$560 \div 14$	$560 \div 28$
(e)	65×1000	65×500	65×250	65×125

3 Match the answers to the questions. One has been done for you.

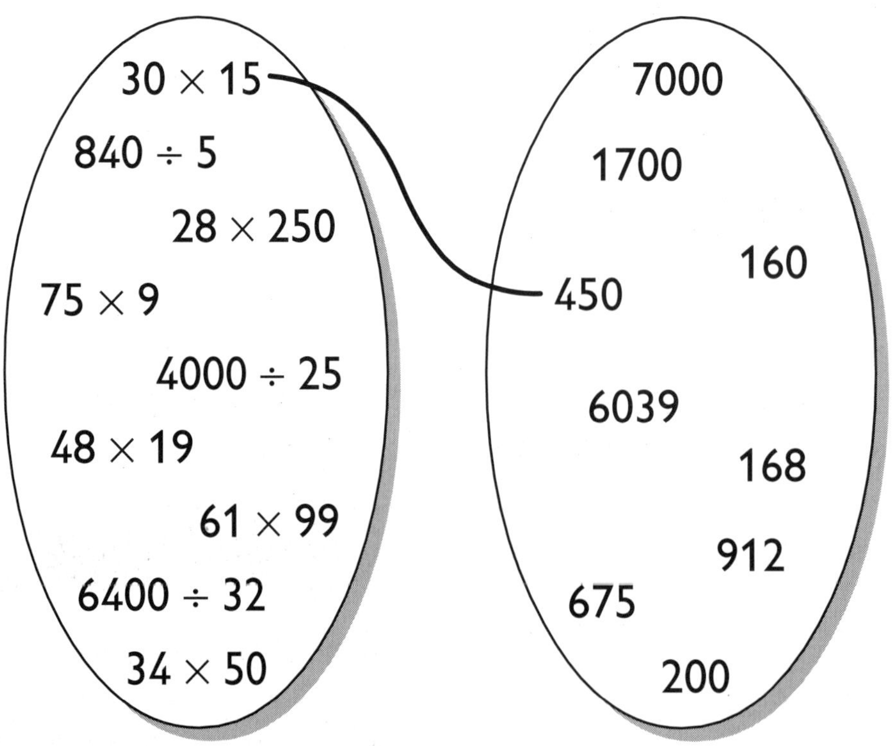

This week's work is about multiplying using a written method.

1 Follow the instructions to put the correct numbers in the circles.

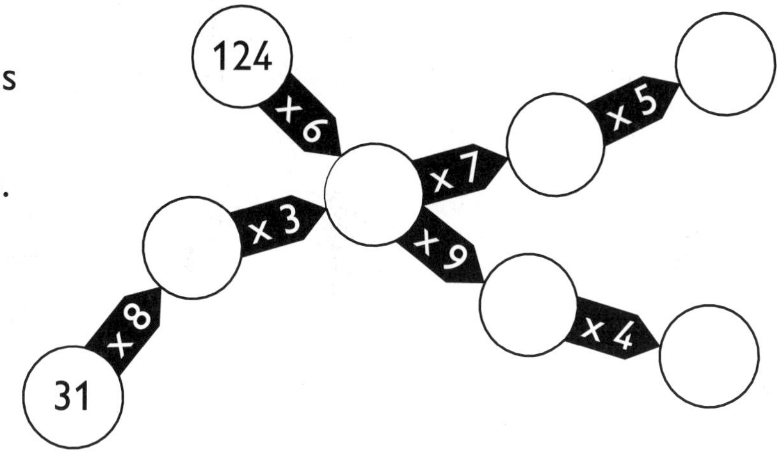

2 Mrs Semple is buying furniture for the school computer room. This is a page from the catalogue.

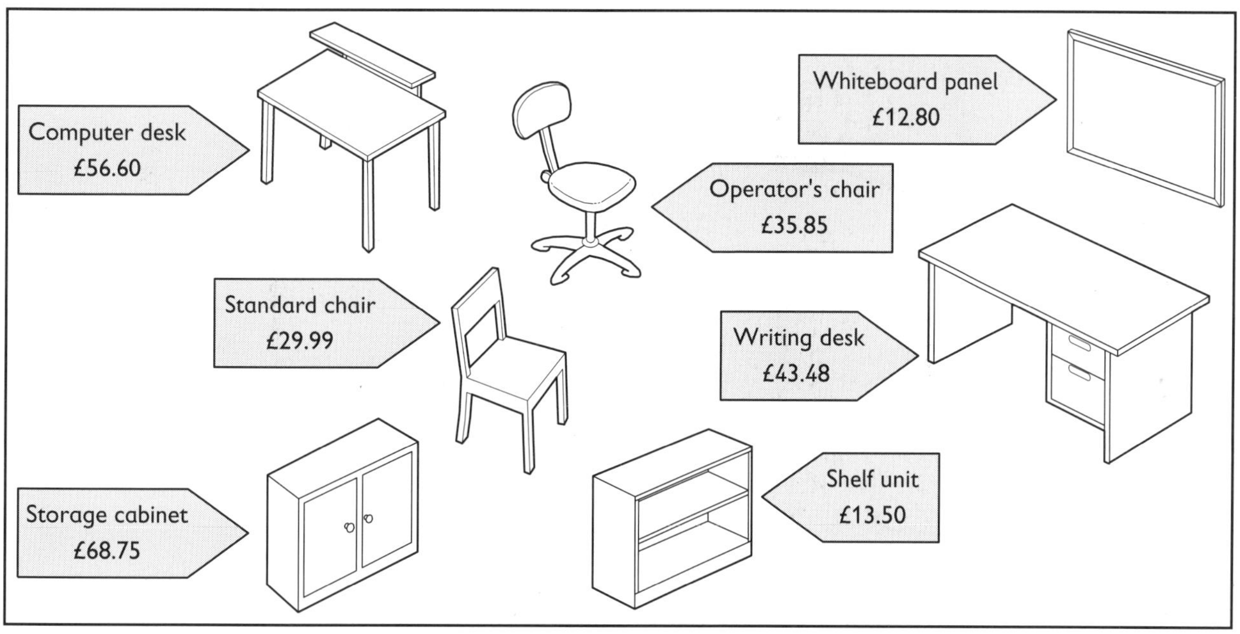

Complete her order form.

Item	Number required	Cost of one item	Item total
Computer desk	*8*		
Writing desk	*6*		
Operator's chair	*7*		
Standard chair	*5*		
Shelf unit	*9*		
Storage cabinet	*3*		
Whiteboard panel	*4*		
		Order Total	

Homework 3

This week's work is about fractions and decimals.

1 There are four different sets of equivalent fractions in the diagram. Join up the ones that are equivalent with straight lines.

$\frac{10}{16}$ $\frac{15}{24}$ $\frac{15}{25}$ $\frac{30}{50}$ $\frac{1}{2}$ $\frac{5}{10}$ $\frac{4}{6}$ $\frac{7}{10}$ $\frac{25}{40}$ $\frac{5}{8}$ $\frac{3}{5}$ $\frac{9}{15}$ $\frac{3}{6}$ $\frac{12}{24}$ $\frac{16}{24}$ $\frac{6}{9}$

2 Change all the mixed numbers to improper fractions. Change all the improper fractions to mixed numbers.

$2\frac{1}{2}$ $\frac{11}{6}$ $\frac{11}{4}$ $3\frac{1}{4}$ $5\frac{1}{3}$ $\frac{19}{8}$ $\frac{70}{9}$ $3\frac{2}{3}$ $4\frac{2}{5}$ $\frac{36}{25}$

3 Label each mark on these number lines.

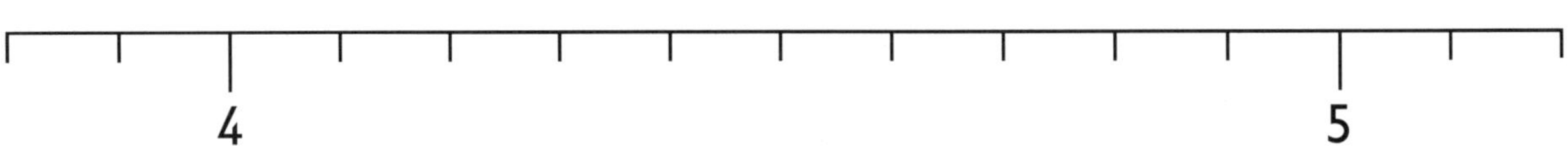

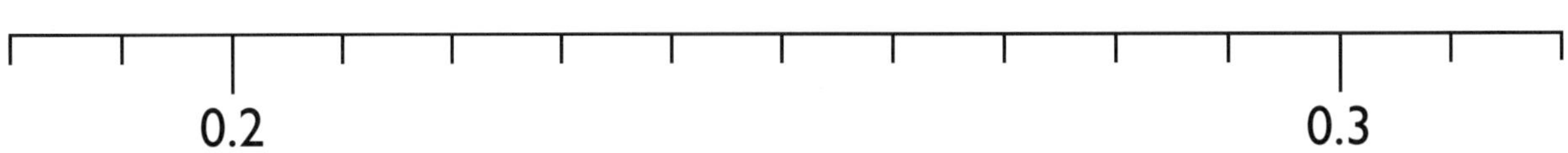

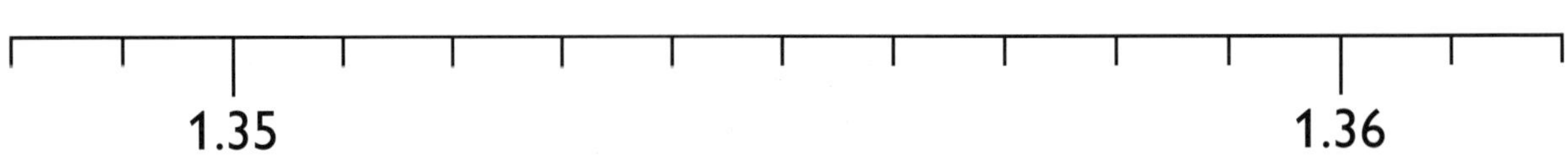

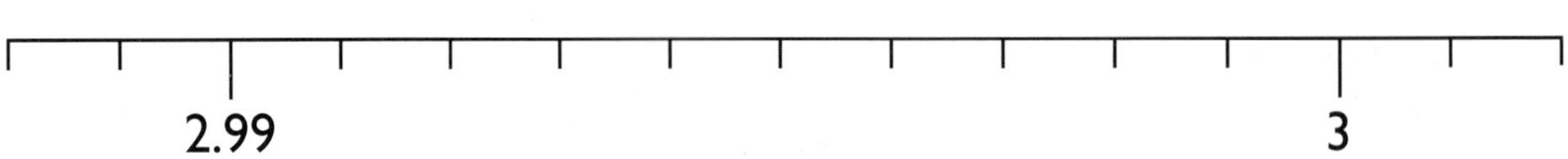

This week's work is about percentages, ratio and proportion.

1 For each pattern, complete these sentences.
There are _____ black squares in every _____ squares.
There are _____ white squares in every _____ squares.
There are _____ white squares to every _____ black squares.

(a)

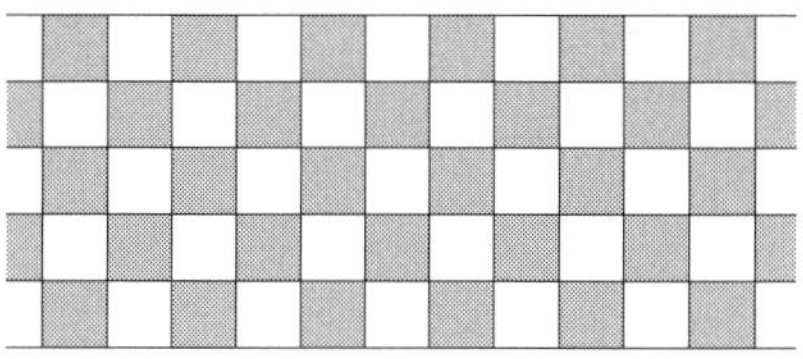

(b)

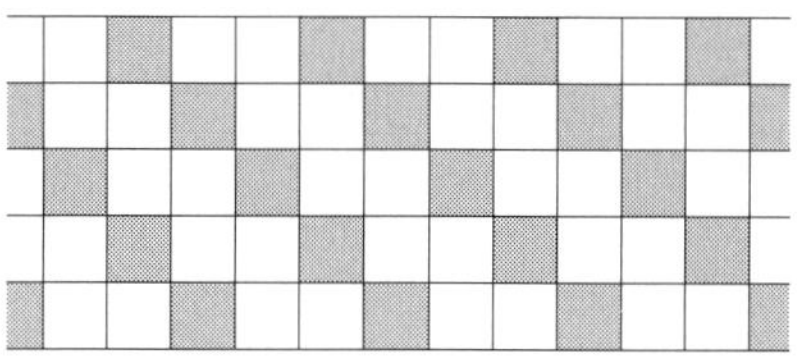

2 Sam, Gina and Fred count their money. They have £12.60 between them. Sam has twice as much as Gina. Gina has twice as much as Fred. How much does each person have?

3 Copy the shapes onto graph paper.
Shade in the correct percentage of each shape.

45% 20% 60% 30%

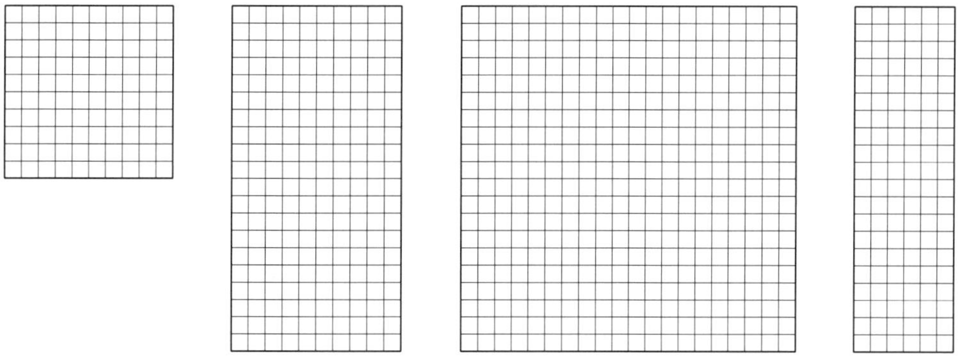

4 This recipe makes 4 servings of Waldorf salad. Rewrite the recipe for 5 servings.

8 sticks of celery

_____ sticks

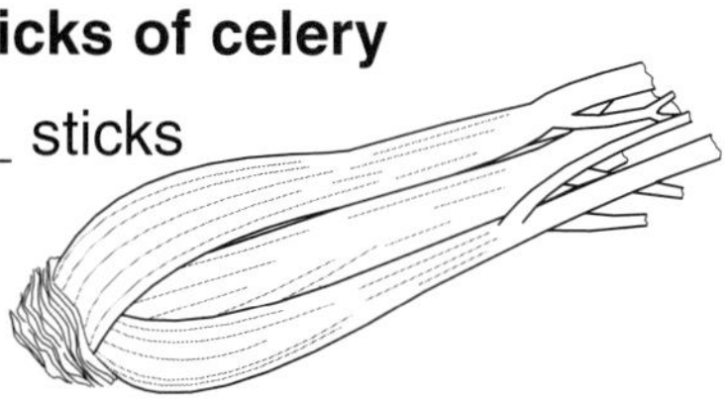

160 ml mayonnaise

_____ ml

100 g seedless raisins

_____ g

60 g chopped walnuts

_____ g

500 g red apples

_____ g

40 ml lemon juice

_____ ml

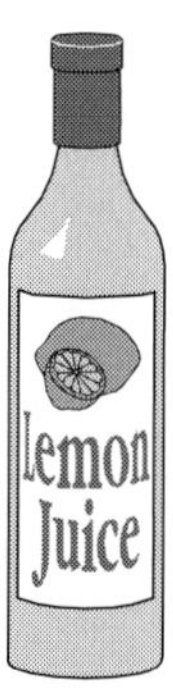

Homework 5

This week's work is about statistics and probability.

You need three coins to do this experiment.

When you flip three coins, two things can happen:

(i) All the coins show the same face (all heads or all tails);

(ii) One coin shows a different face to the other two.

Prepare a tally chart for the results, like this:

Result	**Tally**	**Frequency**
All the same		
Not the same		

Flip the coins 100 times and record the results in your tally chart.

Fill in the **Frequency** column.

Make a bar chart of your results. You will need some squared paper or graph paper. If you have a computer at home, you might be able to use it to make your bar chart.

Which of the two results is more likely?

Can you explain why?

What do you think would happen if you flipped *four* coins? Explain your answer. You do *not* need to do the experiment!

This week's work is about quadrilaterals.

For each question on this sheet:

(a) Draw a coordinate grid with *x*- and *y*-axes from 0 to 10, like this:

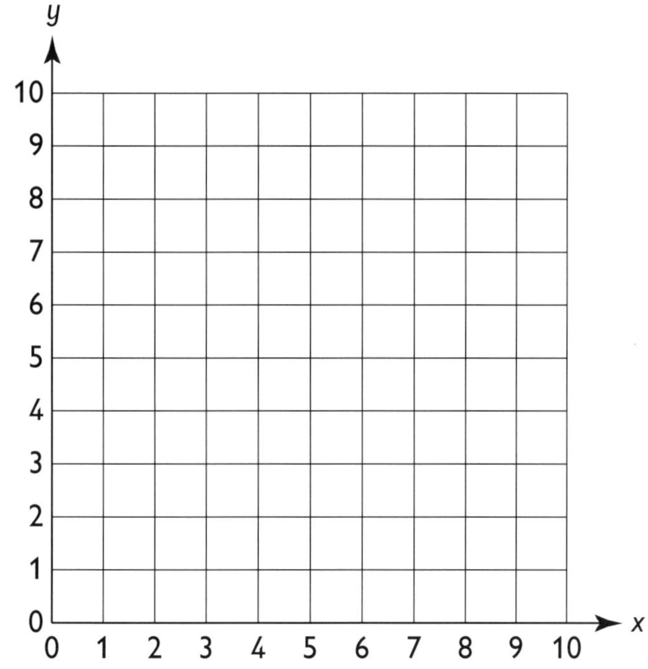

(b) Plot the points given.
(c) Add a fourth point to make the quadrilateral in the question.
(d) Write down the coordinates of your point.
(e) If you think more than one answer is possible, say so.

1	(2, 1)	(2, 8)	(9, 8)	Square
2	(7, 8)	(7, 1)	(4, 1)	Rectangle
3	(5, 3)	(8, 3)	(4, 7)	Parallelogram
4	(3, 6)	(7, 6)	(5, 8)	Kite
5	(5, 7)	(6, 8)	(4, 9)	Rhombus
6	(4, 1)	(8, 2)	(7, 6)	Square
7	(1, 6)	(4, 9)	(9, 4)	Rectangle
8	(1, 2)	(10, 2)	(4, 5)	Trapezium

Homework 7

This week's work is about perimeters.

This rectangle is 2 cm by 1 cm.

You can put three of them together in lots of different ways.

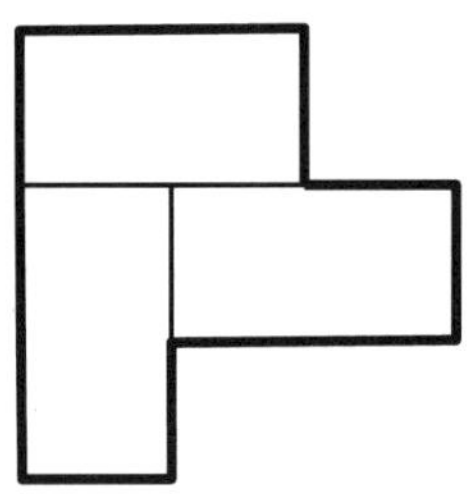

Investigate the perimeter of the shapes you can make.

Are they all the same?

If not, what is the biggest perimeter you can make?

What is the smallest?

What happens if you use rectangles that are 3 cm by 1 cm?

This week's work is about measures and units.

How many times do you clean your teeth in a week?

How long is the squeeze of toothpaste that you use?

What length of toothpaste do you squeeze in a week?

What length of toothpaste do you squeeze in a year?

What length of toothpaste do you squeeze in your whole lifetime?

Suppose you eat spaghetti once a week.

A piece of spaghetti is about 30 cm long.

How many pieces of spaghetti do you think are in a meal?

How long would all the spaghetti in a meal be, if placed end to end?

What length of spaghetti would you eat in a year?

What length would you eat in your whole lifetime?

How many slices of bread do you eat in a week?

An average slice of bread is about 10 cm by 15 cm. What area does a slice cover, roughly?

Remember, the area of a rectangle = length × width.

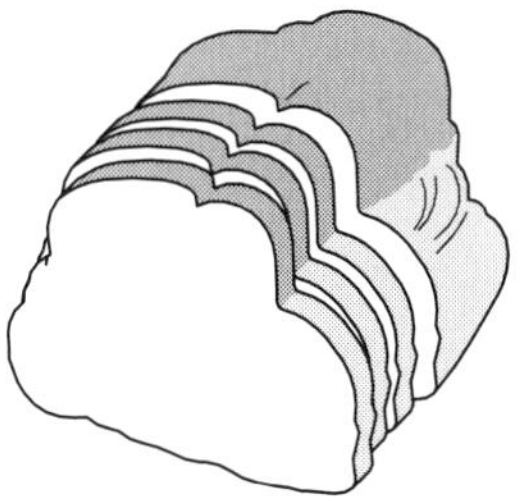

What area could you cover over with bread in a week?

What area could you cover in a year?
It might be useful to know that 10 000 cm^2 = 1 m^2.

What area could you cover in your whole lifetime?

An 800 g loaf of bread has about 20 slices in it. How many loaves do you eat in a year? How much does this weigh?

What weight of bread do you eat in a lifetime?

Homework 9

This week's work is about solving problems.

This square is 5 cm along each side.

What is its area?

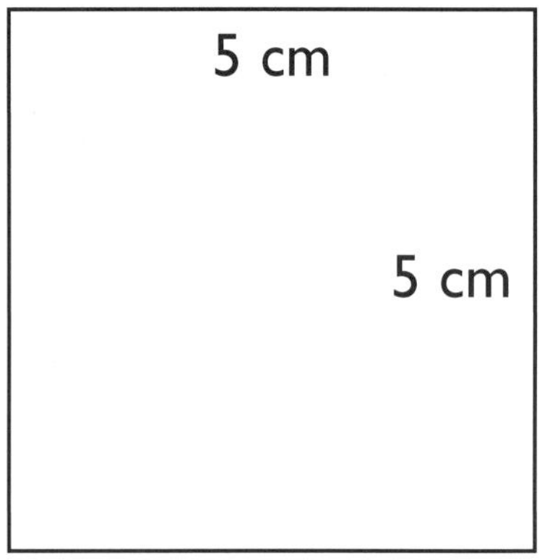

If you add 1 cm to the length and take 1 cm from the width, you get this rectangle.

What is its area?

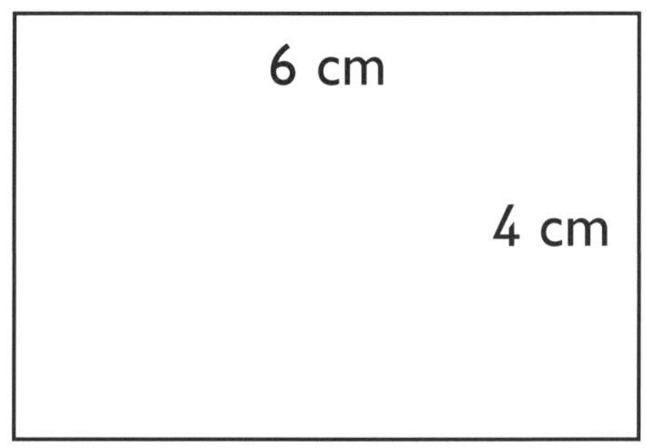

Try this with different-sized squares. Is there a rule about what happens to the area?

Write a sentence to describe it. Does it work if the square's sides aren't a whole number of cm?

What happens if you change a square's measurements by 2 cm? With the original 5 cm square, that would give you this rectangle.

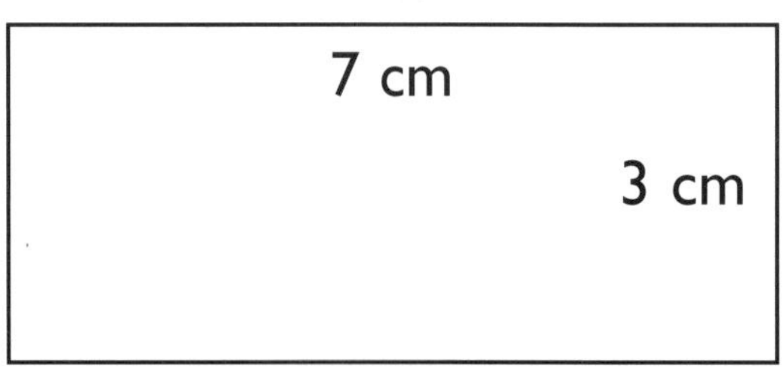

What happens if you change a square's measurements by 3 cm? 4 cm? Investigate.

This week's work is about number sequences and patterns.

This picture shows a stack of cans in a shop.

The rules for making stacks are:

When you make a row, it has one less can than the one it's standing on.

A can rests on two cans underneath it.

There must be at least two rows in a stack.

How many cans can you have in a stack?

The picture shows 3 + 4 + 5 = 12 cans.

Are there some numbers of cans that can be stacked in more than one way?

Are there some numbers of cans that can never make a stack?

Find out as much as you can about stacks.

Homework 11

This week's work is about negative numbers.

1 Find the answers to these additions and subtractions.

(a) 2 − 5 **(b)** 5 − 2

(c) −3 + 8 **(d)** −3 − 8

(e) 11 − 35 **(f)** −11 + 35

(g) 0 − 7 **(h)** 135 − 531

(i) 1.6 − 2.3 **(j)** −1 + 3.56

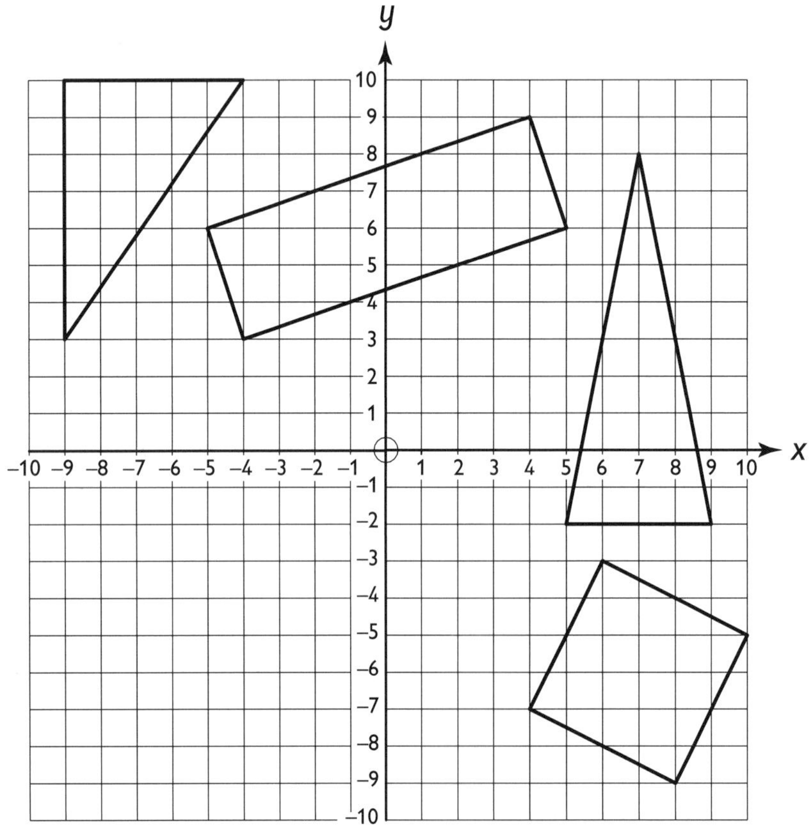

2 Write down the coordinates of the corners of:

(a) the isosceles triangle **(b)** the rectangle

(c) the square **(d)** the right-angled triangle

3 Draw your own grid, or use the one on this sheet if your teacher has said you can.

(a) Plot the following coordinates:
(2, 2), (−2, 2), (1, −10), (−8, 2), (−5, −10), (−4, 2), (−6, −6), (4, 2), (−3, −2), (−10, 2), (−7, −10), (0, −6), (−1, −10)

(b) Join the points up to make a letter of the alphabet. The order is **not** the one given in part **(a)**. What letter is it?

This week's work is about multiplication and division.

Find the missing numbers on the leaves of this tree.

If you have to multiply or divide by a 2-digit number, split the calculation into two stages. So to multiply by 15, multiply by 5, then 3.

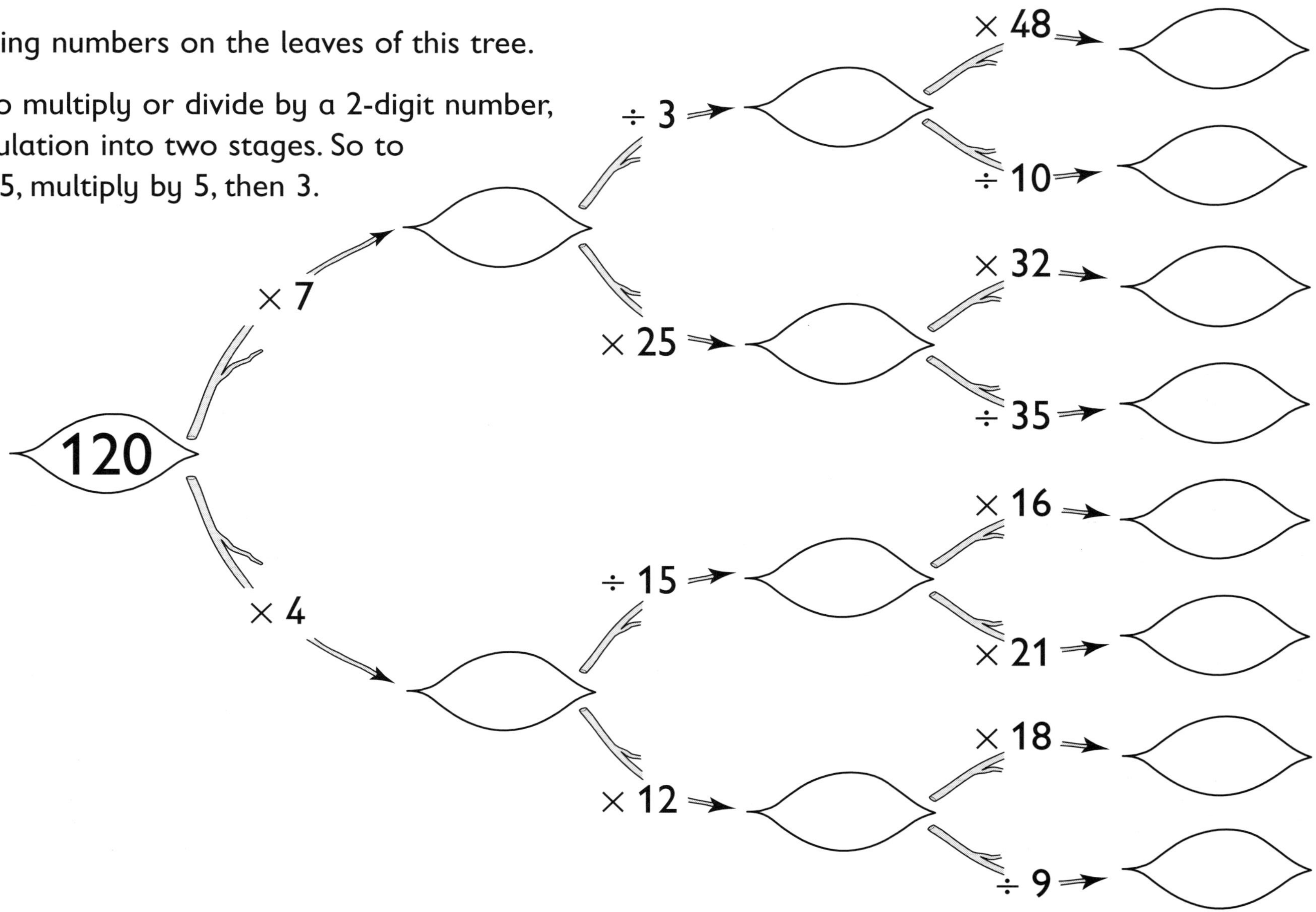

Homework 13

This week's work is about problems involving money.

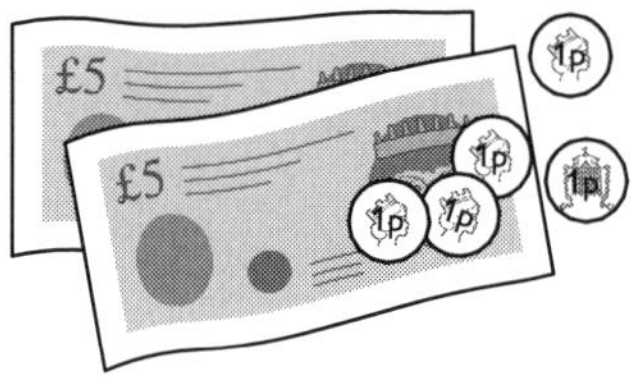

1 Mr Singh bought a car for £14 995. This table shows how much of its value it lost over the years.

New	After 1 year	After 2 years	After 5 years	After 10 years
£0	£2500	£3750	£6725	£9800

Work out what the car was worth at each stage.

2 Sinead bought 3 m of material at £4.95 a metre. How much did she pay?

3 Yusuf works 6 days a week for 8 hours a day. He is paid £6.22 an hour. What does he earn in a week?

4 Which is more expensive: 12 packets of choc chip cookies at 85p a packet, or 15 packets of chocolate digestives at 72p a packet? What is the difference in price?

5 Josh had £3.20 more than April. Between them, they had £10.70. How much did they each have?

6 Margaret's annual earnings are £5226.24. How much does she earn each month?

7 A washing machine costs £329.95 if you pay cash.
Mr Jones pays a deposit of £96.50, followed by 24 monthly payments of £11.85.

(a) How much does Mr Jones pay altogether?
(b) How much would he have saved if he paid cash?

8 How many different combinations of coins will make 10p?

This week's work is about fractions and decimals.

1 What fraction of each diagram is shaded grey?

(a) 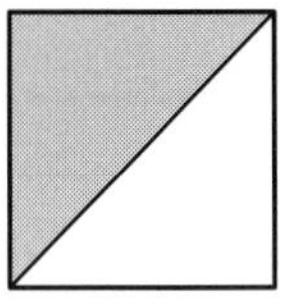 **(b)**  **(c)** 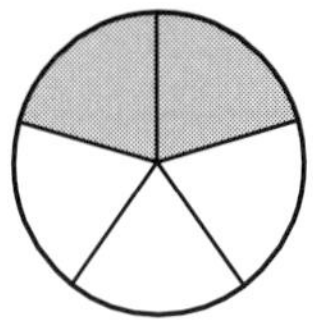 **(d)** 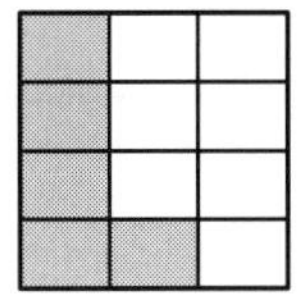

(e) 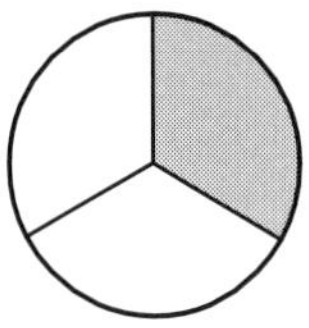 **(f)** 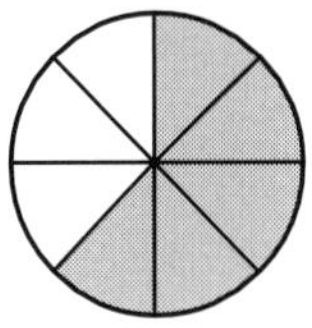 **(g)** 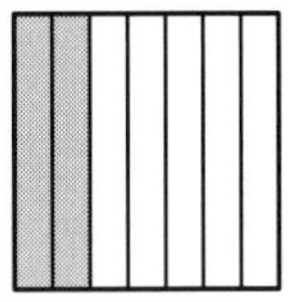 **(h)** 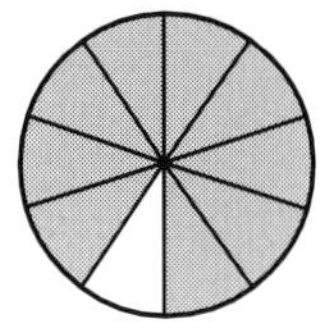

2 Change these fractions to lowest terms.

(a) $\frac{6}{8}$ **(b)** $\frac{12}{15}$ **(c)** $\frac{20}{30}$ **(d)** $\frac{35}{50}$

(e) $\frac{7}{21}$ **(f)** $\frac{45}{55}$ **(g)** $\frac{15}{24}$ **(h)** $\frac{64}{100}$

3 Work out these fractions.

(a) $\frac{1}{3}$ of £27 **(b)** $\frac{1}{8}$ of 160 kg

(c) $\frac{1}{10}$ of 65 km **(d)** $\frac{2}{5}$ of 40 l

(e) $\frac{2}{3}$ of 360° **(f)** $\frac{3}{4}$ of 240 cm^2

(g) $\frac{7}{10}$ of £4.50 **(h)** $\frac{5}{12}$ of 60 cl

4 Put each set of fractions in order, smallest to largest. Remember to change them all to the same type first.

(a) $\frac{7}{12}$ $\frac{2}{3}$ $\frac{1}{6}$ $\frac{1}{2}$ $\frac{5}{6}$ $\frac{11}{12}$

(b) $\frac{7}{10}$ $\frac{13}{50}$ $\frac{2}{5}$ $\frac{3}{5}$ $\frac{7}{20}$ $\frac{3}{10}$

5 Change these decimals to fractions.

(a) 0.1 **(b)** 0.6 **(c)** 0.5 **(d)** 0.25

(e) 0.35 **(f)** 0.88 **(g)** 0.679 **(h)** 0.175

Homework 15

This week's work is about angles.

1 Measure the angles in this quadrilateral.

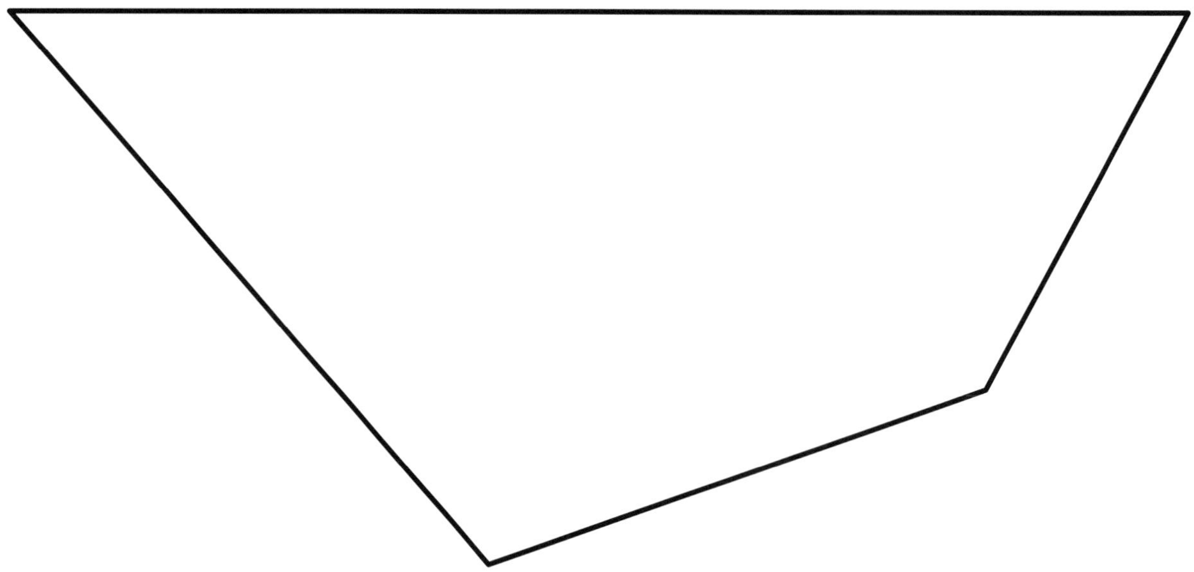

2 Draw these angles:

(a) 35° **(b)** 77° **(c)** 160° **(d)** 98°

3 Use what you know about triangles to work out the missing angles.

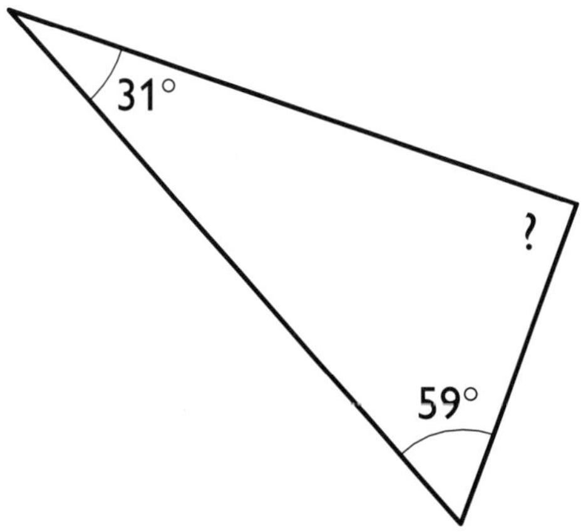

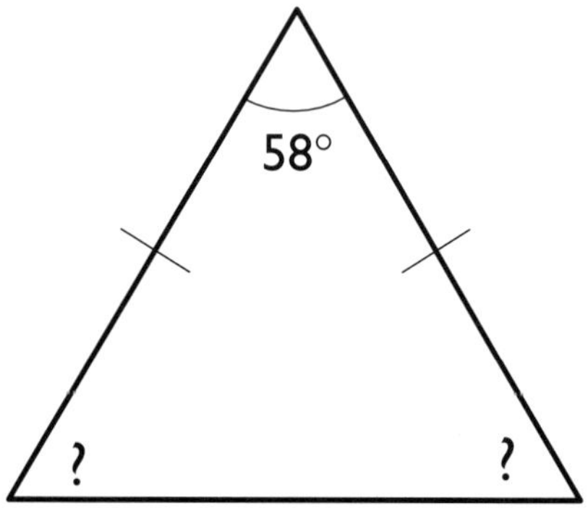

This week's work is about area.

These pentagons are a special type.

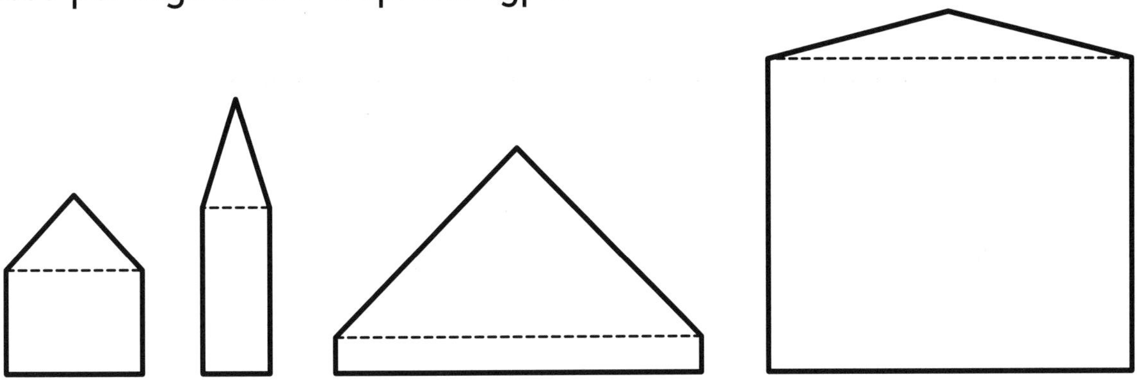

Each one can be split up into a rectangle and an isosceles triangle. Let's call a shape like this a 'house'.

This house shape has an area of 10 cm^2.

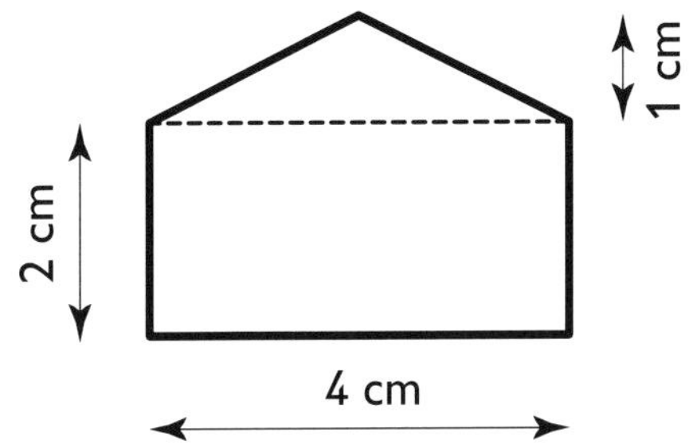

The rectangle's area is $4 \times 2 = 8$ cm^2.

The triangle's area is $4 \times 1 \div 2 = 2$ cm^2.

There are lots of ways to make house shapes with the same area as this one. Find as many as you can.

Challenge question: Design a house shape with an area of 1 cm^2!

Homework 17

This week's work is about mass.

Chocolate Rich Tea biscuits are plain biscuits with chocolate topping. A 300 g packet contains 30 biscuits. 20% of the mass of each biscuit is chocolate.

1 What is the mass of a biscuit?
2 What mass of chocolate is used on a single biscuit?
3 How much chocolate would you eat if you had a whole packet?
4 The chocolate comes in 1 kg blocks. How many biscuits will a block cover?

A packet of Chocolate Rich Tea biscuits is 22 cm long and 6 cm across.

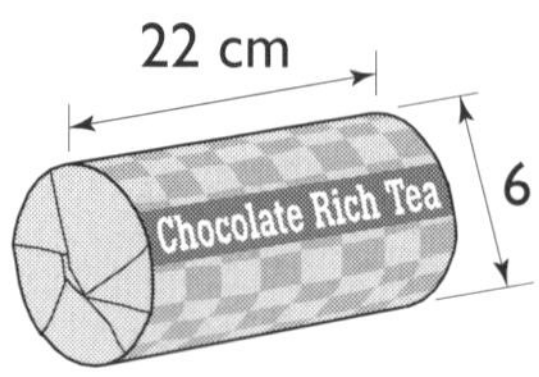

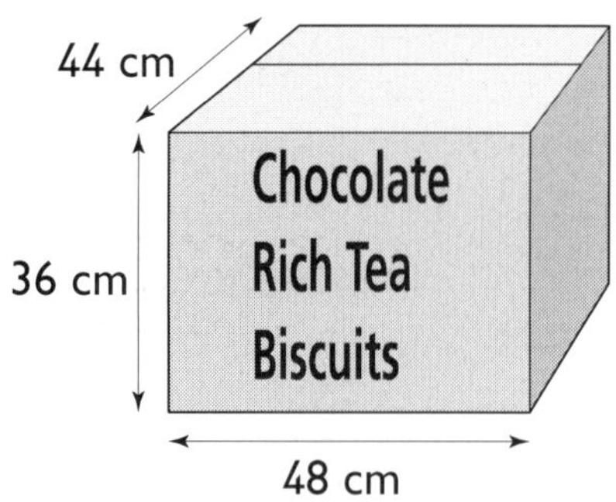

This is the carton they use to transport the biscuits.

5 How many packets fit in this carton?
6 What weight of biscuits are in a carton?

The wooden pallets used to load cartons into the van are 1 m by 1 m. They weigh 10 kg each.

7 How many cartons can fit side-by-side on a pallet?
8 The fork-lift that loads the pallets onto the van can carry half a tonne. How many layers high can the cartons be stacked?
9 The van has a maximum load of 10 tonnes. How many pallets can the van carry?
10 When the van is fully loaded, what is the mass of all the chocolate in all the packets?

This week's work is about calculating with decimals.

1 John recorded the temperature accurately every day for a week. These are his results.

13.3 °C, 12.9 °C, 15.6 °C, 16.8 °C, 17.0 °C, 18.2 °C, 14.7 °C.

Work out the mean temperature for the week.

2 Find the missing numbers.

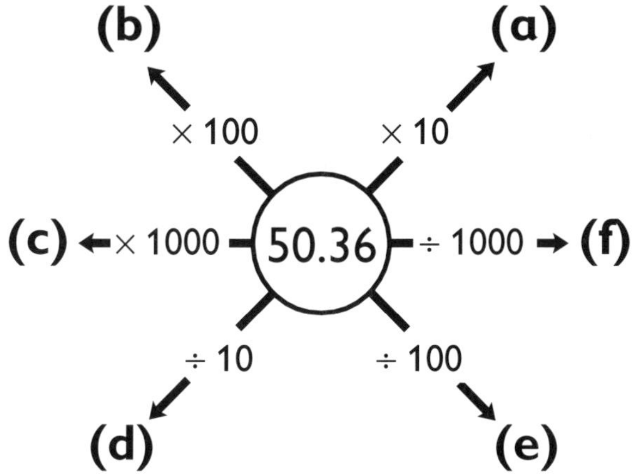

3 Find the missing numbers.

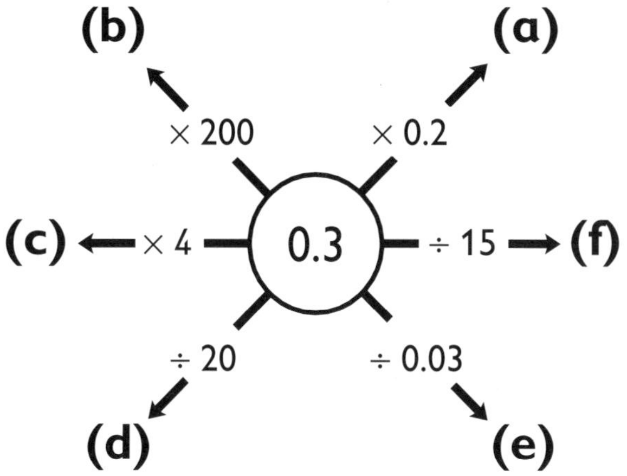

4

(a) Find the pair of numbers from the cloud that have the smallest difference. What is the difference?

(b) Find the pair of numbers with the largest sum.

Homework 19

This week's work is about solving problems.

Shelley the Spider is at corner of the box marked **A**.

She wants to visit her friend Morton, who is at the opposite corner, **B**.

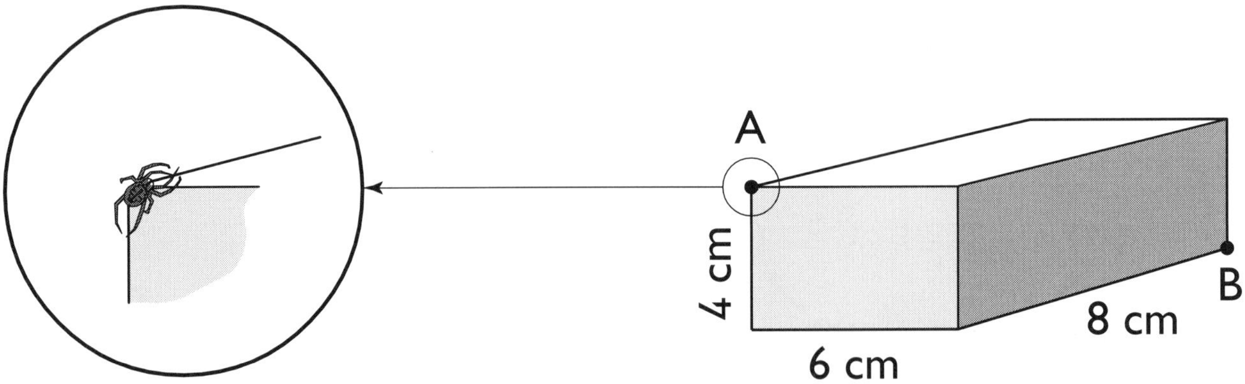

1 If she crawls along the edges of the box and goes the shortest way, how far is it from A to B?

2 Can she make the journey longer by using different edges?

She mustn't use an edge more than once, or go back to A!

3 Suppose she crawls across the faces of the box.

What is the *shortest* distance she has to crawl to get to Morton?

You might find it useful to draw the **net** of the box to answer this question.

Remember: a net is a flat, folded-out version of the box.

4 Suppose that she could go right through the middle of the box in a straight line.

How far is it from A to B?

This week's work is about properties of numbers.

For each question,

either write down an example of the type of number;
or write a sentence to say why it's impossible.

1 An even multiple of 3

2 An odd multiple of 5

3 An odd multiple of 10

4 A square number that is a multiple of 5

5 An even prime number

6 A prime number that is a factor of 15

7 A prime number that is also a square number

8 A number that is a multiple of 8 and also a multiple of 9

9 A number that is a factor of 60 and also a factor of 88

10 A square number that is a factor of 100

11 A number that is a factor of 48, but not a factor of 16

12 A square number that is a multiple of 20

13 A triangular number that is a multiple of 20

14 A number that has three different prime factors

15 A number that has only one prime factor

16 A number whose square is 20

Homework 21

This week's work is about multiplication and division.

1 Multiply the numbers in the circles together. Use any method you can.

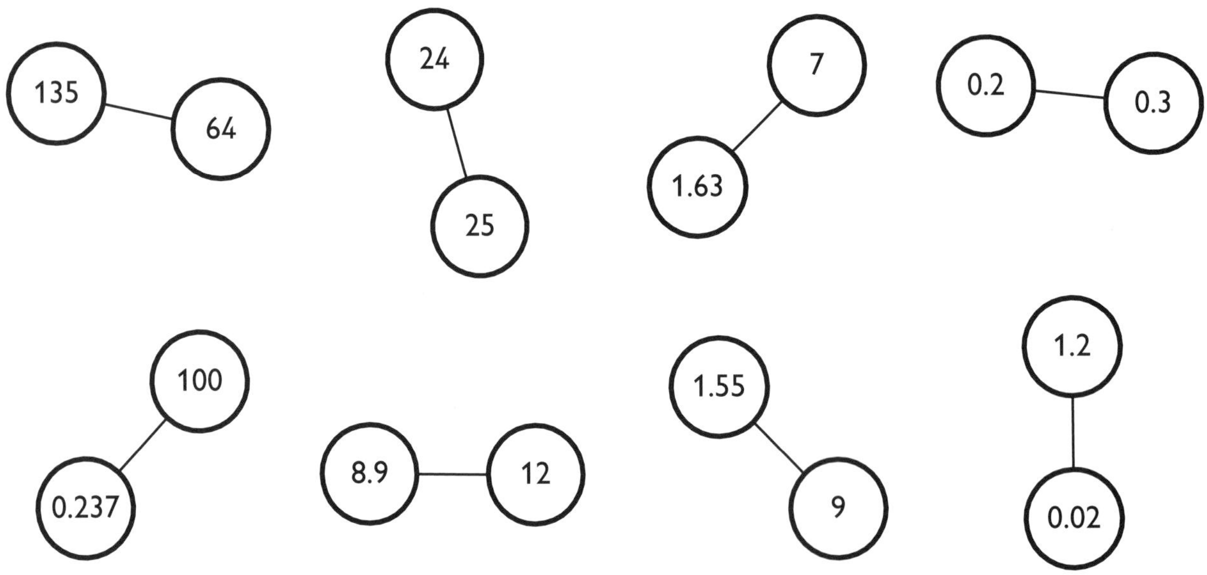

2 Write the answers to these divisions using fractions.

(a) 12 ÷ 5 **(b)** 100 ÷ 6 **(c)** 33 ÷ 7 **(d)** 14 ÷ 3
(e) 81 ÷ 4 **(f)** 44 ÷ 9 **(g)** 125 ÷ 8 **(h)** 400 ÷ 7

3 Write the answers to question **2** as decimals, rounded to 1 decimal place.

4 Find the cost of:

(a) Five CDs costing £13.55 each
(b) Eight books costing £3.99 each
(c) Twelve cans costing £0.58 each
(d) Twenty-four chairs costing £87.36 each

5 The following amounts of money are shared equally. How much does each person receive?

(a) £5000 between 8 people
(b) £120 between 48 people
(c) £235 between 25 people
(d) £150 000 between 75 people

This week's work is about solving problems.

You need: a piece of scrap A4 paper, scissors, glue or sellotape.

Fold the piece of paper in half, so that the fold is parallel to the longest side of the paper. Cut along this fold.

Fold both of these pieces the same way. Cut them both in half.
Now do the same with the four pieces.
You should have 8 strips of paper about $2\frac{1}{2}$ cm wide.

To make a Möbius band, follow these instructions.

Use one of the strips of paper.
Bring the two ends together as if you were making a ring.

Twist one end through a half turn.

Stick the ends together to make a twisted **Möbius band**.

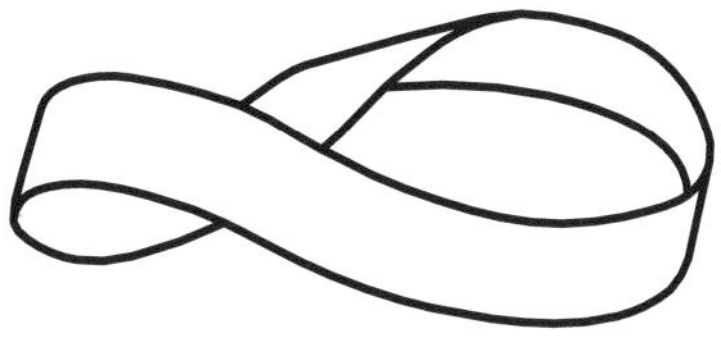

Investigate the results of these experiments. Write down what happens. Use a new Möbius band for each one. Don't try any of these without sticking the band together first.

1 Colour one side of the band red and the other side blue.
2 Draw a red line along one edge of the band and draw a blue line along the other edge.
3 Put your scissors through the band, halfway between the two edges. Cut round the band.
4 Put your scissors through the band, $\frac{1}{3}$ of the way in from one edge. Cut round the band.

Now repeat the experiments, but use a band that has a **double** twist.

Are the results the same?

Homework 23

This week's work is about fractions, decimals and percentages.

1 Fill in the blank spaces in the table. The three entries in each row are equivalent. The first one has been done for you.

Fraction	Decimal	Percentage
$\frac{1}{2}$	0.5	50%
$\frac{1}{10}$		
	0.2	
		25%
$\frac{3}{4}$		
		5%
	0.35	
$\frac{1}{25}$		
	0.125	
		$62\frac{1}{2}\%$
$\frac{31}{50}$		
$\frac{1}{3}$		

2 Work out these percentages.

(a) 50% of £32
(b) 25% of £80
(c) 10% of 6 kg
(d) 20% of 4 km
(e) 4% of £2000
(f) 99% of 250 ml
(g) 75% of £325
(h) 48% of $600

3 Put these fractions, decimals and percentages into order, smallest to largest.

$\frac{2}{5}$ $\frac{9}{20}$ $\frac{4}{9}$ 41% $\frac{21}{50}$ 44%

This week's work is about ratio and proportion.

When two pulleys are connected by a band, they behave like gears. Instead of the number of teeth, look at the diameter of each wheel. For example, the 3 cm wheel in this diagram turns twice as fast as the 6 cm one. The 2 cm wheel turns twice as fast as the 4 cm one. So the 2 cm wheel turns 4 times as fast as the 6 cm one.

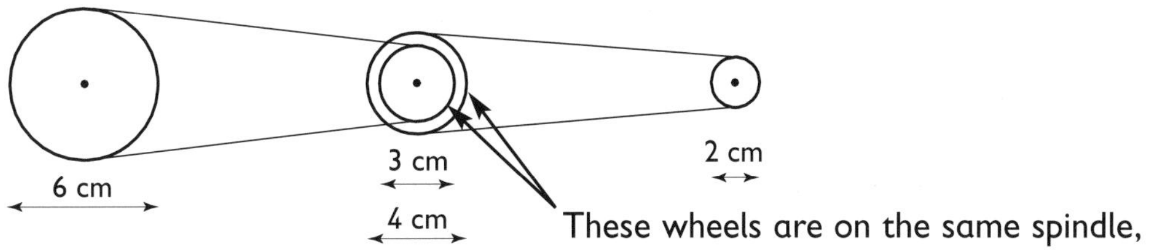

Work out how many turns the wheels in each set make.

1

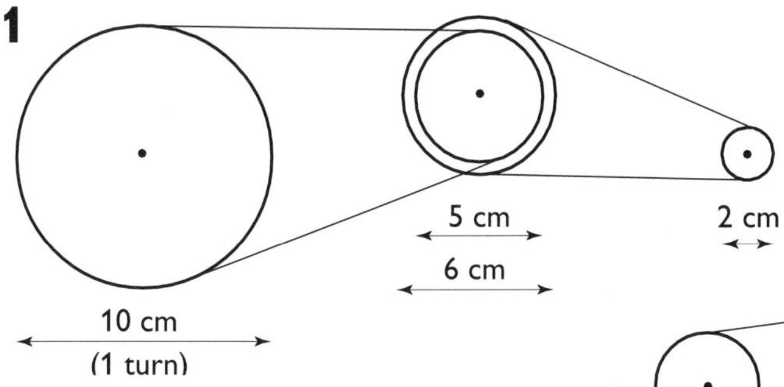

2

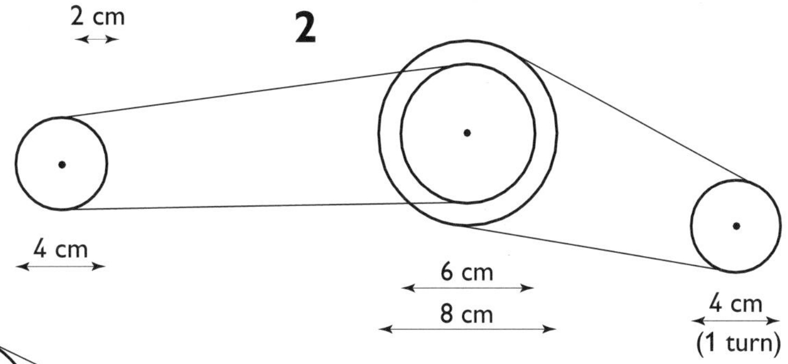

3

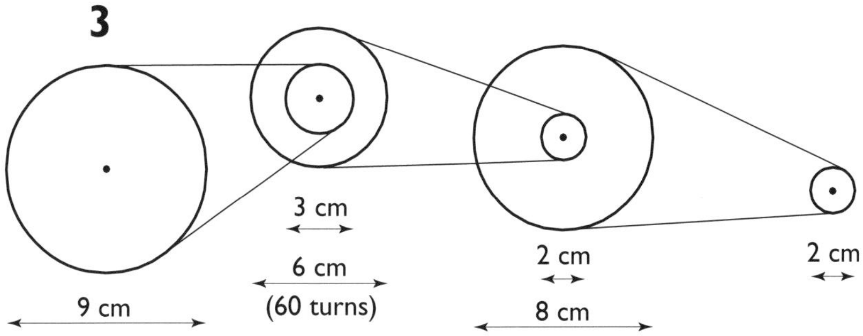

4

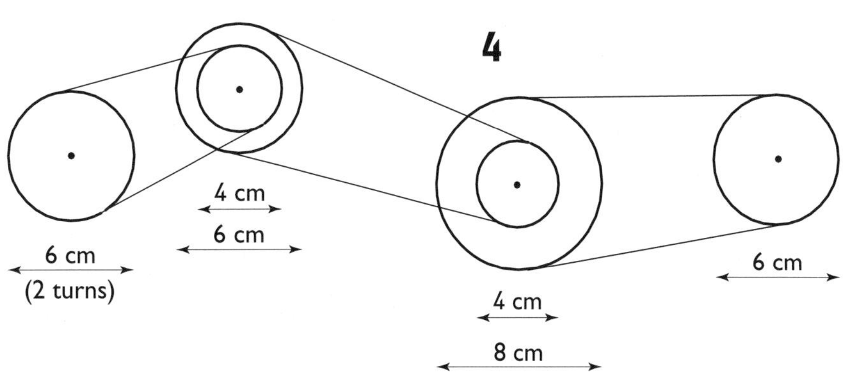

Homework 25

This week's work is about handling data, diagrams and averages.

A group of pupils were asked how many pets they had at home. These were the results.

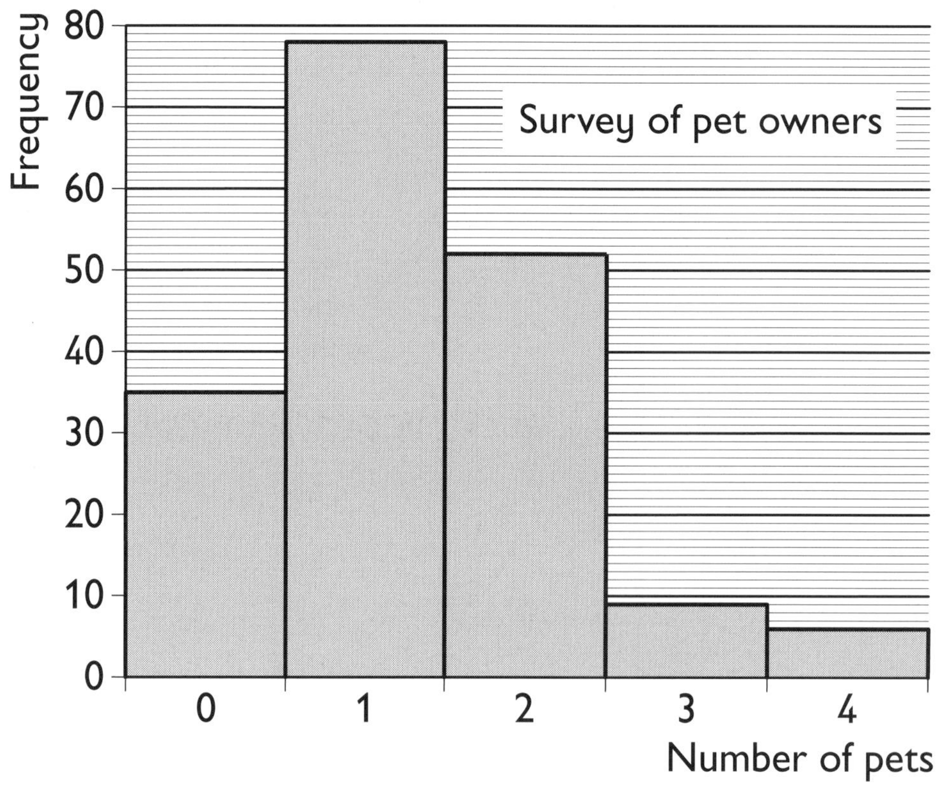

1 Make a frequency table from the bar chart.

2 Work out how many pupils were asked.

3 Work out how many pets belonged to all the people in the survey.

4 Calculate the mean number of pets per person.

5 Draw a pie chart to show this information.

This week's work is about reflection, rotation and translation.

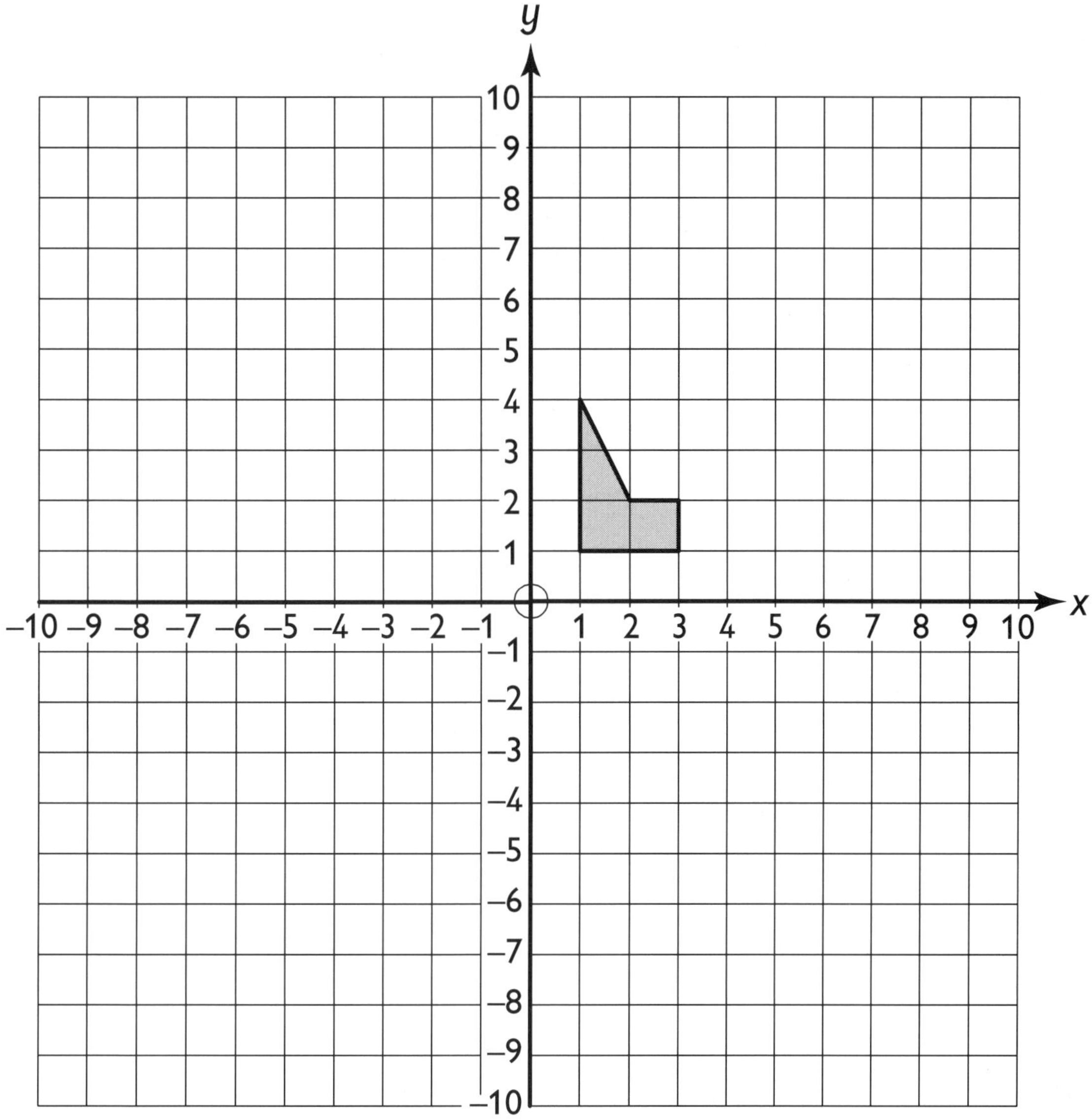

Copy the grid, or use the one on the sheet if your teacher says this is OK.

1 Translate the shape 6 units to the left.

2 Rotate the shape 180° about the corner at (1, 1).

3 Draw a line from (0, −2) to (4, −2). Reflect the shape in this line.

4 Rotate the shape 90° anticlockwise about the corner at (3, 1).

5 Draw a line from (−2, 0) to (−2, 4). Reflect the shape in this line.

6 Translate the shape 5 units to the right and 5 units up.

7 Draw a line from (5, 0) to (0, 5). Reflect the shape in this line.

8 Look at the last two answers. Draw the line of symmetry that would reflect one onto the other.

Homework 27

This week's work is about investigating shapes.

Draw a square 3 cm by 3 cm on squared paper.

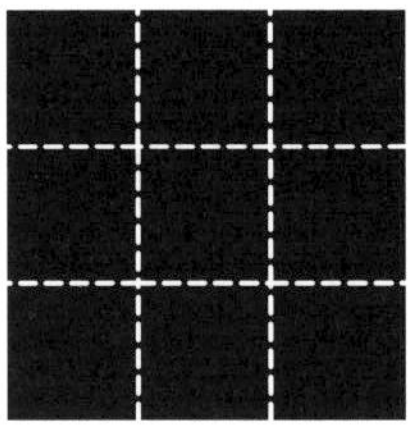

Now take away a square 1 cm by 1 cm from it. You might get something like these:

In fact, these are the *only* possible results. Anything else is just the same as one of these, turned round.

Try this with 4 cm by 4 cm squares. How many different results are there?

What about a 5 cm square? 6 cm? Investigate.

Extension questions:

What happens if you take away 2 cm squares instead?

What happens if the square that's taken away doesn't have to be on the grid lines?

This week's work is about capacity.

Look around the house for objects that have a capacity measurement on them.

These can be bottles, jars, cartons etc.

Try to find as many as possible.

Put them into order of size.

Make a table like this one.

Object	Capacity (metric)	Capacity (imperial)

Convert any metric measurements to imperial, and any imperial measurements to metric, so the table is completely filled in.

Remember: 1 litre = 1.75 pints, 8 pints = 1 gallon and 20 fluid ounces = 1 pint.

Homework 29

This week's work is about addition and subtraction.

1 In a magic square, all the rows, columns and diagonals add up to the same number.

Complete these magic squares.

(a)

8		12
		7
		14

(b)

20		
21		17
16		

(c)

6	11	8	
		14	3
13		15	10
		5	

(d)

20	15		6
11		18	
	21		
9		16	19

2 Investigate what happens to these patterns:

1 + 9	9 − 1
12 + 98	98 − 12
123 + 987 etc.	987 − 123 etc.

3 Pick any 3-digit number *(e.g. 682)*. Reverse its digits *(286)*.

Find the difference between the two numbers *(682 − 286 = 396)*.

Now reverse the digits of this number and find the difference.

Repeat this until you find a pattern.

What happens if you start with a four-digit number? A five-digit number?

This week's work is about functions and formulae.

Follow the instructions on this flow chart.

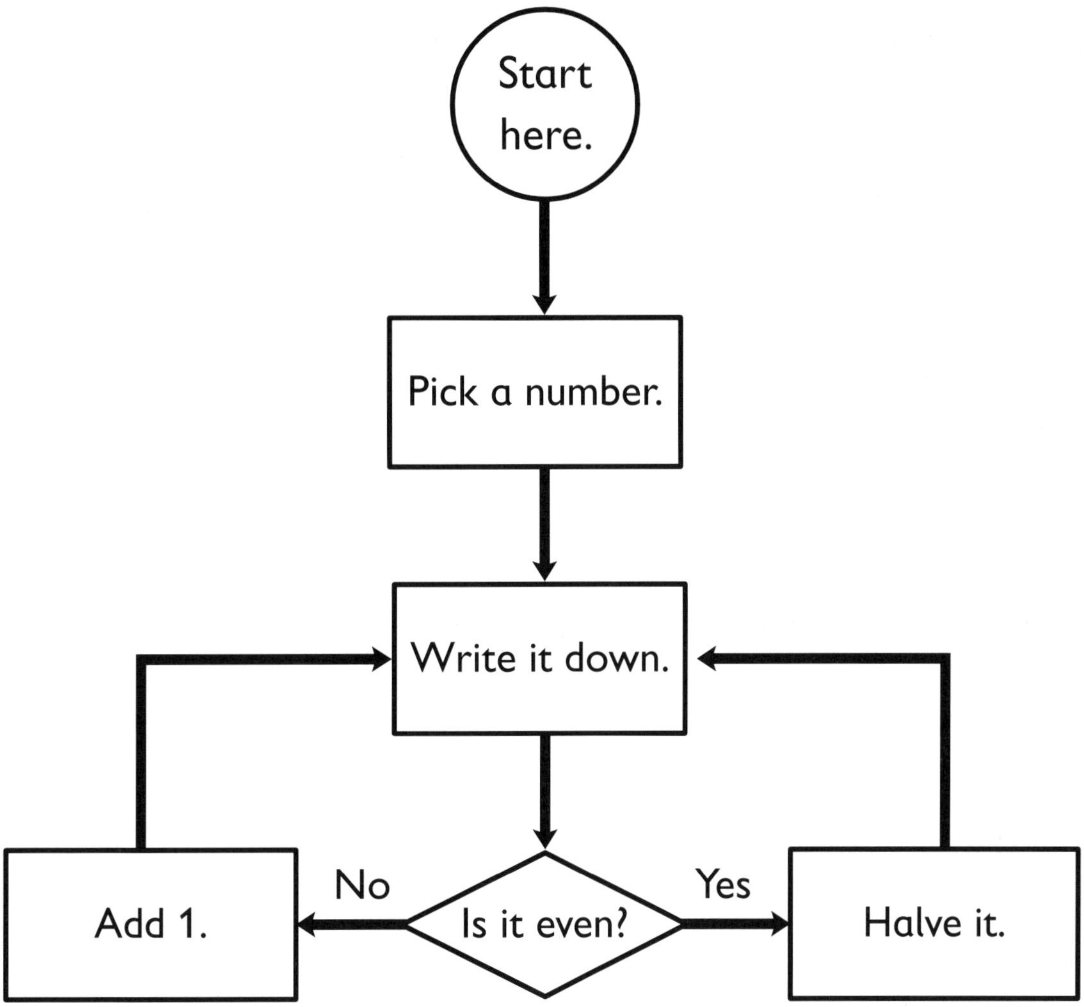

Try this a few times with different starting numbers. Describe what happens.

What if the 'add 1' box is changed to 'subtract 1'? Investigate.

Try changing this box again. You decide what to put there. Investigate what happens.

Copymaster 1: ***Doubling and halving***
1 140, 70, 280
2 192, 96, 384
3 424, 212, 848
4 1568, 784, 3136
5 62, 124, 31
6 144, 288, 72
7 360, 720, 180
8 772, 1544, 386
Roof of house: 25 → 50 → 25 → 50
Wall of house: 79 → 158 → 316 → 632
Trunk of tree: 91 → 182 → 364 → 728
Top of tree: 4 → 8 → 16 → 32 → 64 → 128 → 256
Mark the worksheet and check that the pictures are correct.

Copymaster 2: ***Splitting up calculations***
210, 1050, 148, 62, 1475, 915, 127, 1725, 2400, 1155, 705, 25 350, 625, 15, 3450,123, 6000, 62 500, 105, 7200

Copymaster 3: ***Multiplying with Grids***
1 100 + 40 = 140
2 490 + 21 = 511
3 1200 + 90 + 18 = 1308
4 40 000 + 1600 + 80 + 72 = 41 752
5 875
6 2540
7 5184
8 71 104
9 94 533
10 376 375
11 3 817 416
12 13 333 329

Copymaster 4: ***Catalogue***

Item	Number required	Cost of one item	Item total
Multimedia PC	2	£899.95	£1,799.90
Replacement keyboard	3	£36.46	£109.38
Software CDs	9	£9.72	£87.48
Inkjet printer	2	£108.95	£217.90
Ink cartridges	4	£12.55	£50.20
A4 paper (pack of 250 sheets)	5	£10.40	£52.00
Mouse mat	7	£2.51	£17.57
Floppy disks (box of 10)	6	£1.90	£11.40
		Order Total	£2,345.83

Copymaster 5: ***Fraction Diagrams***
Allow answers that have been cancelled to lowest terms.
1 $\frac{1}{4}$
2 $\frac{1}{8}$
3 $\frac{1}{6}$
4 $\frac{1}{15}$
5 $\frac{1}{25}$
6 $\frac{5}{16}$
7 $\frac{3}{5}$
8 $\frac{7}{8}$
9 $\frac{6}{16}$
10 $\frac{5}{9}$
11 $\frac{4}{9}$
12 $\frac{6}{12}$
13 $\frac{3}{4}$
14 $\frac{2}{9}$
15 $\frac{23}{24}$
16 $\frac{1}{6}$
17 $\frac{4}{5}$
18 $\frac{3}{10}$
19 $\frac{4}{7}$
20 $\frac{27}{100}$
21 $\frac{4}{36}$
22 $\frac{7}{14}$
23 $\frac{12}{25}$
24 $\frac{12}{20}$

Copymaster 6: ***Converting Units***
1 120 mm = (12 cm) = 0.12 m = 0.000 12 km
2 (5 ml) = 0.5 cl = 0.005 l
3 1500 g = (1.5 kg) = 0.0015 t
4 35 000 mm = 3500 cm = (35 m) = 0.035 km
5 (1 mm) = 0.1 cm = 0.001 m = 0.000 001 km
6 4 000 000 g = 4000 kg = (4 t)
7 14 000 ml = 1400 cl = (14 l)
8 10 g = (0.01 kg) = 0.000 01 t
9 700 ml = (70 cl) = 0.7 l
10 12 000 000mm = 1 200 000 cm = 12 000 m = (12 km)
11 30 000 g = (30 kg) = 0.03 t
12 2500 mm = (250 cm) = 2.5 m = 0.0025 km
13 50 000 ml = (5000 cl) = 50 l
14 (1 g) = 0.001 kg = 0.000 001 t
15 200 ml = 20 cl = (0.2 l)
16 2000 g = 2 kg = (0.002 t)
17 (300 mm) = 30 cm = 0.3 m = 0.0003 km
18 (454 ml) = 45.4 cl = 0.454 l
19 25 500 000 g = (25 500 kg) = 25.5 t
20 3000 mm = 300 cm = 3 m = (0.003 km)

Copymaster 7: ***Matching ratios***
1 2 in every 6 = 1 to every 2 = 6 in every 18 = 15 to every 30
6 in every 8 = 6 to every 2 = 15 to every 5 = 3 in every 4
2 1 to every 5 = 10 in every 60 = 2 to every 10 = 2 in every 12
10 to every 10 = 5 to every 5 = 1 in every 2 = 3 in every 6
3 7 to every 3 = 7 in every 10 = 14 to every 6 = 3 in every 10
9 to every 21 = 21 in every 30 = 30 to every 70 = 15 in every 50
4 10 to every 14 = 5 in every 12 = 5 to every 7 = 15 in every 36
5 to every 3 = 15 to every 9 = 15 in every 24 = 10 in every 16
5 3 in every 30 = 10 in every 100 = 10 to every 90 = 2 to every 18
5 in every 45 = 10 to every 80 = 2 in every 18 = 2 to every 16

Copymaster 8: ***Ratio problems***
1 (a) 30 g ginger
9 cloves garlic
6 tbsp almonds
1.5 kg chicken
12 cardamom pods
3 bay leaves
225 g onions
120 ml yogurt
450 ml cream

(b) 50 g ginger
15 cloves garlic
10 tbsp almonds
2.5 kg chicken
20 cardamom pods
5 bay leaves
375 g onions
200 ml yogurt
750 ml cream

2 (a) 5400 **(b)** 450 **(c)** 4950
3 (a) 45 **(b)** 75 **(c)** 96 **(d)** 60
4 (a) 80 **(b)** 120 **(c)** 450 **(d)** 250
5 (a) 10 days **(b)** 5

Copymaster 11: ***Plotting quadrilaterals***
1 rectangle
2 parallelogram
3 kite
4 trapezium
5 rhombus
6 isosceles trapezium
7 square
8 kite (reflex)
9 rectangle
10 parallelogram

Copymaster 13: ***Perimeters and rectangles***
1 70 cm
2 27.6 cm
3 162 cm
4 36 cm
5 32 m
6 1120 m
7 53 cm
8 32 mm
9 112.2 cm
10 50 cm
11 3 cm
12 4.25 m
13 1.5 km
14 7 mm

Copymaster 14: ***Perimeters of shapes***
1 24 cm
2 60 cm
3 80 cm
4 10.5 cm
5 204 m
6 20 km
7 344 cm
8 98 m
9 5.5 mm
10 30 cm
11 (a) 29 cm **(b)** 40 cm **(c)** 32 cm **(d)** 57.5 cm **(e)** 54.5 cm **(f)** 50 cm

Copymaster 18: ***Bank Statements***

Statement of Account — Megabank Limited
MR. N. E. BODDY ACCOUNT NO 12345678 — THE HIGH STREET

Date	Details	Debits	Credits	Balance
1 JUN	BROUGHT FORWARD FROM MAY			£300.24
	CHEQUE NO 000123	£31.50		£268.74
6 JUN	CASH MACHINE WITHDRAWAL	£20.00		£248.74
	$$ W H SMITH	£8.95		£239.79
7 JUN	$$ TOXACO FUEL SERVS	£27.18		£212.61
10 JUN	BANK GIRO CREDIT		£14.30	£226.91
13 JUN	DD MORTGAGES DIRECT	£198.55		£28.36
19 JUN	$$ SHIRTS R US	£24.99		£3.37
	CHEQUE NO 000124	£21.75		−£18.38
20 JUN	DD POWERGEN PLC	£86.04		−£104.42
22 JUN	DD THE NEWSBOX	£12.60		−£117.02
	$$ SPINADISC LTD	£14.95		−£131.97
23 JUN	SALARY PAYMENT		£647.08	£515.11
27 JUN	TRANSFER (SAVINGS ACCOUNT)	£100.00		£415.11
30 JUN	$$ SAFEBURY'S FOODSTORE	£54.62		£360.49

Statement of Account — BST Bank
MS. LENDA POUND ACCOUNT NO 98765432 — MAIN STREET

Date	Details	Debits	Credits	Balance
1 FEB	BROUGHT FORWARD FROM JAN			£45.17
2 FEB	SALARY PAYMENT		£430.56	£475.73
	$$ MARRISON'S FOODSTORE	£98.19		£377.54
4 FEB	CASH MACHINE WITHDRAWAL	£20.00		£357.54
5 FEB	DD RENTAFLAT PROPERTY SERVICES	£210.95		£146.59
8 FEB	BANK CHARGES	£8.50		£138.09
12 FEB	CHEQUE CREDIT		£45.00	£183.09
14 FEB	CASH MACHINE WITHDRAWAL	£40.00		£143.09
18 FEB	$$ GAPS	£51.98		£91.11
23 FEB	$$ EXTRAFLORA	£14.32		£76.79
27 FEB	CASH MACHINE WITHDRAWAL	£30.00		£46.79
28 FEB	DD SUPER GAS	£65.00		−£18.21

Copymaster 20: ***MathHopper's staircase***
The staircases generate the Fibonacci sequence

Staircase number	1	2	3	4	5	6	7	8	9	10	11	12	13	14	15	16	17	18	19	20
Number of ways	1	2	3	5	8	13	21	34	55	89	144	233	377	610	987	1597	2584	4181	6765	10 946

1 + 2 = 3, 2 + 3 = 5, 3 + 5 = 8, etc.

Copymaster 22: ***Co-ordinate Grid***
1 A (6,8) B (8,3) C (6,−6) D (3,−9) E (−4,−8) F (−6,2) G (−5,7)
3 (a) rectangle **(b)** square **(c)** hexagon **(d)** trapezium

Copymaster 23: ***Chain multiplication***

Operation	Possible method	86 × …	3027 × …	1.45 × …
× 12	× 4 × 3	1032	36 324	17.4
× 15	× 5 × 3	1290	45 405	21.75
× 16	× 4 × 4	1376	48 432	23.2
× 21	× 3 × 7	1806	63 567	30.45
× 35	× 5 × 7	3010	105 945	50.75
× 48	× 6 × 8	4128	145 296	69.6
× 49	× 7 × 7	4214	148 323	71.05
× 56	× 7 × 8	4816	169 512	81.2
× 60	× 6 × 10	5160	181 620	87
× 63	× 7 × 9	5418	190 701	91.35
× 72	× 8 × 9	6192	217 944	104.4
× 80	× 8 × 10	6880	242 160	116

Answers

Copymaster 24: ***Chain division***

1 (a) 127 (b) $31\frac{3}{4}$
2 (a) 81 (b) $16\frac{1}{5}$
3 (a) 348 (b) $69\frac{3}{5}$
4 (a) 27 (b) $13\frac{1}{2}$
5 (a) 318 (b) $45\frac{3}{7}$
6 (a) 422 (b) $70\frac{1}{3}$
7 (a) 23 (b) $4\frac{3}{5}$
8 (a) 39 (b) 13
9 (a) 492 (b) $70\frac{2}{7}$
10 (a) 730 (b) $91\frac{1}{4}$
11 (a) 177 (b) $35\frac{2}{5}$
12 (a) 88 (b) $8\frac{4}{5}$

Copymaster 25(a): ***Balance Sheet***

Date	Details	Income	Expenditure	Balance
01 Oct	Starting Balance			£1235.50
07 Oct	Shop sales, week 1	£3022.40		£4257.90
08 Oct	Order: PCs and monitors		£2589.95	£1667.95
08 Oct	Order: blank disks		£250.50	£1417.45
14 Oct	Shop sales, week 2	£2480.85		£3898.30
15 Oct	Order: business software		£399.62	£3498.68
19 Oct	Order: games		£488.25	£3010.43
21 Oct	Shop sales, week 3	£2261.53		£5271.96
21 Oct	Order: Games console + Joypads		£855.32	£4386.64
28 Oct	Pay for advertising		£45.50	£4341.14
28 Oct	Shop sales, week 4	£2622.54		£6963.68
29 Oct	Order paper supplies		£175.30	£6788.38
31 Oct	Mail order sales, October	£595.20		£7383.58

Copymaster 25(b): ***Order Form***

Item	Quantity	Item price	Item total
Large Tin Baked Beans (4 pack)	4	£1.05	£4.20
Variety Pack Breakfast Cereals	12	£1.98	£22.68
Sparkling Spring Water (6 pack)	10	£1.32	£13.20
Biscuits for Cheese (giant tin)	8	£4.98	£39.84
Rainbow Ice Lolly (10 pack)	6	£2.12	£12.72
Cheese Selection Pack	5	£5.68	£28.40
Potatoes (large bag)	7	£1.51	£10.57
Pitta Bread (catering pack)	9	£3.18	£28.62
Vegetable Soup (12 large tins)	3	£3.35	£10.05
Coffee Whitener (jumbo tin)	2	£4.29	£8.58
$1^1/_2$ kg Sugar	11	£0.74	£8.14
		Grand Total	£187.00

Copymaster 26(a): ***Lottery Syndicates***

1 £2666.67
2 £6250
3 £1 166 666.67
4 £66 666.67
5 £27.50
6 £8571.43
7 £500 000
8 £3343.75

Copymaster 26(b): ***Funny Money***

M̶0.01 = 1.27p = 1p to nearest penny
M̶0.02 = 2.54p = 3p to nearest penny
M̶0.05 = 6.35p = 6p to nearest penny
M̶0.10 = 12.7p = 13p to nearest penny
M̶0.25 = 31.75p = 32p to nearest penny
M̶0.50 = 63.5p = 64p to nearest penny
£1 = M̶0.79 to nearest centar
£5 = M̶3.94 to nearest centar
£10 = M̶7.87 to nearest centar
CD: M̶11.42 to nearest centar

Copymaster 27: ***Fraction flags***

1

$\frac{1}{6}$	$\frac{1}{4}$	$\frac{1}{3}$	$\frac{3}{8}$	$\frac{5}{12}$

2

$\frac{5}{8}$	$\frac{3}{4}$	$\frac{4}{5}$	$\frac{7}{8}$	$\frac{9}{10}$

3

$\frac{1}{4}$	$\frac{3}{8}$	$\frac{1}{2}$	$\frac{5}{8}$	$\frac{3}{4}$

4

$\frac{1}{10}$	$\frac{1}{5}$	$\frac{2}{5}$	$\frac{1}{2}$	$\frac{7}{10}$

5

$\frac{1}{6}$	$\frac{1}{3}$	$\frac{1}{2}$	$\frac{2}{3}$	$\frac{5}{6}$

6

$\frac{1}{10}$	$\frac{1}{8}$	$\frac{3}{20}$	$\frac{7}{40}$	$\frac{1}{4}$

7

$\frac{1}{8}$	$\frac{1}{6}$	$\frac{1}{4}$	$\frac{5}{12}$	$\frac{11}{24}$

8

$\frac{2}{5}$	$\frac{1}{2}$	$\frac{2}{3}$	$\frac{7}{10}$	$\frac{5}{6}$

9

$\frac{2}{5}$	$\frac{3}{7}$	$\frac{4}{7}$	$\frac{3}{5}$	$\frac{5}{7}$

10

$\frac{1}{25}$	$\frac{1}{12}$	$\frac{7}{60}$	$\frac{3}{25}$	$\frac{11}{75}$

11

$\frac{9}{10}$	$\frac{89}{90}$	$1\frac{1}{100}$	$1\frac{1}{4}$	$1\frac{1}{2}$

12

$\frac{28}{27}$	$\frac{19}{18}$	$\frac{10}{9}$	$\frac{7}{6}$	$\frac{4}{3}$

Copymaster 28: ***Conveyor belts***

1

$\frac{3}{8}$	$\frac{2}{5}$	0.42	$\frac{11}{25}$	0.45
$\frac{75}{200}$	$\frac{80}{200}$	$\frac{84}{200}$	$\frac{88}{200}$	$\frac{90}{200}$

2

0.1	$\frac{3}{25}$	$\frac{3}{20}$	0.16	0.17
$\frac{10}{100}$	$\frac{12}{100}$	$\frac{15}{100}$	$\frac{16}{100}$	$\frac{17}{100}$

3

$\frac{1}{2}$	0.51	0.53	$\frac{11}{20}$	$\frac{14}{25}$
$\frac{50}{100}$	$\frac{51}{100}$	$\frac{53}{100}$	$\frac{55}{100}$	$\frac{56}{100}$

4

$\frac{9}{25}$	0.38	$\frac{2}{5}$	0.42	0.45
$\frac{36}{100}$	$\frac{38}{100}$	$\frac{40}{100}$	$\frac{42}{100}$	$\frac{45}{100}$

5

$\frac{3}{10}$	$\frac{1}{3}$	$\frac{11}{30}$	$\frac{2}{5}$	$\frac{3}{5}$
$\frac{90}{300}$	$\frac{100}{300}$	$\frac{110}{300}$	$\frac{120}{300}$	$\frac{180}{300}$

6

$\frac{9}{22}$	$\frac{23}{55}$	$\frac{5}{11}$	0.5	0.7
$\frac{45}{110}$	$\frac{46}{110}$	$\frac{50}{110}$	$\frac{55}{110}$	$\frac{77}{110}$

7

$\frac{1}{5}$	0.25	$\frac{1}{3}$	0.4	$\frac{5}{12}$
$\frac{12}{60}$	$\frac{15}{60}$	$\frac{20}{60}$	$\frac{24}{60}$	$\frac{25}{60}$

8

1.14	$1\frac{1}{4}$	$1\frac{2}{5}$	1.44	1.5
$\frac{114}{100}$	$\frac{125}{100}$	$\frac{140}{100}$	$\frac{144}{100}$	$\frac{150}{100}$

9

$\frac{21}{20}$	$1\frac{3}{40}$	1.1	1.15	$1\frac{1}{5}$
$\frac{42}{40}$	$\frac{43}{40}$	$\frac{44}{40}$	$\frac{46}{40}$	$\frac{48}{40}$

Copymaster 29: ***Triangles***

The three triangles have the following angles:
40°, 50°, 90°
45°, 35°, 105°
44°, 68°, 68°

1 110°
2 30°
3 50°
4 25°
5 57°
6 49°
7 30°, 30°
8 74°, 74°
9 16°
10 60°, 60°, 60°

Copymaster 31: ***Lengths and widths***

1 3 cm
2 5 cm
3 16 m
4 12 cm
5 1 mm
6 3.5 cm
7 5 m
8 16 m
9 62.5 cm
10 20 cm
11 1.25 mm
12 1000 km

Copymaster 32: ***Triangles***

1 40 cm^2
2 3 cm^2
3 30 cm^2
4 36 m^2
5 39 mm^2
6 7500 m^2
7 480 mm^2
8 0.2 km^2
9 0.5 m^2
10 32 cm^2
11 65 cm^2
12 65 cm^2

Copymaster 33: ***Food facts***

CORN FLAKES	per pack (750 g)	per 100 g	per serving (30 g)
Protein	60 g	**8 g**	**2.4 g**
Carbohydrates	615 g	**82 g**	**24.6 g**
Fat	6 g	**0.8 g**	**0.24 g**
Fibre	22.5 g	**3 g**	**0.9 g**
Energy	2775 kcal	**370 kcal**	**111 kcal**

ORANGE JUICE	per carton (1 l)	per 100 ml	per serving (250 ml)
Protein	7 g	**0.7 g**	**1.75 g**
Carbohydrates	90 g	**9 g**	**22.5 g**
Fat	0 g	**0 g**	**0 g**
Fibre	5 g	**0.5 g**	**1.25 g**
Energy	430 kcal	**43 kcal**	**107.5 kcal**

BAKED BEANS	per tin (415 g)	per 100 g	per serving (207 g)
Protein	19.505 g	**4.7 g**	**9.729 g**
Carbohydrates	56.44 g	**13.6 g**	**28.152 g**
Fat	0.83 g	**0.2 g**	**0.414 g**
Fibre	15.355 g	**3.7 g**	**7.659 g**
Energy	311.25 kcal	**75 kcal**	**155.25 kcal**

STRAWBERRY JAM	per jar (454 g)	per 100 g	per serving (18 g)
Protein	1.362 g	**0.3 g**	**0.054 g**
Carbohydrates	59.02 g	**13 g**	**2.34 g**
Fat	0.454 g	**0.1 g**	**0.018 g**
Fibre	0.454 g	**0.1 g**	**0.018 g**
Energy	1271.2 kcal	**280 kcal**	**50.4 kcal**

Protein	flakes, beans, juice, jam
Carbohydrates	flakes, beans, jam, juice
Fat	flakes, beans, jam, juice
Fibre	beans, flakes, juice, jam
Energy	flakes, jam, beans, juice

Flakes: 1333 packs
Beans: 2409 tins
Juice: 1000 cartons
Jam: 2202 jars
These wouldn't be exactly right, as the extra packaging (boxes, pallets, etc.) isn't taken into account.

Copymaster 34: ***Units of mass***

Object	Given mass	Answer
pack of butter	1 lb	453 g
jar of jam	$\frac{1}{2}$ lb	227 g
thick marker	4 oz	113 g
envelope containing greeting card	1 oz	28.3 g
bag of chips	6 oz	170 g
fizzy drink can	10 oz	283 g
bag of sugar	2 lb	0.91 kg
girl about 10 years old	7 st	44 kg
small one-hand dumbell	12 lb	5.4 kg
small van	$1\frac{1}{2}$ tons	1515 kg
litre bottle of pop	1 kg	2.2 lb
pack of cheese	500 g	1.1 lb
CD in its case	120 g	4.24 oz
large bag of crisps	50 g	1.77 oz
1 stick of chewing gum	1 g	0.035 oz
sheet of A4 paper (eg this worksheet!)	5 g	0.18 oz
large bag of potatoes	5 kg	11 lb
petrol lawnmower	20 kg	44 lb
man	55 kg	121 lb
articulated lorry	44 t	44.44 tons

Copymaster 35: ***Adding and subtracting decimals***

1 5.9 **3** 4.28 **5** 5.22 **7** 11.16 **9** 28.227
2 18 **4** 3.08 **6** 10 **8** 3.785 **10** 13.999

Difference		Right-hand kite			
		3	4.2	1.7	0.615
Left-hand kite	16	13	11.8	14.3	15.385
	6.85	3.85	2.65	5.15	6.235
	9.2	6.2	5	7.5	8.585

Copymaster 36: ***Place value calculations***

1 **(1) 2.8:** 2800, 280, 28, 0.28, 0.028
(2) 1.45: 1450, 145, 14.5, 0.145, 0.0145
(3) 5.06: 5060, 506, 50.6, 0.506, 0.0506
(4) 0.56: 560, 56, 5.6, 0.056, 0.0056
(5) 3.5: 3500, 350, 35, 0.35, 0.035
(6) 7: 700, 70, 0.7, 0.07, 0.007
(7) 1.002: 1002, 100.2, 10.02, 0.1002, 0.01002
(8) 14.56: 14 560, 1456, 145.6, 1.456, 0.1456
(9) 305.3: 30.53, 3.053, 0.3053, 0.030 53, 0.003 053
(10) 0.0035: 0.000 35, 0.035, 0.35, 3.5, 3500

2 (1)

Product		Right-hand box		
		2	200	0.02
Left-hand box	6	12	1200	0.12
	0.6	1.2	120	0.012
	0.06	0.12	12	0.0012

(2)

Product		Right-hand box		
		4	0.4	0.04
Left-hand box	4	16	1.6	0.16
	0.4	1.6	0.16	0.016
	0.04	0.16	0.016	0.0016

(3)

Product		Right-hand box		
		5	0.5	50
Left-hand box	11	55	5.5	550
	0.11	0.55	0.055	5.5
	1.1	5.5	0.55	55

(4)

Product		Right-hand box		
		8	80	0.8
Left-hand box	12	96	960	9.6
	1.2	9.6	96	0.96
	0.12	0.96	9.6	0.096

(5)

Product		Right-hand box		
		3	0.3	0.03
Left-hand box	0.7	2.1	0.21	0.021
	0.07	0.21	0.021	0.0021
	0.007	0.021	0.0021	0.000 21

(6)

Product		Right-hand box		
		15	1.5	0.015
Left-hand box	15	225	22.5	0.225
	0.15	2.25	0.225	0.002 25
	1.5	22.5	2.25	0.0225

Copymaster 37: Astronomical facts

Object	Distance (au)
Mercury	0.39
Venus	0.72
Earth	1
Mars	1.53
Jupiter	5.23
Saturn	9.40
Uranus	19.46
Neptune	30.20
Pluto	39.60
Comet cloud	63 800
Alpha Centauri	275 000
Galactic centre	2 billion
Andromeda spiral	1.2 trillion

Copymaster 38: ***House and garden***

Area of plot = 300 m^2, so area of house = 100 m^2.
L-shapes therefore have to consist of two rectangles whose areas sum to 100 m^2. Many different combinations are possible. Rectangles less than 3 m wide should be disregarded from practical considerations.

Pupils need their calculators. Pupils should then be asked the question: How much do the walls of the house that they designed in Lesson 3 weigh? They should be encouraged to think first about what additional information they will need in order to answer the question.

Assuming that the visible face of a brick with its mortar measures 24 cm by 9 cm and that mortar is of similar density to brick, a single-thickness unit weighs approximately 2.9 kg.

Thus 1 m^2 of wall contains 46.3 such units and weighs 135 kg.

A house plan 10 m square can be converted into many suitable L-shapes by removing one rectangular corner. The perimeter of such an L-shape will be 40 m. Assuming the height of the walls to be a uniform 7 m, the surface are of the brickwork is about 280 m^2. The mass of the exterior brickwork is therefore about 38 tonnes. If the walls are double thickness, this should be effectively doubled, and if interior walls are taken into account, could be tripled.

Discussions about the roof and timbers could follow.

Copymaster 39: ***Prime numbers and prime factors***

1 The prime numbers are: 2, 3, 5, 7, 11, 13, 17, 19, 23, 29, 31, 37, 41, 61, 71, 101, 163, 199, 211.
2 The composite numbers have the following prime factors:

18: 2, 3	45: 3, 5	66: 2, 3, 11	96: 2, 3	124: 2, 31	202: 2, 101	208: 2, 13
21: 3, 7	55: 5, 11	68: 2, 17	98: 2, 7	171: 3, 19	203: 7, 29	210: 2, 3, 5, 7
25: 5	64: 2	70: 2, 5, 7	116: 2, 29	200: 2, 5	205: 5, 41	333: 3, 37
35: 5, 7	65: 5, 13	72: 2, 3	117: 3, 13	201: 3, 67	207: 3, 23	404: 2, 101

Copymaster 40: ***Number puzzles***

1 31
2 4
3 9
4 24
5 37
6 4
7 66
8 4 and 56
9 47 and 59
10 2, 37 or any number made by adding 2 to a multiple of 35
11 50 or any number made by adding a multiple of 72 to it
12 4 (1) or 144 (36)

Give out Copymaster 41: ***Finding pairs***

1

×		Right-hand box		
		6	60	6000
Left-hand box	4	24	240	24 000
	40	240	2400	240 000
	400	2400	24 000	2 400 000

2

×		Right-hand box		
		11	110	1100
Left-hand box	20	220	2200	22 000
	200	2200	22 000	220 000
	2000	22 000	220 000	2 200 000

3

÷		Right-hand box		
		2	20	200
Left-hand box	800	400	40	4
	8000	4000	400	40
	800 000	400 000	40 000	4000

4

÷		Right-hand box		
		7	70	700
Left-hand box	5600	800	80	8
	56 000	8000	800	80
	5 600 000	800 000	80 000	8000

5

×		Right-hand box		
		9	90	9000
Left-hand box	80	720	7200	720 000
	800	7200	72 000	7 200 00
	8000	72 000	720 000	72 000 000

6

÷		Right-hand box		
		30	300	3000
Left-hand box	27 000	900	90	9
	270 000	9000	900	90
	27 000 000	900 000	90 000	9000

7

÷		Right-hand box		
		40	60	400
Left-hand box	36	0.8	0.6	0.08
	360	8	6	0.8
	36 000	800	600	80

8

×		Right-hand box		
		0.9	9	90
Left-hand box	0.5	0.45	4.5	45
	5	4.5	45	450
	500	450	4500	45 000

9

6	× 5	30	× 7	210
			× 7000	210 000
	× 50	300	× 7	2100
			× 7000	2 100 000
600	× 5	3000	× 7	21 000
			× 7000	21 000 000
	× 50	30 000	× 7	210 000
			× 7000	210 000 000

10

8	× 6	48	÷ 40	1.2
			÷ 400	0.12
	× 600	4800	÷ 40	120
			÷ 400	12
80	× 6	480	÷ 40	12
			÷ 400	1.2
	× 600	48 000	÷ 40	1200
			÷ 400	120

Copymaster 42: *Clothes Shop*

Item	Number required	Wholesale price of one item	Item total
T-shirt	48	£13.50	**£648.00**
Pair of Socks	16	£2.60	**£41.60**
Polo Shirt	25	£12.48	**312.00**
Coat	32	£65.00	**£2,080.00**
Suit	24	£149.99	**£3,599.76**
Sweatshirt	49	£25.12	**£1,230.88**
Shirt	99	£15.60	**£1,544.40**
Sweater	28	£31.35	**£877.80**
Skirt	44	£25.64	**£1,128.16**
Jacket	56	£45.86	**£2,568.16**
Leggings	71	£5.73	**£406.83**
Handkerchiefs	63	£1.28	**£80.64**
		Order Total	£14,518.23

Item	Number sold	Selling price of one item	Total sales for this item
T-shirt	16	**£18.90**	£302.40
Pair of Socks	5	**£3.64**	£18.20
Polo Shirt	8	**£17.47**	£139.76
Coat	10	**£91.00**	£910.00
Suit	8	**£209.99**	£1,679.92
Sweatshirt	16	**£35.17**	£562.72
Shirt	33	**£21.84**	£720.72
Sweater	9	**£43.89**	£395.01
Skirt	14	**£35.90**	£502.60
Jacket	18	**£64.20**	£1,155.60
Leggings	23	**£7.99**	£183.77
Handkerchiefs	21	**£1.79**	£37.59

Copymaster 43: *Density*

helium	0.00017 g/cm^2	sea water	1.025 g/cm^2	diamond	3.2 g/cm^2
air	0.0013 g/cm^2	milk	1.03 g/cm^2	iron	7.86 g/cm^2
balsa wood	0.097 g/cm^2	beer	1.042 g/cm^2	silver	21.5 g/cm^2
ice	0.92 g/cm^2	salt	2.2 g/cm^2	osmium	22.6 g/cm^2
water	1 g/cm^2	jet	2.5 g/cm^2	white dwarf	1 000 000 g/cm^2

Copymaster 44: *MegaPark*

The pupils should work through the questions on the worksheet. You may have to point out to them that in questions 1 and 3, the number of child ride tickets is '6 or more'. Watch out for pupils who miss out the volume discounts.

Question 2 deliberately doesn't mention whether Toni is an adult or a child. The answer covers both cases.

1 The Scotts

Admission Tickets	1 family + 1 child	£18.50
Parking	6 hours	£3.00
Meals	2 adult + 3 child	£16.50
Rides	12 @ 30p + 4 @ 60p	£6.00
Discounts	*none*	—
	Total	£44.00

2 Toni (child)

Admission Tickets	1 child	£3.50
Bus fare		£4.00
Rides	5 @ 35p	£1.75
	Total	£9.25

Toni (adult)

Admission Tickets	1 adult	£5.00
Bus fare		£4.00
Rides	5 @ 50p	£2.50
	Total	£11.50

1 Miss Zahar's class

(a)

Admission Tickets	2 family + 22 child	*£107.00
Coach hire		£80.00
Parking	1 day	£9.00
Meals	4 adult + 26 child	*£83.00
Rides	78 @ 30p	£23.40
	Total	£302.40
*Discounts	*admission*	*−£10.70*
	meals	*−£4.15*
	Total less discounts	£287.55

(b) £287.55 ÷ 30 = £9.585 = £9.59 to the nearest penny.
A sensible rounding is £9.60 per person, or even £10.

Copymaster 45: *Ordering fractions*

1 $\frac{1}{3} > \frac{3}{10}$ (0.333… > 0.3)
2 $\frac{3}{8} > \frac{7}{20}$ (0.375 > 0.35)
3 $\frac{2}{3} < \frac{3}{4}$ (0.666… < 0.75)
4 $\frac{1}{5} > \frac{3}{16}$ (0.2 > 0.1875)
5 $\frac{4}{5} > \frac{7}{9}$ (0.8 > 0.777…)
6 $\frac{9}{14} > \frac{7}{12}$ (0.642… > 0.583…)
7 $\frac{7}{10} > \frac{9}{13}$ (0.7 > 0.692…)
8 $\frac{5}{8} > \frac{31}{50}$ (0.625 > 0.62)
9 $\frac{17}{32} > \frac{133}{250}$ (0.53125 > 0.532)
10 $\frac{4}{7} > \frac{21}{38}$ (0.571… > 0.552…)
11 $\frac{131}{423} > \frac{29}{95}$ (0.309… > 0.305…)
12 $\frac{68}{69} < \frac{205}{208}$ (0.98550… < 0.98557…)

13

$\frac{3}{10}$	$\frac{13}{40}$	$\frac{33}{100}$	$\frac{1}{3}$	$\frac{17}{50}$	$\frac{3}{8}$
0.3	0.325	0.33	0.333…	0.34	0.375

14

$\frac{2}{3}$	$\frac{7}{10}$	$\frac{5}{7}$	$\frac{3}{4}$	$\frac{49}{64}$	$\frac{4}{5}$
0.666…	0.7	0.714…	0.75	0.765625	0.8

15

$\frac{3}{40}$	$\frac{9}{100}$	$\frac{1}{11}$	$\frac{1}{10}$	$\frac{5}{48}$	$\frac{1}{8}$
0.075	0.09	0.0909…	0.1	0.104166	0.125

16

$\frac{5}{11}$	$\frac{1}{2}$	$\frac{25}{47}$	$\frac{27}{50}$	$\frac{11}{20}$	$\frac{5}{9}$
0.4545…	0.5	0.531…	0.54	0.55	0.555…

Copymaster 46: *Calculating percentages*

1 60 kg
2 £10
3 45 pence
4 11 tonnes
5 1200 people
6 4.1 litres
7 0.8 km
8 39.2 m^2
9 £5.28
10 25 homes
11 Board game: £10 − £3 = £7; Construction set: £25 − £7.50 = £17.50
Computer game: £17.50 − £5.25 = £12.25; Soft toy: £8.90 − £2.67 = £6.23
Action figure: £5.25 − £1.58 = £3.67
12 All of these people got a 12% pay rise. Work out how much extra they earn, and their new pay.
Alex: £300 + £36 = £336/week
Ranjit: £580 + £69.60 = £649.60/month
Molly: £1250 + £150 = £1400/month
Dafydd: £65 + £7.80 = £72.80/day
Sky: £15 500 + £1860 = £17 360/year

Copymaster 47: *Sharing*

1 (a) 60 **(b)** 40
2 (a) 25 **(b)** 120
3 (a) 15 **(b)** 135
4 (a) £1 in the current account to every £5 in the savings account
(b) £15 to current account, £75 to savings account
(c) £315 in current account, £1575 in savings account
5 Sanjeev 54, Allen 72
6 14 classical, 42 pop
7 Andy £32, Beatrice £40, Colin £48
8 Louis 360, Geri 300, Marco 400

Copymaster 50: *Pie Charts II*

Cows White 10, brown 19, spotted 11
Breakfast Toast 89, cereals 78, cooked 8, drink only 5
Entertainment Film 25, play/show 3, concert 10, dancing 7

Copymaster 51: *Lines of symmetry*

The number of lines of symmetry is given for each shape.

1 1
2 1
3 2
4 5
5 2
6 1
7 2
8 0
9 2
10 2
11 1
12 0
13 4
14 8
15 4
16 0
17 1
18 0
19 3
20 0

Copymaster 52: *Rotational symmetry*

The order of rotational symmetry is given for each shape.

1 2
2 3
3 2
4 5
5 2
6 0
7 2
8 6
9 2
10 4
11 0
12 2
13 2
14 8
15 4
16 2
17 3
18 0
19 0
20 4

Copymaster 53: *Angles in triangles*

1 50°
2 10°
3 40°
4 158°
5 83°
6 50°
7 70°, 70°
8 90°
9 30°, 30°
10 60°, 60°, 60°
11 135°

Copymaster 54: *Diagonals*

Sides of polygon	3	4	5	6	7	8	9	10	11	12
Diagonals	0	2	5	9	14	20	27	35	44	54

Copymaster 55: *Reading Scales*

	(a)	(b)	(c)	(d)
1	5	6.5	2.3	3.05
2	700	750	840	625
3	4	2.5	6.75	0.375
4	35	10	24	49.5
5	800	280	650	475
6	2	2.5	0.6	1.45

The table shows which scale should be used for each question.

3 l **scale 1**	680 ml **scale 2**	6 cl **scale 4**	40.5 cl **scale 4**	24 pints **scale 3**	350 l **scale 5**
$\frac{1}{4}$ pint **scale 6**	525 l **scale 5**	$1\frac{1}{2}$ gallons **scale 3**	875 ml **scale 2**	4.5 l **scale 1**	22 fl. oz. **scale 6**

Copymaster 56: *Capacity problems*
1 (a) 20 ml **(b)** 50 **(c)** 200 **(d)** 4 **(e)** £2.40 **(f)** 90% **(g)** 40 l **(h)** 17 times **(i)** 85 **(j)** £2.97 (3 boxes) **(k)** £53.88
2 (a) 800 m^2 **(b)** 800 000 l **(c)** 3 hours 10 minutes **(d)** 2 hours 46 minutes 40 seconds
(e) 1 minute 40 seconds
(f) The outflow rate is 5000 l/min but only 4800 l/min was being pumped in. The pool wouldn't even have started to fill.

Copymaster 57: *Money problems*
1 (a) £82 976 **(b)** Cathy's and Ashok's: £317 **(c)** Ashok's and Dipa's: £13 405 **(d)** Yes

2 Cost of 2 CDs

		2nd CD			
		Full	Budget	Special	Bargain
1st CD	Full	£27.90	£20.94	£24.45	£17.20
	Budget	£20.94	£13.98	£17.49	£10.24
	Special	£24.45	£17.49	£21.00	£13.75
	Bargain	£17.20	£10.24	£13.75	£6.50

3 (a) £9.26 **(b)** 74p
4 (a) £511.77 **(b)** £85.29$\frac{1}{2}$ **(c)** £287.23 **(d)** Sometime in December

Copymaster 58: *Addition and subtraction problems*
1 (a) S + M − 35 cm **(b)** 2M − 20 cm, or 4S **(c)** L + 3S − 50 cm **(d)** 3L − 5 cm **(e)** 7L + M − 5 cm

2

Left Pan	Right Pan	Balances (on right pan)
I	—	130 g
B	—	555 g
L	—	1.38 kg
I + B	—	685 g
I + L	—	1.51 kg
B + L	—	1.935 kg
I + B + L	—	2.065 kg
B	I	425 g
L	I	1.25 kg
B + L	I	1.805 kg
L	B	825 g
I + L	B	955 g
L	I + B	695 g

3

	Amount in A	Amount in B	Amount in C	Amount in D
(a)	0.45	0	0	2.04
(b)	0.45	0	1.25	0.79
(c)	0.45	0.88	0.37	0.79
(d)	0.45	0.88	1.16	0
(e)	0.36	0.88	1.25	0
(f)	0	0	1.25	1.24
(g)	0.45	0	0.8	1.24
(h)	0.45	0.8	0	1.24
(i)	0.37	0.88	0	1.24
(j)	0.37	0.08	0	2.04

Empty B into A.

Copymaster 60: *Mathematical puzzles*

Pascal's Triangle
The next three rows read:
1-5-10-10-5-1
1-6-15-20-15-6-1
1-7-21-35-35-21-7-1
Each row adds up to a power of 2.

Series of fractions
First series: partial sums approach 1 as more terms are added.
Second series: this grows without limit as more terms are added.

Compound Interest
The year was 2000.

Strange sequence
3, the number of letters in *ten*. The sequence is the number of letters in *one, two, three…*

Square grid
Squares: **16** 1-cm squares, **9** 2-cm squares, **4** 3-cm squares and **1** 4-cm square makes **30** altogether.
Rectangles: **24** 2 × 1, **16** 3 × 1, **8** 4 × 1, **12** 3 × 2, **6** 4 × 2, **4** 4 × 3 makes **70** altogether, though technically, squares are rectangles too, making **100**!

Mounting money
There would be ($2^{20} - 1$) pence altogether, making £10 485.75!

Supplies
This is impossible without crossing lines.

Answers

Homework Copymaster 1

1

×	2	4	8	16
12	24	48	96	192
32	64	128	256	512
57	114	228	456	912
105	210	420	840	1680

2 (a) 260, 520, 1040, 2080 **(b)** 430, 4300, 2150, 1075 **(c)** 5, 50, 25, 125 **(d)** 8, 80, 40, 20
(e) 65 000, 32 500, 16 250, 8125
3 $30 \times 15 = 450$ $840 \div 5 = 168$ $28 \times 250 = 7000$ $75 \times 9 = 675$ $4000 \div 25 = 160$ $48 \times 19 = 912$
$61 \times 99 = 6039$ $6400 \div 32 = 200$ $34 \times 50 = 1700$

Homework Copymaster 2

1 31 → 248 → 744 → 5208 → 26 040 124 → 744 → 6696 → 26 784

2

Item	Number required	Cost of one item	Item total
Computer desk	*8*	*£56.60*	*£452.80*
Writing desk	*6*	*£43.48*	*£260.88*
Operator's chair	*7*	*£35.85*	*£250.95*
Standard chair	*5*	*£29.99*	*£149.95*
Shelf unit	*9*	*£13.50*	*£121.50*
Storage cabinet	*3*	*£68.75*	*£206.25*
Whiteboard panel	*4*	*£12.80*	*£51.20*
		Order Total	*£1,493.53*

Homework Copymaster 3

1 $(\frac{1}{2}, \frac{3}{6}, \frac{5}{10}, \frac{12}{24})$ $(\frac{3}{5}, \frac{9}{15}, \frac{15}{25}, \frac{30}{50})$ $(\frac{5}{8}, \frac{10}{16}, \frac{15}{24}, \frac{25}{40})$ $(\frac{4}{6}, \frac{6}{9}, \frac{16}{24})$
2 $2\frac{1}{2} = \frac{5}{2}$, $3\frac{1}{4} = \frac{13}{4}$, $5\frac{1}{3} = \frac{16}{3}$, $3\frac{2}{3} = \frac{11}{3}$, $4\frac{2}{5} = \frac{22}{5}$ $\frac{11}{6} = 1\frac{5}{6}$, $\frac{11}{4} = 2\frac{3}{4}$, $\frac{19}{8} = 2\frac{3}{8}$, $\frac{70}{9} = 7\frac{7}{9}$, $\frac{36}{25} = 1\frac{11}{25}$
3 3.8, 3.9, **4**, 4.1, 4.2, 4.3, 4.4, 4.5, 4.6, 4.7, 4.8, 4.9, **5**, 5.1, 5.2
0.18, 0.19, **0.2**, 0.21, 0.22, 0.23, 0.24, 0.25, 0.26, 0.27, 0.28, 0.29, **0.3**, 0.31, 0.32
1.348, 1.349, **1.35**, 1.351, 1.352, 1.353, 1.354, 1.355, 1.356, 1.357, 1.358, 1.359, **1.36**, 1.361, 1.362
2.988, 2.989, **2.99**, 2.991, 2.992, 2.993, 2.994, 2.995, 2.996, 2.997, 2.998, 2.999, **3**, 3.001, 3.002

Homework Copymaster 4

1 (a) There is 1 black squares in every 2 squares.
There is 1 white square in every 2 squares.
There is 1 white square to every 1 black square.
(b) There is 1 black square in every 3 squares.
There are 2 white squares in every 3 squares.
There are 2 white squares to every 1 black square.
2 Fred : Gina : Sam = 1 : 2 : 4, so there are 7 "shares".
Fred : Gina : Sam = £1.80 : £3.60 : £7.20.
3 45% of 100 squares = 45 squares
20% of 200 squares = 40 squares
60% of 400 squares = 240 squares
30% of 120 squares = 36 squares
625 g red apples
4 10 sticks of celery; 75 g chopped walnuts; 125 g seedless raisins; 200 ml mayonnaise;
50 ml lemon juice

Homework Copymaster 5

The probability of obtaining all heads or all tails is $\frac{2}{8} = \frac{1}{4}$, and the results should reflect this.
Direct the pupils to writing down all 8 combinations for the three coins.
The probability of obtaining the same face on all four coins is $\frac{2}{16} = \frac{1}{8}$.

Homework Copymaster 6

1 (9, 1)
2 (4, 8)
3 (1, 7) or (7, 7)
4 any co-ordinate of the form (5, *y*), as long as *y* is not 8.
5 (7, 6)
6 (3, 5)
7 (6, 1)
8 Only considering points with integer co-ordinates, the following are allowed:
any co-ordinate of the form (*x*, 5), as long as *x* is not 4; (1, 2), (3, 1), (5, 0); (8, 0), (9, 1), (10, 2).

Homework Copymaster 7

2×1 rectangles: maximum 14 cm, minimum 10 cm.
3×1 rectangles: maximum 20 cm, minimum 12 cm.
Discuss very briefly how problems involving length and mass are solved: make sure you have enough information, plan what calculations will be needed, that answers are sensible, etc.
So one person must carry a tent and nothing else.
The remaining three must therefore carry 34 kg between them.

Homework Copymaster 8

Answers given here use typical values to give an idea of the correct orders of magnitude.
An average life span has been assumed to be 70 years.

Toothpaste
10 times/week
2.5 cm
25 cm
25 cm × 52 = 13 m
13 m × 70 = 910 m

Spaghetti
About 40 pieces in a meal
30 cm × 40 = 12 m
12 m × 52 = 624 m
624 m × 70 = 43.68 km

Bread
Guess about 30 slices a week
150 cm^2 per slice
150 cm^2 × 30 = 4500 cm^2
4500 cm^2 × 52 = 23.4 m^2
23.4 m^2 × 70 = 1638 m^2
30 × 52 ÷ 20 = 78 loaves/year
800 g × 78 = 62.4 kg
62.4 kg × 70 = 4.368 tonnes

Homework Copymaster 9

25cm^2 24cm^2
When 1 cm is added/subtracted, the area of the rectangle is 1 cm^2 less than that of the square.
When *x* cm are added/subtracted, the area of the rectangle is x^2 cm^2 less than that of the square.

Homework Copymaster 10

Some results are as follows:
All odd numbers can be written as 2-row stacks.
All multiples of 3 can be made into 3-row stacks.
All numbers that are 6 more than a multiple of 4 are 4-row stacks.
Multiples of 5 above 10 are 5-row stacks.
Numbers stack in more than one way when they fit more than one of the above criteria.
Examples: 9 = 4 + 5 = 2 + 3 + 4.
15 = 7 + 8 = 4 + 5 + 6 = 1 + 2 + 3 + 4 + 5.
Powers of 2 are *never* stacks.

Homework Copymaster 11

1 (a) −3 **(b)** 3 **(c)** 5 **(d)** −11 **(e)** −24 **(f)** 24 **(g)** −7 **(h)** −396 **(i)** −0.7 **(j)** 2.56
2 (a) (7, 8), (9, −2), (5, −2) **(b)** (4, 9), (5, 6), (−4, 3), (−5, 6) **(c)** (6, −3), (10, −5), (8, −9), (4, −7)
(d) (−4, 10), (−9, 3), (−9, 10)
3 A symmetrical capital 'W'.

Homework Copymaster 12

<table>
<tr><td rowspan="8">120</td><td rowspan="4">840</td><td rowspan="2">280</td><td>13 440</td></tr>
<tr><td>28</td></tr>
<tr><td rowspan="2">21 000</td><td>672 000</td></tr>
<tr><td>600</td></tr>
<tr><td rowspan="4">480</td><td rowspan="2">32</td><td>512</td></tr>
<tr><td>672</td></tr>
<tr><td rowspan="2">5760</td><td>103 680</td></tr>
<tr><td>640</td></tr>
</table>

Homework Copymaster 13

1

New	After 1 year	After 2 years	After 5 years	After 10 years
£14 995	£12 495	£11 245	£8270	£5195

2 £14.85
3 £298.56
4 Choc chip cookies: £10.20; chocolate digestives: £10.80; difference: £0.60.
5 Josh £6.95; April £3.75.
6 £435.52
7 (a) £380.90 **(b)** £50.95
8 10p
5p 5p
5p 2p 2p 1p
5p 2p 1p 1p 1p
5p 1p 1p 1p 1p 1p
2p 2p 2p 2p 2p
2p 2p 2p 2p 1p 1p
2p 2p 2p 1p 1p 1p 1p
2p 2p 1p 1p 1p 1p 1p 1p
2p 1p 1p 1p 1p 1p 1p 1p 1p
1p 1p 1p 1p 1p 1p 1p 1p 1p 1p

Homework Copymaster 14

1 (a) $\frac{1}{2}$ **(b)** $\frac{3}{4}$ **(c)** $\frac{2}{5}$ **(d)** $\frac{5}{12}$ **(e)** $\frac{1}{3}$ **(f)** $\frac{5}{8}$ **(g)** $\frac{2}{7}$ **(h)** $\frac{9}{10}$
2 (a) $\frac{3}{4}$ **(b)** $\frac{4}{5}$ **(c)** $\frac{2}{3}$ **(d)** $\frac{7}{10}$ **(e)** $\frac{1}{3}$ **(f)** $\frac{9}{11}$ **(g)** $\frac{5}{8}$ **(h)** $\frac{16}{25}$
3 (a) £9 **(b)** 20 kg **(c)** 6.5 km **(d)** 16 l **(e)** 240° **(f)** 180 cm^2 **(g)** £3.15 **(h)** 25 cl
4 (a)

$\frac{1}{6}$	$\frac{1}{2}$	$\frac{7}{12}$	$\frac{2}{3}$	$\frac{5}{6}$	$\frac{11}{12}$
$\frac{2}{12}$	$\frac{6}{12}$	$\frac{7}{12}$	$\frac{8}{12}$	$\frac{10}{12}$	$\frac{11}{12}$

(b)

$\frac{13}{50}$	$\frac{3}{10}$	$\frac{7}{20}$	$\frac{2}{5}$	$\frac{3}{5}$	$\frac{7}{10}$
$\frac{26}{100}$	$\frac{30}{100}$	$\frac{35}{100}$	$\frac{40}{100}$	$\frac{60}{100}$	$\frac{70}{100}$

5 (a) $\frac{1}{10}$ **(b)** $\frac{3}{5}$ **(c)** $\frac{1}{2}$ **(d)** $\frac{1}{4}$ **(e)** $\frac{7}{20}$ **(f)** $\frac{22}{25}$ **(g)** $\frac{679}{1000}$ **(h)** $\frac{7}{40}$

Homework Copymaster 15

1 48°, 61°, 138°, 113°
2 Allow suitable tolerances.
3 90°, 61°, 61°.

Homework Copymaster 16

The integer solutions are:

Base	**Height** (wall + roof)								
1	9 + 2	8 + 4	7 + 6	6 + 8	5 + 10	4 + 12	3 + 14	2 + 16	1 + 18
2	4 + 2	3 + 4	2 + 6	1 + 8					
4	2 + 1	1 + 3							
5	1 + 2								

Homework Copymaster 17

1 10 g
2 2 g
3 60 g
4 500
5 96
6 28.8 kg
7 4
8 8
9 10
10 61.44 kg

Homework Copymaster 18

1 15.5°C
2 (a) 503.6 **(b)** 5036 **(c)** 50 360 **(d)** 5.036 **(e)** 0.5036 **(f)** 0.050 36
3 (a) 0.06 **(b)** 60 **(c)** 1.2 **(d)** 0.015 **(e)** 10 **(f)** 0.02
4 (a) 1.01 − 0.994 = 0.016 **(b)** 3.53 + 3.506 = 7.036

Homework Copymaster 19

1 4 + 6 + 8 = 18 cm
2 8 + 6 + 8 + 4 + 6 + 8 + 6 = 46 cm
3 A straight route round the 'front' of the box as seen in the diagram is 14.6 cm; however, across the 'top' first and down the side is only 14.4 cm.
4 Pupils might attempt to draw the internal triangle involved to measure it: the answer is 10.8 cm.

Homework Copymaster 20

1 6, 12, 18, etc.
2 5, 15, 25, etc.
3 Impossible. 10 is even, so all its multiples are even,
4 25, 100, 225, etc.
5 2
6 3 or 5
7 Impossible. Square numbers have a double factor. Prime numbers don't.

8 72, 144, etc.
9 1, 2 or 4
10 1, 4, 25 or 100
11 24 or 48
12 100, 400, 900, etc.
13 120, 300, 780, etc.
14 $2 \times 3 \times 5 = 30$
15 Any prime number, or a power of a prime number: 4, 8, 16, etc; 9, 27, 81, etc.
16 There isn't a whole number, but 20 does have a square root! $\sqrt{20} = 4.47$ to 2 d.p.

Homework Copymaster 21

1 (a) 8640 **(b)** 600 **(c)** 11.41 **(d)** 0.06 **(e)** 23.7 **(f)** 106.8 **(g)** 13.95 **(h)** 0.024
2 (a) $2\frac{2}{5}$ **(b)** $16\frac{2}{3}$ **(c)** $4\frac{5}{7}$ **(d)** $4\frac{2}{3}$ **(e)** $20\frac{1}{4}$ **(f)** $4\frac{8}{9}$ **(g)** $15\frac{5}{8}$ **(h)** $57\frac{1}{7}$
3 (a) 2.4 **(b)** 16.7 **(c)** 4.7 **(d)** 4.7 **(e)** 20.3 **(f)** 4.9 **(g)** 15.6 **(h)** 57.1
4 (a) £67.75 **(b)** £31.92 **(c)** £6.96 **(d)** £2096.64
5 (a) £625 **(b)** £2.50 **(c)** £9.40 **(d)** £2000

Homework Copymaster 22

For the single-twist Möbius band:
1 It is impossible to colour one side red and the other blue, because the band only has one side.
2 It is impossible to draw a red line along one edge and a blue line along the other, because the band only has one edge.
3 A single band results.
4 Two linked bands are produced.
For the double-twist Möbius band:
1 This works.
2 This works.
3 Two linked bands are produced.
4 Two linked bands are produced, one twice the width of the other.

Homework Copymaster 23

1

Fraction	Decimal	Percentage
$\frac{1}{2}$	0.5	50%
$\frac{1}{10}$	**0.1**	**10%**
$\frac{1}{5}$	0.2	%
$\frac{1}{4}$	**0.25**	25%
$\frac{3}{4}$	**0.75**	**75%**
$\frac{1}{20}$	**0.05**	5%
$\frac{7}{20}$	0.35	**35%**
$\frac{1}{25}$	**0.04**	**4%**
$\frac{1}{8}$	0.125	**$12\frac{1}{2}$%**
$\frac{5}{8}$	**0.625**	$62\frac{1}{2}$%
$\frac{31}{50}$	**0.62**	**62%**
$\frac{1}{3}$	**0.333...**	**$33\frac{1}{3}$%**

2 (a) £16 **(b)** £20 **(c)** 0.6 kg **(d)** 0.8 km **(e)** £80 **(f)** 247.5 ml **(g)** £243.75 **(h)** $288

3

$\frac{2}{5}$	41%	$\frac{21}{50}$	44%	$\frac{4}{9}$	$\frac{9}{20}$
0.4	0.41	0.42	0.44	0.444...	0.45

Homework Copymaster 24

1

Spindle	1	2	3
Pulleys (cm)	10	5, 6	2
Turns	1	**2**	**6**

2

Spindle	1	2	3
Pulleys (cm)	4	8, 6	4
Turns	1	**0.5**	**0.75**

3

Spindle	1	2	3	4
Pulleys (cm)	9	3, 6	2, 8	2
Turns	**20**	60	**180**	**720**

4

Spindle	1	2	3	4
Pulleys (cm)	6	4, 6	4, 8	6
Turns	2	**3**	**4.5**	**6**

Homework Copymaster 25

1

Number of pets	0	1	2	3	4
Number of owners	35	78	52	9	6
Total pets	0	78	104	27	24

2 180
3 233
4 1.29 to 2 d.p.

5

Number of people in car	1	2	3	4	5
Pie chart angle	70°	156°	104°	18°	12°

Homework Copymaster 26

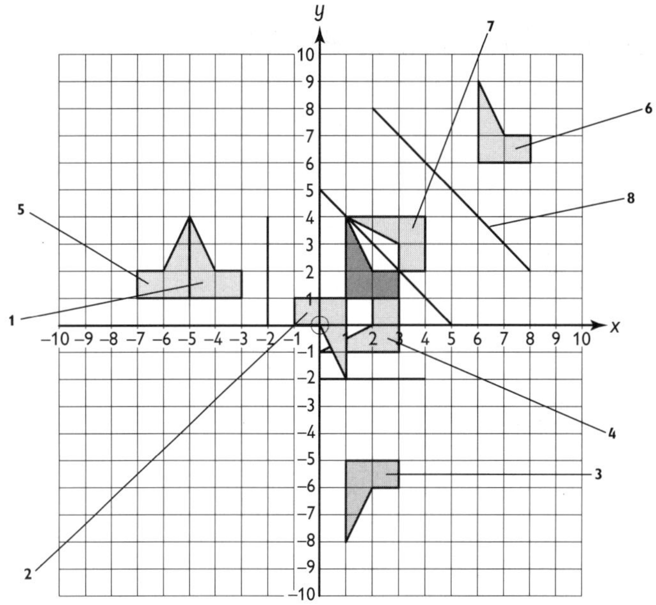

Homework Copymaster 27

Size of square	1	2	3	4	5	6	7	8	9	10
Positions	1	1	3	3	6	6	10	10	15	15

The number of positions is represented by triangular numbers as shown.
If larger squares are removed, the same sequence occurs, translated along the table.
If the squares removed do not have to be on grid lines, an infinite number of possibilities exists.

Homework Copymaster 28

Answers depend on what pupils have found at home.

Homework Copymaster 29

1 In a magic square, all the rows, columns and diagonals add up to the same number.

(a)

8	13	12
15	11	7
10	9	14

(b)

20	15	22
21	19	17
16	23	18

(c)

6	11	8	17
16	9	14	3
13	4	15	10
7	18	5	12

(d)

20	15	13	6
11	8	18	17
14	21	7	12
9	10	16	19

2 $1 + 9 = 10$; $12 + 98 = 110$; $123 + 987 = 1110$; $1234 + 9876 = 11110$, etc.
$9 - 1 = 8$; $98 - 12 = 86$; $987 - 123 = 864$; $9876 - 1234 = 8642$, etc.
3 3-digit numbers eventually arrive at 99, and then 0.
4-digit numbers eventually arrive at 999, and then 0. The pattern continues.

Homework Copymaster 30

The given flowchart always ends up with a cycle of 2s and 1s.
When +1 is changed to −1, all numbers end up at 0.
Other results will depend on what pupils chose, but are similar in character when odd numbers are added or subtracted.

Notes

Notes